APPALACHIAN ENGLISHES IN THE TWENTY-FIRST CENTURY

Appalachian Englishes in the Twenty-First Century

Edited by Kirk Hazen

WEST VIRGINIA UNIVERSITY PRESS / MORGANTOWN

Copyright © 2020 by West Virginia University Press
All rights reserved
First edition published 2020 by West Virginia University Press
Printed in the United States of America

ISBN
Cloth 978-1-949199-54-3
Paper 978-1-949199-55-0
Ebook 978-1-949199-56-7

Library of Congress Cataloging-in-Publication Data
Names: Hazen, Kirk, editor.
Title: Appalachian Englishes in the twenty-first century / edited by Kirk Hazen.
Description: First edition. | Morgantown : West Virginia University Press, 2020. | Includes bibliographical references and index.
Identifiers: LCCN 2020008819 | ISBN 9781949199543 (cloth) | ISBN 9781949199550 (paperback) | ISBN 9781949199567 (ebook)
Subjects: LCSH: English language—Dialects—Appalachian Region. | English language—Variation—United States. | Americanisms—Appalachian Region. | Appalachian Region—Languages. | Language and culture—Appalachian Region.
Classification: LCC PE2970.A6 A67 2020 | DDC 427/.975—dc23
LC record available at https://lccn.loc.gov/2020008819

Book and cover design by Than Saffel / WVU Press

*For our Appalachian students who have taught us
so much about language and life*

i can't say the landscape of me is all honeysuckle and clover cause there have always been mines in these lily-covered valleys. you have to risk the briar bush to reach the sweet dark fruit, and ain't no country woman all church and piney woods. there is pluck and cayenne pepper. there is juke joint gyrations in the youngun-bearing girth of this belly and these supple hips. all roads lead me back across the waters of blood and breast milk, from ocean, to river, to the lake, to the creek, to branch and stream, back to the sweet rain, to the cold water in the glass i drink when i thirst to know where i belong.

—Crystal Wilkinson, "Terrain"

I suspect my children will not exist or else become legendary in their silences, mute puttocks scrimmed from the sourmash. And yet the mountain rain, all kinds of spectacular dying, Biblical black leather, going to town, hair that won't stop growing, a mosquito stealthing blood, the asylum inmates buried vertically. I shall play my toothpick. I shall eat yonder cabin. I shall ride yonder donkey. I shall ho yander cake. I shall be wrought from my own particular orality.

—Tim Earley, *Poems Descriptive of Rural Life and Scenery*

Contents

Foreword by Donna Christian   ix
Preface   xv

PART I
Linguistic and Regional Boundaries

1. Just What and Where Are Appalachian Englishes?   3
   J. Daniel Hasty

2. Phonological Possibilities in Appalachian Englishes   20
   Paul E. Reed

3. Grammar across Appalachia   36
   Kirk Hazen

PART II
Language in Society

4. Discourse in Appalachia   55
   Allison Burkette

5. Identity and Representation in Appalachia   69
   Jennifer Cramer

6. Language, Gender, and Sexuality in Appalachia   84
   Christine Mallinson and J. Inscoe

7. Language and Ethnicity in Appalachia   99
   Becky Childs

PART III
Language in the Wider World

8   Redneck Memes as an Appalachian Reclamation of   115
    Vernacular Authority, Language, and Identity
    Jordan Lovejoy

9   Intersections of Literature and Dialect in Appalachia   130
    Isabelle Shepherd and Kirk Hazen

10 Teachers and Teens Making Sense of Identity, Place,   145
    and Language in Appalachian Secondary Schools
    Audra Slocum

11 Appalachian Englishes and the College Campus   160
    Stephany Brett Dunstan and Audrey J. Jaeger

   Afterword by Walt Wolfram   177
   Contributors   193
   Index   197

Foreword

As we wrapped up the report of our study of the English spoken in two counties in West Virginia, Walt Wolfram and I commented: "We look forward to looking at the development of AE [Appalachian English] in the years to come as it preserves some features while changing others" (Wolfram and Christian 1976, 162). That was not a very risky prediction, and, not surprisingly, in the years since then, the English varieties used by speakers in Appalachia have evolved, as have the demographic and sociocultural characteristics of the region. Furthermore, our understanding of how language works in its social context, and how it varies according to linguistic and social environments, has expanded dramatically. The scope of linguistic inquiry has broadened and deepened, and technology has given us new tools for investigation.

Given the amount of change on many fronts, we are indebted to Kirk Hazen for bringing together the expert contributors to this volume on Appalachian Englishes to chart the development of our knowledge base and bring us well into the twenty-first century with their research. It is significant that they have chosen to recognize the diversity in the region both linguistically and socially by adopting the plural label (appropriately echoing the term *World Englishes* for the diverse varieties of English around the world). As Hazen observes in his preface, the plural form allows us to ensure that "all speakers of English in Appalachia are part of the picture." This choice is more than just the selection of a term. Earlier studies (from the previous century!) provided a baseline for describing the varieties of English in Appalachia by focusing on speakers from working-class and primarily rural families, seeking to identify and explore the language features that differed the most from standard varieties of English. The studies tended to emphasize the isolation of communities in mountainous areas (a factor mentioned in the title of our comparative study of Ozark and Appalachian varieties of English [Christian, Wolfram, and Dube 1988]) and may have created an impression of homogeneity of language in the region.

Building on this base, researchers such as the authors represented in this collection have moved ahead to study a wide range of speakers residing in the region, covering an expanded set of groups by age, ethnic background, socioeconomic status, and other social factors. Their examination of the geographical coverage of the term *Appalachia* shows us how complex that term really is, especially on linguistic grounds. They lead us to consider subregions of northern and southern Appalachia (see Hasty chapter 1) and how the subregions relate to neighboring communities. The contributors also include speakers from communities of newer arrivals (including immigrant families) and those who were not typically part of the earlier studies (such as African Americans and Native Americans). This volume presents a welcome overview of the diversity of Englishes and of communities in today's Appalachia.

In some ways, the situation in Appalachia is a reflection of a global phenomenon being discussed in multilingual contexts as "superdiversity" (Blommaert and Rampton 2011). The situation is characterized by an enormous increase in the numbers and types of migrants settling in new communities, creating demographic and social changes along with greater linguistic diversity. This trend has coincided with a rapid expansion of new technologies, particularly those that affect possibilities of interaction and the cultural life of groups (mobile phones, the internet, and so on). Relative ease of movement and communication has increased the amount of contact between people from diverse backgrounds (and set the stage for the linguistic consequences that occur when speakers interact). While Appalachia may not yet have the extent of international migration that characterizes these multilingual, multicultural areas, the region is experiencing the same forces. Attending to the diversity of Englishes recognizes the need to include all voices and consider the role of language in the social, political, and cultural lives of the speakers.

One direction of expansion has been to focus attention on previously neglected groups, such as African Americans, Native Americans (see Childs chapter 7), and those identified by gender and sexuality (see Mallinson and Inscoe chapter 6). In so doing, we learn about the likely influence of ancestral languages, such as Cherokee, on speech patterns that diverge from other local varieties. We also find out how African American speakers in Appalachia incorporate some grammatical features from African American English varieties in other areas but tend to adopt local patterns in many cases. Finally, the growing presence of Latinx populations brings the opportunity to study the dynamic interplay of ancestral language, local English varieties, and competing social forces that will shape new Englishes in the region.

At the same time, it is very interesting to observe how the English varieties that were previously studied have changed over time by comparing current speech patterns to those documented in previous decades. It is also important to distinguish the evidence of empirical research from the stereotypes that have proliferated in popular media about "mountain folk," often featured in caricatures and cartoons. Both of these themes are well treated in the chapters in this volume. As Hazen and his colleagues have demonstrated in numerous studies of speakers in West Virginia (such as Hazen, Butcher, and King 2010), many of the features that characterized the vernacular described in earlier studies have diminished in frequency and are much less often observed in the speech of younger groups. This fact points to possible language change in progress. Considering, for example, some of the grammatical patterns documented in earlier studies, we learn that a pattern like the use of *was* with a plural subject (e.g., *we* was *tired*) has declined significantly in usage, from a 50–80 percent level in earlier studies and with older subjects to less than 10 percent among younger speakers in more recent studies (Hazen chapter 3). It turns out that this pattern of change occurs not just with one feature but with many, an indication that the varieties are evolving (as all varieties of language do). Southern Appalachia appears to retain more of the characteristics that typify Southern varieties of English, pointing to the power of regional influences. Furthermore, new language features are also being introduced, such as quotative *be like* (as in *She's like, "What's his problem?"*). This usage is increasing in frequency among younger members of the speech communities (Hazen chapter 3), demonstrating how Appalachian Englishes are also incorporating new elements from other regions. As studies document specific linguistic features and how their use has changed, we gain a perspective on linguistic, sociological, and cultural movements as well.

While the vernacular varieties were evolving, the field of linguistics and allied disciplines were as well. In linguistics, there continues to be a strong interest in the structural elements (phonology, morphology, syntax, and so on), but this volume testifies to the broadening of our paths of inquiry. We're now looking at not only how people use the variable structures of their language but also how language works in a broader context and the social meaning it conveys. This perspective includes looking at larger stretches of language and interaction (discourse) and exploring how language reflects a speaker's identity, including gender and ethnicity. The developments also move us from speech to perception, as we consider how users of varieties of a language, and those who hear them, react to the language and to the speakers. These domains are several of the more recent directions of investigation that are followed in this volume.

In one of many memorable exchanges in our data, a sixty-seven-year-old retired miner in West Virginia, who was interviewed for our study in 1974, showed a keen sense of how language and identity relate (and what "outsiders" might be focusing on when they listen to the language of the community):

Fieldworker: What are some of the things people grow here in their gardens?

Respondent: Oh, potatoes and tomatoes—or did you want me to say 'maters and 'taters? (Wolfram and Christian 1976, 170)

He was an eloquent storyteller, and his language variety included many vernacular features that he employed both naturally and purposefully. For example, in discussing the value of spending time with your children, he used a number of vernacular features that have since declined in usage among residents of West Virginia, such as *a*-prefixing: "Grow up a-hunting with them instead a-hunting for them. . . . We like to hunt and we done fished, we done 'at together. Me and the boys and the dog" (Wolfram and Christian 1976, 179). Of course, it's not clear that this individual would have identified himself as "Appalachian" or considered the relationship between his language and that of others in that region or other areas, even though he was clearly aware of stereotypes (we didn't ask the question at the time!).

Studies of identity and perception, such as those in this volume, highlight the social forces that may be shaping the vernacular. Burkette (chapter 4) finds that *a*-prefixing and other similar vernacular features are becoming more associated with narratives than other types of discourse (especially with younger speakers). Thus, while the vernacular forms may continue to be used, their function has changed, as they appear to be used as a rhetorical strategy. These changes can be understood in part by looking at perceptions of varieties of English in Appalachia that often reflect negative stereotypes about speakers of these varieties, leading to a reduction in usage of salient features. However, to complicate matters, the lack of overt prestige is often accompanied by covert prestige, where speech patterns, while considered "incorrect," may also be perceived as "pleasant" and linked to a community's heritage (Cramer chapter 5). They may also be used purposefully to challenge stereotypes, as in social media groups like those described by Lovejoy (chapter 8). Overall, the broadening of our inquiry beyond the structural aspects of language gives us a much fuller picture of the linguistic patterns and what they mean in the life of communities.

Finally, it is important to consider the impact of varieties of English on the lives of individual speakers, particularly in critical areas like education. Walt Wolfram and I conducted our research, with funding from the US Department of Education, looking for possible consequences of vernacular dialect background in education, in areas like teaching reading and assessing achievement and intelligence. Language has been recognized as a central factor in educational access and success, and understanding that "difference" in language does not mean that there is a "deficit" (linguistic or intellectual) is critical in providing equity for students from diverse language backgrounds (Reaser et al. 2017). In the work of applying linguistic research to societal concerns, the horizons have expanded as well, with research on higher levels of education (secondary and postsecondary) and on dimensions such as identity development and dialect appreciation. In other words, the language variety one brings to an educational setting, particularly for adolescents and young adults, is not only a factor in learning and in the evaluations and expectations of teachers; it is also a central part of identity formation and the self-image that students are developing. As the contributors to this volume demonstrate, educators need information about language variation and its social evaluation in order to support students as they navigate the educational system and their relationships with members of home and school communities.

In conclusion, our knowledge of the language of Appalachia has grown in both depth and breadth as research has explored the rich diversity of the region. This volume brings into focus the current stage in the evolution of our study of language variation evidenced through studies of Appalachian Englishes. The editor and authors are to be congratulated for preparing a set of chapters grounded in innovative research that can help us counter the myths and stereotypes about the language and people of Appalachia, understand the current state of knowledge, and inspire the next generation of research. With its companion website, the collection sets us on a path of exploration of the continuum of language varieties spoken in Appalachia, these Appalachian Englishes, and their social impact, and it will help to guide us toward a greater understanding of language itself.

Donna Christian
Center for Applied Linguistics

References

Blommaert, Jan, and Ben Rampton. 2011. "Language and Superdiversity." *Diversities* 13, no. 2: 1–22.

Christian, Donna, Walt Wolfram, and Nanjo Dube. 1988. *Variation and Change in Geographically Isolated Communities: Appalachian English and Ozark English*. Publication of the American Dialect Society 74. Tuscaloosa: University of Alabama Press.

Hazen, Kirk, Paige Butcher, and Ashley King. 2010. "Unvernacular Appalachia: An Empirical Perspective on West Virginia Dialect Variation." *English Today* 26, no. 4: 13–22.

Reaser, Jeffrey, Carolyn Temple Adger, Walt Wolfram, and Donna Christian. 2017. *Dialects at School: Educating Linguistically Diverse Students*. New York: Routledge.

Wolfram, Walt and Donna Christian. 1976. *Appalachian Speech*. Arlington, VA: Center for Applied Linguistics.

Preface

WHAT IS IN THIS BOOK?

This book discusses many of the qualities of the varieties of English that are part of everyday life in Appalachia. Appalachia is a big place. It resists definition, and for many people it is as much a state of mind as it is a place. For natives of the region, what they call the heart of Appalachia varies widely. For most Appalachians, home is a special place, no matter what part of Appalachia it falls in. Many of the authors in this book are linguists, although some are from other academic fields. All of the authors talk about language variation. In doing so, these authors examine language change over time and dialects today. Through these studies, we both distill and present years of scholarship on Appalachian Englishes as well as provide new analyses. At every turn, the authors have been frustrated by the dearth of scholarship on our respective topics, but we are both aware and resolved about the need for future scholarship. Instead of this book purporting to be a stopping point for the decades of research on English variation in Appalachia, it should be seen as a wayside rest point to reflect on what we know and what all we need to find out.

WHAT'S IN A TERM?

For decades of scholarship on the kind of English spoken in Appalachia, the main term was *Appalachian English*. It is a sturdy term, and it was accepted without question. In the first decade of this century, scholars began to discuss among themselves the idea of abandoning the term. Several concerns about the term prompted the switch. The primary one was that the term *Appalachian English* denoted a single, monolithic variety, as if one dialect of English stretched across the entire region. At no point was such a situation true, but the term led both scholars and the general public to believe there was only one kind of English in Appalachia. The second problem was that, in order to keep the unity of this monolithic content, the term was at times applied to some speakers in Appalachia but not others. Folk in the country might speak Appalachian English, but people in town would not. Such an assumption goes against the basic sociolinguistic tenet to investigate language variation across communities. For these reasons, we have opted to refer to the plurality of varieties in Appalachia and to assume that all speakers of English in Appalachia are part of the picture.

In the same way, people speak several different standard Englishes in the United States, and the number of standard Englishes increases greatly when we consider the hundreds of English varieties around the world. Differences in standard Englishes range from vowels to past tense forms (e.g., *sneak* vs. *snuck*). In the United States, varieties that are not stigmatized are considered standard. The standard English of any one region is defined by what it is not; it does not contain vernacular features. The judgment of what might be vernacular depends entirely on how speakers are viewed socially. Southerners and African Americans have been viewed as socially lesser for a long time, and, as a result, any differences in their speech have been judged as flaws and stigmatized. Appalachians have also been derided since at least the Civil War (Catte 2018), and any variation in their speech has been taken as evidence to justify that derision. This book takes apart that justification by showing the systematic patterns to English varieties in Appalachia and combating the stereotypes laid upon them.

In this kind of work, previous studies are regularly cited. In reviewing the work of those studies, one question that arises is: How do we cast the named varieties in the previous research? If an author in this book is citing an article from the 1960s that investigated Negro English, should that term be carried forward in the review or should it be recast as African American Language? If this book were designed exclusively for other linguistic scholars, retaining older names of varieties would be a valid approach because all scholars have experienced them before: those scholars would already realize the nuances between names like African American Language and African American Vernacular English. As this book is aimed at a broader audience than just linguists, names of varieties from previous studies have been standardized.

WHERE TO FIND THE HISTORY OF APPALACHIA AND ITS ENGLISH VARIETIES

When considering histories of Appalachia, even language histories, too many scholarly works before the late 1990s incorporated myths about Appalachia into their scholarship. After Lewis and Billings (1997) focused scholars' attention on the kinds of scholarly myths that had been reified over the previous decades, the extent of the mythologization of Appalachia in academia was there for all to see. There is a growing body of modern scholarship, and it looks to be gaining momentum. For a good history of Appalachia, read John Williams's *Appalachia* (2002), although there are other histories available. For a language-specific account of contributing dialects to the English varieties found in Appalachia today, see Michael Montgomery's essay in *Talking Appalachia* (Clark and Hayward 2013). For a concise overview of the history of Appalachian scholarship and definitions of Appalachia, see William Schumann's "Place and Place-Making in Appalachia" in *Appalachia Revisited* (Schumann and Fletcher 2016). Relatedly, a new volume recharacterizes Appalachia in light of recent scholarship and reassesses its place in the United States. The volume *Appalachia in Regional Context: Place Matters* challenges conventional representations of Appalachia through studies of activism, foodways, representations of Appalachia, and the experiences of rural LGBTQ youth (Billings and Kingsolver 2018). Another important essay to consult to assess where scholarship has gone recently in regard to language, Appalachia, and the South is Reaser's introduction to *Language Variety in the New South* (Reaser et al. 2018).

The book that has most impacted how I think about Appalachia while editing this book is Elizabeth Catte's *What You Are Getting Wrong about Appalachia* (2018). If you only read one other book about Appalachia, read that one. For any language scholar who is relatively new to scholarship on Appalachia, her book characterizes the history of activism in Appalachia and corrects the ways Appalachia has been maligned, even by those that purport to be helping its people.

OTHER LANGUAGES IN APPALACHIA?

In writing a book of this type, we find plenty of areas where we want to see improved scholarship. One area that many of the authors in this book would like to see improved is the study of *other* languages in Appalachia. Spanish has been part of Appalachia for decades now, but we know of no such studies in Appalachia itself. It has been studied in lowland areas in the South, such as North Carolina and Texas (e.g., Callahan 2017; Thomas 2019). Future studies of the rise of Spanish in Appalachia are much needed, and some advanced planning is already in the works. German has been part of Pennsylvanian Appalachia since the first European settlement (e.g., Keiser 2012; Louden 2016), and it continues unabated today. Native American languages like Cherokee have been part of Appalachia for far longer than English has, and Childs (chapter 7) discusses some of the scholarly efforts. A book that dealt with the entirety of the language complexity in Appalachia would take into account all these languages and characterize their sociolinguistic patterns.

ARE WE INCLUDING ALL THE REFERENCES AVAILABLE?

References in the chapters are what we consider "gateway" references. These are the citations that will get readers to most of the relevant literature. We have not included the top five most important citations for each claim, nor have we provided an exhaustive list for each topic. Academic writing is infamous for citation-laden prose, especially in linguistics. Linguists traditionally add in all the possible relevant references to demonstrate our knowledge and perhaps appease potential reviewers that their favorite people (or they themselves) are properly recognized for their contributions. In this volume, we purposefully avoid that writing style. There are many works written about English varieties in Appalachia. The online bibliography for Appalachian Englishes can be found at http://artsandsciences.sc.edu/appalachianenglish/. It is built by the "dean" of this scholarship, Michael Montgomery, and Paul Reed (author of chapter 2). That bibliography is thematically grouped, which makes the thousands of citations vastly more useful for more people. The citations in this volume will only represent a smidgen of those citations, but we hope they provide the path to find the works readers are most interested in.

THE COMPANION WEBSITE

Like a bedroom closet, space is always limited in a book with sixteen authors. With those limitations, we have not been able to include the images, maps, memes, and related media many of our authors relate to with their chapters. We have a companion website (http://dialects.wvu.edu/appalachian-englishes) that provides these materials along with links to other resources that our authors wanted to share. The website will evolve and be updated as new material becomes available, so if you have relevant curriculum material to share, please contact me at Kirk.Hazen@mail.wvu.edu.

WHO ARE THESE AUTHORS?

Professionally, these authors are a diverse mix of the academic timeline. As authors, we have two graduate students, two assistant professors, three associate professors, three full professors, an alumni distinguished professor, an endowed named professor, an emeritus president of the Center for Applied Linguistics, an assistant vice provost, and a nonprofit development specialist. Academically, many of us are linguists of one stripe or another, but we do have people who instead focus on folklore or poetry. Three of us are education specialists. Some of the more elder authors have various subspecialties, as sociolinguists are wont to examine related areas that guide the paths of language variation and change. Unfortunately, there are no authors of color in this volume, and I sincerely hope that, in the second edition, a wider ethnic diversity of scholars will join this evolving conversation.

AN OVERVIEW

In the foreword, Donna Christian examines how both the study of Appalachian Englishes and the language itself have evolved since her 1974 research for *Appalachian Speech*. Considering the growing scope of linguistic inquiry and the advances in linguistic tools and technology, she writes about how this book addresses the evolving and diverse facets that come together to form Appalachia. In particular, she comments on the plural labeling of Appalachian English varieties and its representation of the region's diversity demographically, ethnically, socially, and culturally. She also considers the evolution of grammatical patterns in Appalachia, the decline of certain features such as *was*-leveling, and the development of new language features such as quotative *be like*. Finally, she writes about the implications of Appalachian identity and perception on speakers themselves, and she discusses how this book speaks to the concerns of education and identity formation in Appalachia.

Linguistic and Regional Boundaries

The first section of the book covers some of the linguistic and regional patterns found in Appalachia. Each of these chapters could be divided into several fully different chapters, and full dissertations have been written on some of these topics (Hasty 2012; Reed 2016). This section also lays out some of the major regional divisions found in Appalachia.

In chapter 1, J. Daniel Hasty writes about the regional divides in Appalachia. One of the persistent challenges in scholarship on Appalachia is that no consensus exists as to what Appalachia might be. Hasty describes the different definitions in relation to dialect boundaries and relates some of the most diagnostic dialect features that delineate different regions. His chapter also points out the gaps in what we know about regional language variation in Appalachia. Hasty emphasizes the diversity found in Appalachian varieties and illustrates that diversity across the levels of language and the contrasts found within the region. The contrasts can be found in many parts of Appalachian life, including economic differences between urban and rural areas and any one area's association to other dialect regions. Hasty draws major distinctions between Northern Appalachia and Southern Appalachia. Within these regions, dialect variation and language change are headed in different directions.

In chapter 2, Paul Reed explains some of the most prominent sound patterns in Appalachia. He directly confronts the idea that differences found in Appalachia come from fossilized, archaic pronunciations. The ideas of dialects frozen in time or accents left unchanging for centuries have been propagated for well over one hundred years. Reed describes the innovations and continued evolution of sound patterns in Appalachian varieties across vowels and consonants. In exploring similarities to other regions, Reed describes how many Appalachian dialect features are also found in Southern or Midland dialects. Reed's work comes from the variationist paradigm within sociolinguistics, and with those methodologies he is able to draw distinctions in both the quantitative and qualitative patterns. With the quantitative patterns, systematic sound differences can happen more or less often and correlate with social motivations; with qualitative distinctions, the sound systems can have different constraints on certain forms. Within Appalachia, both kinds of distinctions arise for phonological patterns.

In chapter 3, I write about some of the grammatical possibilities in Appalachia. Grammar for linguists contains two areas of study: morphology, which examines how words are put together (*un + happy + ness*), and syntax, which examines how phrases are put together (Determiner + Adjective + Noun; *This unhappy squid*). The chapter reviews the scholarship on morphological and syntactic variation in Appalachia, but it also focuses on the language variation patterns that are part of current varieties. Some of the grammatical patterns from decades past have faded away to become infrequently used or only used in performance of an Appalachian identity. Both language change and dialect diversity illustrate the uneven distribution of these grammatical patterns in Appalachia. In popular portrayals of Appalachia, writers use the most vernacular types of grammatical variation, but those dialect features are not the norm. Areas for future research are discussed because, despite the popular attention paid to grammatical variation in Appalachia, little quantitative research has been done on grammatical patterns and their social associations.

Language in Society

In this section, the authors foreground the social connections upheld through language variation in Appalachia. The section starts with swaths of language larger than a phrase, namely the conversations that Appalachians weave together. It then progresses into the ways Appalachians use language to represent themselves both inside and outside their communities. The last two chapters in the section address the ways Appalachians represent their gender and ethnicity through language and how these specific identities guide language variation in Appalachia.

In chapter 4, Allison Burkette investigates discourse in Appalachia. After a review of what actually constitutes discourse, she reviews previous research on discourse in Appalachia in order to highlight the natural connection between discourse and the construction of social meaning. Burkette also works through important concepts for Appalachian discourse, including how interaction and emergence can be used and how nonlinguistic elements can be tools for analysis of discourse.

In chapter 5, Jennifer Cramer explains how Appalachians use language to craft their identities and represent themselves. Perceptions from outside and inside the region play a part in how language is heard and spoken in Appalachia. Cramer uses perceptual dialectology to examine how perceptions reflect local understandings of language varieties. The perceived prestige of a variety, or lack thereof, plays a major role in the qualities of a variety, such as whether it sounds educated or friendly or honest. Cramer's work connects dialect variation to notions of culture, heritage, home, and family.

In chapter 6, Christine Mallinson and J. Inscoe pull together all the known research on language and gender in Appalachia. The downside is that not much exists. The upside is that they explore all that is out there and provide a clear path forward for all future work on language and gender in Appalachia. In addition, their chapter emphasizes the diversity of Appalachian speakers' lived experiences along the lines of sexuality, ethnicity, class, age, and identity. Because gender studies involve so much interdisciplinary scholarship, Mallinson and Inscoe reach outside linguistics to fields such as anthropology, sociology, education, and communications studies. They also emphasize the need for more research on language and gender among diverse communities in Appalachia.

In chapter 7, Becky Childs reviews the literature on language and ethnicity in Appalachia. Like the previous chapter, this chapter's topic has not been at the forefront of previous scholarship. Yet despite persistent myths about the ethnic homogeneity of Appalachia, the region has always had ethnic diversity. Native Americans inhabited the region long before Europeans forcefully settled the area. Along with European settlement, African Americans have had a continuous and growing population in Appalachia. In addition, the Latinx community is growing in both urban and rural areas of Appalachia. All of these ethnic groups are part of Appalachia, and Childs illustrates their influence on language variation in the region.

Language in the Wider World

In the final section, these authors explore how Appalachian varieties play out in various language-rich realms, from folklore to literature to classrooms.

In chapter 8, Jordan Lovejoy demonstrates the roles that language plays in Appalachian folklore. She explains the modern folklore scholarship in this chapter and characterizes two main identity types of *redneck*. Lovejoy illustrates how folklorists study social groups that use language for both identification and differentiation. As she notes, Appalachian Englishes are ripe for the study of negative language stereotypes and how speakers take ownership and pride in traditional Appalachian language features.

In chapter 9, Isabelle Shepherd and I illustrate how language variation has been used in Appalachian literature. Our chapter explores literary uses of grammatical and orthographic variation by writers from Appalachia. We work through examples from novels, short stories, and poems to show the creation of identity and place. Appalachian literature is multifaceted, and its complexity is reflected in the language variation authors bring to its pages.

In chapter 10, Audra Slocum explores how students and teachers use and perceive language in secondary schools in Appalachia. As with any region, teenagers in Appalachia use language to do their identity work in school. Like gender and ethnicity language–related studies, research on adolescents' language varieties in Appalachia is lacking. Slocum discusses the ways language intersects with identity and culture. For quality education to be crafted, teachers and students co-construct the language of the classroom, and Slocum highlights the important role that schools play as a social institution in the regulation of language variation.

In chapter 11, Stephany Brett Dunstan and Audrey J. Jaeger report on what happens when Appalachians bring their varieties of English to college campuses. Appalachians most often face a wall of linguistic hegemony and the burden of standard language ideology, both of which influence who has power in any speaking situation. For college students from rural southern Appalachia, speaking a stigmatized dialect influences whether they feel marginalized or accepted on campus and whether or not the college campus embraces linguistic diversity. Dunstan and Jaeger report that fewer rural Appalachian students either attend or graduate college than students from any other region. They explore how dialect variation interacts with a sense of belonging on a college campus. With their findings, they then lay out the practical implications for scholars and teachers to foster inclusive environments that support successful educational outcomes.

In the afterword, Walt Wolfram reflects on nearly fifty years of scholarship on Appalachia. He reviews the progress made since the early 1970s but also critiques the missed opportunities and the sometimes myopic views sociolinguists have presented about the region. Tying together linguistic scholarship with proactive educational outreach, Wolfram describes the symbiotic relationships between language and Appalachia that fuel modern sociolinguistic work.

ACKNOWLEDGEMENTS

The authors would like to thank the language scholars who made our scholarship possible and taught us about studying language in communities. These scholars include Walt Wolfram, Michael Montgomery, Jeff Reaser, and all the other authors in this book.

As editor, I thank all the authors for working so hard to turn in quality drafts on time at every stage. I thank the WVU Press for their astute editing and smooth publishing process; they are a joy to work with. I thank Maggie McDonald for assistance getting the project started with abstracts, conceptualization, and a system of accountability. I thank Jordan Miller for extensive work copyediting the book and transmogrifying it to WVU Press standards for the external reviews. I also thank Mary Werner, Caroline Toler, and Taylor Miller for their diligent work copyediting the final draft with revised WVU Press guidelines and preparing the index.

References

Billings, Dwight B., and Ann E. Kingsolver. 2018. *Appalachia in Regional Context: Place Matters*. Lexington: University of Kentucky Press.

Callahan, Erin. 2017. "Interlanguage and Cross-Generational Assimilation: Past Tense Unmarking in Hispanicized English." *Journal of English Linguistics*: 45, no. 2: 103–29.

Catte, Elizabeth. 2018. *What You Are Getting Wrong about Appalachia*. Cleveland, OH: Belt Publishing.

Clark, Amy D., and Nancy M. Hayward, ed. 2013. *Talking Appalachian: Voice, Identity, and Community*. Lexington: University Press of Kentucky.

Hasty, Daniel. 2012. "This Might Could Help Us Better Understand Syntactic Variation: The Double Modal Construction in Tennessee English." Unpublished PhD diss., Michigan State University.

Keiser, Steven Hartman. 2012. *Pennsylvania German in the American Midwest*. Durham, NC: Duke University Press.

Lewis, Ronald L., and Dwight B. Billings. 1997. "Appalachian Culture and Economic Development: A Retrospective View on the Theory and Literature." *Journal of Appalachian Studies* 3, no. 1: 3–42.

Louden, Mark L. 2016. *Pennsylvania Dutch: The Story of an American Language*. Baltimore: Johns Hopkins University Press.

Reaser, Jeffrey, Eric Willbanks, Karissa Wojcik, and Walt Wolfram. 2018. *Language Variety in the New South: Contemporary Perspectives on Change and Variation*. Chapel Hill: University of North Carolina Press.

Reed, Paul E. 2016. "Sounding Appalachian: /aɪ/ Monophthongization, Rising Pitch Accents, and Rootedness." Unpublished PhD diss., University of South Carolina.

Schumann, William, and Rebecca Adkins Fletcher. 2016. *Appalachia Revisited: New Perspectives on Place, Tradition, and Progress*. Lexington: University of Kentucky Press.

Thomas, Erik R., ed. 2019. *Mexican American English: Substrate Influence and the Birth of an Ethnolect*. Cambridge: Cambridge University Press.

Williams, John Alexander. 2002. *Appalachia: A History*. Chapel Hill: University of North Carolina Press.

PART I
Linguistic and Regional Boundaries

CHAPTER 1

Just What and Where Are Appalachian Englishes?: Subregional Language Variation in Appalachia

J. Daniel Hasty

SUMMARY

This chapter focuses on the regional divides in Appalachia. By describing the varying definitions in relation to dialect boundaries, along with the most diagnostic dialect features, the chapter also points out the gaps in scholarship on regional language variation in Appalachia. It is important to show the range of diversity across the levels of language and the contrasts found within the region. The contrasts can be found in many parts of Appalachian life, including economic differences between urban and rural areas and connections between dialect regions. The most major division is between Northern Appalachia and Southern Appalachia. Within these regions, dialect variation and language change are headed in different directions.

INTRODUCTION

One of the first questions to answer regarding language in Appalachia is this: Just what exactly are these things we are calling *Appalachian Englishes*? How do Appalachian Englishes differ from other varieties of English? And what is the extent of language variation within Appalachia, as illustrated by our use of the pluralized Appalachian English*es*? While Appalachia is often perceived to be merely a part of the larger South, this characterization may not be the case for all of the region. Thus, we need to explore Appalachia's relationship to and distinctiveness from other varieties of English, which can be quite complex and variable. This chapter then attempts to provide some direction on regional and subregional language variation in Appalachia.

APPALACHIA AND OTHER REGIONS

Perhaps the best place to start is to situate Appalachian Englishes in relation to other varieties of English. First, it is important to realize that, when used by linguists, terms like *language* and *dialect* are not as exclusive as when used by the general public and that these terms are socially rather than linguistically defined. That is, separating varieties commonly considered dialects (e.g., Southern English or African American English) is not straightforward because they are often connected. Further, even attempting to divide up varieties of related languages (e.g., Spanish or Portuguese) is not as easy as many would initially believe. Because of this complexity, any discussion of language variety should take the question of scope into consideration, since at some level of abstraction all Englishes spoken in America are similar in some ways (e.g., in contrast to English spoken in Great Britain). However, at the same time it cannot be denied that there are differences within American English, which can be measured both linguistically and perceptually. So, at some level, in the United States and thus in Appalachia as well, we are all speaking what could at least broadly be labeled American English, yet there are also clear regional (and other social) differences that have created different varieties of this English.

The most widely accepted understanding of the major regional dialects in the United States is illustrated in figure 1.1 indicating at least four major dialect regions: North, South, Midwest, and West. This delineation of dialects is also paralleled through the general public's perception of where regional variation exists. Dennis Preston has investigated laypeople's perceptions of dialect boundaries in the United States by asking them to indicate on a map where people speak differently (cf. Preston 1997). Respondents to Preston's studies have shown the same basic agreement seen in the maps drawn from the usage studies like Carver (1987) and Labov, Ash, and Boberg (2006).

However, these large speech regions also have a degree of subregional variation within them. While Appalachia does not show up as one of the major regional varieties, it is certainly an important area between some of these larger regions. Carver's map divides up larger areas like the South into several smaller subregions including an Upper South and a Lower North in Appalachia. Others divide up these regions even further, for example Pederson (2001) delineates

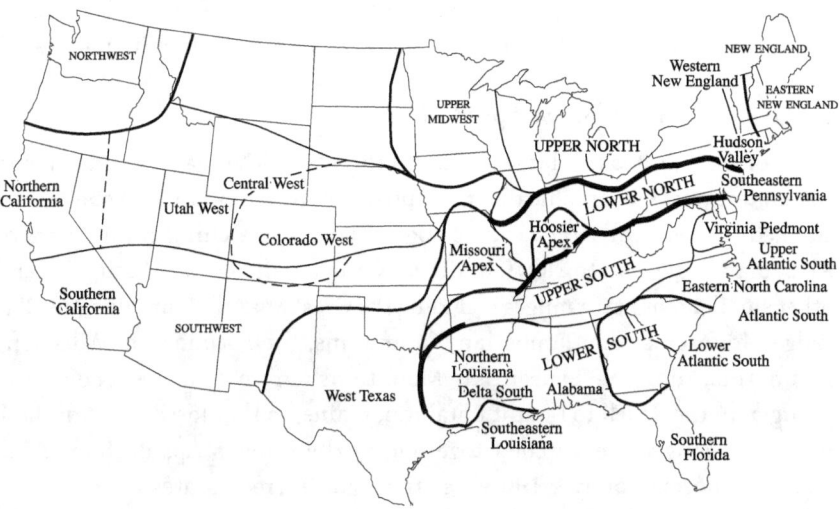

Figure 1.1. US Regional Dialects according to Carver (1987). From "The Major Dialect Regions Summarized" (figure 8.1) in *American Regional Dialects: A Word Geography* by Craig M. Carver, © University of Michigan Press, 1987.

---

eighteen subregions within the South, including some version of Appalachia that he calls the eastern South Midland Highlands. Preston (1997) also shows evidence for perceptually distinct subregions, including at least a part of Appalachia. Other language attitude studies show measurable perceived differences between subregional varieties (cf. Hasty 2018 for Southern subregional differences), and Cramer (2016, chapter 5 this volume) indicates perceived differences specifically within Appalachia.

So, coming back to our question of just what Appalachian Englishes are, the answer must be that Appalachian Englishes are many things depending on the level of abstraction you are using. Appalachian Englishes are certainly part of American English. Some of them may be part of other regions like Southern English or Midwestern English. But there is also both a perceptual and linguistic truth to the idea that they are distinct—something unique from those larger categories.

DEFINING APPALACHIA

We can now move on to the more specific question of where these other regions end and Appalachia begins. This question is quite difficult to answer, and it seems to really depend on who you ask. That is, are we talking about Appalachia geographically, politically, socially, perceptually, or linguistically?

Geographic Definitions of Appalachia

Much of what unites this large subregion together is the shared connection to the mountains. Geographically, the Appalachian Mountains are sometimes claimed (Fenneman 1917) as a geological whole stretching from northern Alabama all the way to Newfoundland, Canada, and encompassing several other smaller mountain ranges including the Great Smoky Mountains, the Blue Ridge Mountains, the Cumberland Mountains, the Poconos, the Allegheny Mountains, and the Laurentian Mountains. From Springer Mountain, Georgia, in the South to Mount Katahdin, Maine, in the North, most of these mountain ranges are stitched together by the famous Appalachian Trail, running approximately 2,190 miles through fourteen states (Appalachian Trail Conservancy 2018). This area is quite an expanse, but perhaps we can shorten it a bit since many geologists would place the northern boundary of the Appalachian Mountains in southern New York, given the differences in the structure and estimated age of the mountains north of this line (i.e., the Laurentians, Alleghenies, and Poconos) compared to the rest of these mountain ranges (Goddard Earth Sciences Data 2009). With this geographic definition of Appalachia, the region would be massive, stretching across at least part of nine or ten states. Even so, just having a common geographic form like a mountain range or a famous hiking trail does not necessarily give rise to the determination of a region, at least not a sociocultural region.

Political Definitions of Appalachia

In 1960, as a reaction to social problems of low income, high unemployment, low educational levels, and slow population growth in many parts of their states, governors from West Virginia, Maryland, Kentucky, Virginia, Tennessee, North Carolina, Alabama, and Georgia formed the Conference of Appalachian Governors and petitioned President Kennedy for federal aid (Roosevelt 1964). Therefore, one official definition of Appalachia could include at least parts of just those states. In an attempt to understand the scope of the problem and propose a plan for federal aid, in 1963 President Kennedy formed the President's Appalachian Regional Commission (PARC), which, along with cabinet officials, included governors from the states of Pennsylvania and Ohio. So, these two states could be added to the definition of Appalachia. Further, the original PARC report itself provided a description of what was officially meant by the term *Appalachia*: "a mountain land boldly upthrust between the prosperous Eastern seaboard and the industrial Middle West—a highland region which sweeps diagonally across ten states from northern Pennsylvania to northern Alabama" (Roosevelt 1964, xv).

Based on the PARC report, in 1965 President Johnson submitted legislation to Congress that was passed as the Appalachian Regional Development Act and formally established the Appalachian Regional Commission (ARC) to carry out the programs and plans contained in the legislation. Within this act, a final legal definition of Appalachia is given. The act lists specific counties within the states that are to be considered part of this legal definition of Appalachia that would be able to receive aid from the ARC. Counties in part of all of the states from the original PARC are included: West Virginia, Maryland, Kentucky, Virginia, Tennessee, North Carolina, Alabama, Georgia, Pennsylvania, and Ohio, as well as the addition of certain counties in New York, South Carolina, and Mississippi (Appalachian Regional Development Act 1965). This final, legal definition including 420 counties in thirteen states is the definition currently being followed by the ARC (ARC 2018).

While these political definitions may make the boundaries of Appalachia appear rather clear cut, there were questions from early on whether this prescribed thirteen-state area actually constituted a region socially. To account for these differences, based on "contiguous regions of relatively homogeneous characteristics (topography, demographics, and economics)" (ARC 2009), the ARC currently maintains a five-way subregional distinction within the official definition of Appalachian: Northern (Pennsylvania and New York), North Central (West Virginia and Ohio), Central (eastern Kentucky, extreme southwestern Virginia, northcentral Tennessee), South Central (southwest Virginia, northeast Tennessee, and North Carolina), and Southern (South Carolina, Georgia, Alabama, and Mississippi) (see fig. 1.2). However, ARC is a politically created organization, and thus their definition of the region should be considered with that mindset. For example, Watts (1978, 7) notes that the additions of counties in New York and Mississippi were for "political reasons" rather than cultural or geographic cohesion and that these additions "resulted in a loss of both physical and socio-economic uniformity."

Perceptual Definitions of Appalachia

Using different measures of cultural unity, sociologists and geographers have shown an Appalachian cultural area somewhat different from the ARC political definition, with different subregional breakdowns. These studies have attempted to gain a more accurate picture of Appalachia by studying people's perceptions of Appalachia and its location, for as Batteau (1990) argues, in

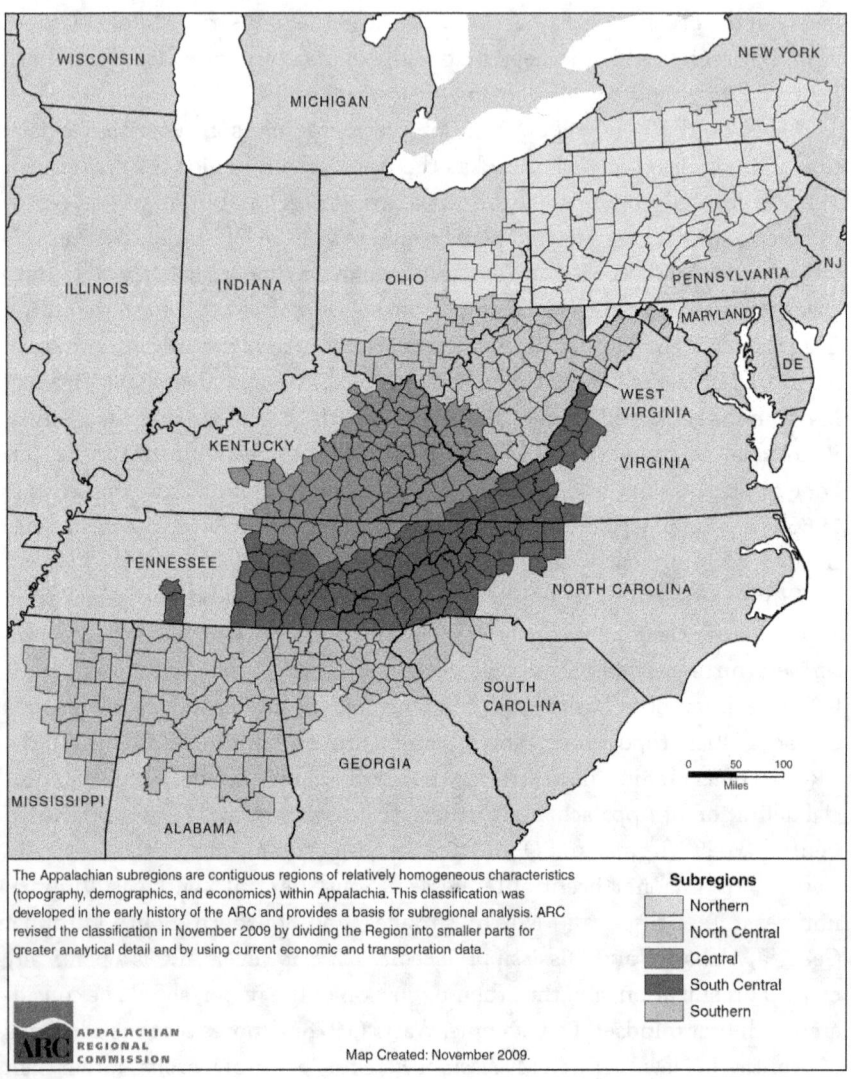

Figure 1.2. ARC Appalachian Subregions. From the Appalachian Regional Commission (www.arc.gov).

many ways Appalachia is a social construct. In a large-scale study (*N* 2,397), Ulack and Raitz (1981) ask college students from both within and outside the region where Appalachia exists. They find a much smaller perceived Appalachian region, with only a 10 percent overall agreement with the ARC delineation, which excludes Mississippi, and with less than 20 percent of the respondents including Alabama, Georgia, Pennsylvania, or New York, calling into question the far northern and southern edges from the ARC definition. Ulack and Raitz show a very small core of 80 percent agreement centered on southern West Virginia (basically Mercer County); a larger 60 percent agreement line including West Virginia, southeast Kentucky, southwest Virginia, northeast Tennessee, and Western North Carolina; and lastly a 40 percent agreement adding in small portions of southern Pennsylvania, northwest South Carolina, and northern Georgia. Thus, their study describes a perceptual center in the central Southern parts of Appalachia, indicating a northern and southern subregional distinction.

Cooper, Knotts, and Elders (2011) take a different approach and study respondents' self-proclaimed Appalachian identity by counting the names of businesses including *Appalachia(n)*. From this self-naming of Appalachia, Cooper, Knotts, and Elders find a three-way distinction similar to Ulack and Raitz, with a core area of Appalachia in northeast Tennessee, Western North Carolina, southeast Kentucky, southwest Virginia, and extreme southern West Virginia. Next, they identify a larger area including more of North Carolina, Tennessee, Kentucky, and Virginia along with south and middle West Virginia. Finally, they identify a third area on the southern and northern edges including parts of northern Georgia, northeast Alabama, northern Mississippi, and northwest South Carolina in the south as well as southeast Ohio, northern West Virginia, central Pennsylvania, and southern New York in the north. Thus, they find a self-defined, major perceptual area of Appalachia positioned in the central Southern states (which here notably excludes most of West Virginia), a second area including slightly more of these core states as well as most of West Virginia, and a marginal perceptual area on the far southern and northern edges. So, while the media and the general public may lump all of Appalachia together, it is clear from the research that there are differences throughout Appalachia.

The people within this region may even hold quite different beliefs about being considered part of Appalachia. Hazen and Fluharty (2004) mention how many of their northern West Virginian respondents do not necessarily identify with the label of *Appalachian*, perhaps from the great stigma attached to the region or, as discussed below, from competing ideological associations with nearby northern urban regions. Additionally, people in southern parts of Appalachia may not realize that they live in an area believed to be different from the rest of the South until they travel outside it. For example, I grew up in a small farming community in northeast Tennessee. Though I could see the Appalachian Mountains from my bedroom window and lived just a few miles from the Appalachian Fairground and many local businesses with *Appalachia* in their name,[1] it was not until I went to college outside Appalachia in Middle Tennessee (on the western side of the Cumberland Plateau) and then later to graduate school in Auburn, Alabama, that I realized I was from somewhere more than just Southern. People in Middle Tennessee and Alabama, who I believed to be "fellow Southerners," consistently pointed out how differently I talked from them, specifically mentioning how I pronounced words like *price* (see /aɪ/ ungliding below and in Reed chapter 2). Thus, the perception of Appalachia and differences within it may be driven by factors such as proximity to other contrasting regions, and perceptions of Appalachia are also intimately tied to personal identity construction (Greene 2010; Reed 2014; Cramer 2016).

Linguistic Definitions of Appalachian English(es)

While these geographic and political perceptions of Appalachia are important, this book is primarily interested in understanding the language differences in the region. Wolfram and Christian's (1975, 1976) pioneering work *Appalachian Speech* is the first and most extensive discussion of language within Appalachia. Wolfram and Christian describe close to eighty different linguistic features cutting across all the levels of grammar: phonological (sounds), lexical (words), and morphosyntactic (sentences).

As Wolfram and Christian note, many of these features were either known at the time or have been found since to be present in other varieties of American English, especially Southern English but also other nonstandard varieties of American English (e.g., nonstandard agreement, regularization of verbs, multiple negation). From the beginning, Wolfram and Christian (1976, 29–30) note that their definition of English in Appalachia should be qualified by the region they were focused on (specifically Mercer and Monroe Counties in southern West Virginia) and that other social factors (since they were focused solely on rural, working-class speakers) would certainly show variation with other Appalachian varieties. However, given its breadth of coverage, their work has often been taken as emblematic of a homogenous Appalachian English containing every feature described in their book.

Wolfram (1984) explicitly tries to head off such monolithic views, stating that, like all language, Appalachian Englishes would exhibit variation and change governed by social factors like class, age, gender, rurality, and style. While Wolfram and Christian (1976) and others have suggested that there may be some small set of linguistic features that could be identified as uniquely Appalachian, Wolfram (1984, 223) notes that what is perceived as Appalachian is probably best understood as implicational sets of features rather than a unique group of features not shared with other varieties. Thus, Appalachian Englishes on the whole should be thought of as some quantitative combination of the features mentioned in the present work, and linguistic variation within Appalachia should be expected. See the later chapters of this book for other categories of variation, especially by ethnicity and gender. The remainder of this chapter will outline some of the subregional differences within Appalachian Englishes.

SUBREGIONAL VARIATION IN APPALACHIAN ENGLISHES

In light of the discussion above, I understand why scholars divide Appalachia into at least three parts following the distinctions made in Ulack and Raitz (1981) and Cooper, Knotts, and Elders (2011). Yet given that the far edges of what the ARC has called Appalachia (New York in the North and Mississippi, Alabama, and Georgia in the South) have been called into question in the perceptual studies of geographers, sociologists, and linguists, this discussion will not consider these outer edges to be a major part of the region. Rather, I limit my understanding of the subregions of Appalachia into a more basic two-way distinction between what I call *Northern Appalachia,* including West Virginia and southern Pennsylvania, and *Southern Appalachia,* including southeast Kentucky, southwest Virginia, northeast Tennessee, and Western North Carolina. This distinction combines the ARC subregions of Central and South Central together as Southern Appalachia and North Central and Northern together as Northern Appalachia.

Major Phonological Differences

/aɪ/ **Ungliding**

When discussing specific Appalachian features involved in subregional variation, /aɪ/ ungliding is perhaps the most clear cut and recognizable. /aɪ/ ungliding involves the reduction or deletion of the upglide in the vowel in words like *pride* [praɪd], pronounced as something like "prahd" [praɪd] (see Reed chapter 2). This feature is not confined to Appalachia as it is also a prominent feature of Southern English and one of the most noticeable features identifying a speaker as Southern in general. Because of the salience of this feature, in the *Atlas of North American English,* Labov, Ash, and Boberg (2006) use /aɪ/ ungliding to define the boundary of Southern English. In modern Southern English, the ungliding of /aɪ/ is primarily confined to words where it occurs before voiced consonants (like *pride*) or at the end of a word (like *pry*). However, one of the socially distinguishing features of at least some Appalachian varieties is the ungliding of /aɪ/ before voiceless consonants like in the word *price* (Thomas 2001).

Labov, Ash, and Boberg (2006) primarily confine prevoiceless /aɪ/ ungliding to what they call the Inland South (southeast Kentucky, southwest Virginia, northeast Tennessee, Western North Carolina, and some parts of extreme southern West Virginia), which is what I have called Southern Appalachia. Several studies of Appalachian Englishes note prevoiceless /aɪ/ ungliding in Southern Appalachia (Wolfram and Christian 1976; Irons 2007b; Greene 2010; Reed 2014), while in Northern Appalachia /aɪ/ ungliding is confined primarily to prevoiced and word-final environments (Hazen and Fluharty 2004). /aɪ/ ungliding has been shown to be sensitive to variation in age (Irons 2007b; Reed 2014), urban/rural distinction (Labov, Ash, and Boberg 2006; Irons 2007b), as well as Appalachian identity (Greene 2010; Reed 2014). Therefore, it is understandable that this feature would be one of the most recognizable differences between Northern Appalachia and Southern Appalachia.

/æ/ Breaking

Another major distinction between Northern and Southern Appalachian speech is the "breaking" of the vowel sound in words like *pass* [pæs] into a diphthong pronunciation including an additional upglide, resulting in a pronunciation with two or even three syllables. For example, *pass* is pronounced as "pa.ahs" [pæːʲæs]. This breaking of /æ/ is primarily what people perceive as the "Southern Drawl" (Feagin 1987). This feature, as well as the vowel lengthening in other parts of the Southern Vowel Shift (Reed chapter 2), has given rise to the popular stereotype that Southerners talk slow.

Labov, Ash, and Boberg (2006) show /æ/ breaking confined to the South and going no farther north than Tennessee and North Carolina. While /æ/ breaking is not specifically unique to Appalachia, it does help to create another important distinction between Northern and Southern Appalachia since Southern Appalachia participates in /æ/ breaking while Northern Appalachia does not.

Low-Back Vowel Merger

A third major phonological difference between Northern and Southern Appalachia is participation in the low-back vowel merger, where the vowel sounds in words like *cot* [kɑt] and *caught* [kɔt] are merged together and both pronounced as *cot* [kɑt]. The low-back vowel merger is quite widespread across the West and some areas of the North but generally not in the Midwest or the South (Labov, Ash, and Boberg 2006). With Appalachia in the middle of these regions, participation in the merger is variable.

Earlier studies (Hartman 1985) did not indicate Appalachian participation in the low-back vowel merger; however, the current situation has changed with this feature showing subregional variation. Hazen (2005) reports extensive adoption of the low-back vowel merger in West Virginia, and Labov, Ash, and Boberg (2006) show this merger in most of the area I have labeled as Northern Appalachia. Southern Appalachia shows much less participation in the low-back vowel merger. However, Irons (2007a) indicates that participation in the merger may be changing for at least parts of Southern Appalachia. His study in Kentucky shows that, while there is still some resistance, the low-back vowel merger is gaining ground, especially with younger speakers. Thus, this phonological feature points to variation within Appalachian Englishes as well as some unity, for perhaps Southern Appalachia is just a few generations behind Northern Appalachia in fully adopting the merger.

Subregional Comparisons

Beyond these phonological distinctions, little formal study has directly compared subregional Appalachian varieties to each other. This hole in the scholarship is partly because of the logistical constraints on collecting sociolinguistic data in an area as large as Appalachia. Many studies have confined themselves to a single community of Appalachia (e.g., Wolfram and Christian 1976) in order to have the adequate time and resources to devote to the study. As Hazen and Fluharty (2004) point out, it is not necessarily a problem that previous studies have only focused on a single area within Appalachia; however, they call for studies of other areas within Appalachia in order to gain a complete picture of the region. In an attempt to add to our understanding of Appalachian subregional variation, Becky Childs and I set out to do a large-scale survey of variation within Appalachia, comparing Northern and Southern Appalachia, as well as Southern English. The following is a brief report of the preliminary results of that study (see Hasty and Childs 2016 for the specifics).

Our study utilized an online survey[2] that presented respondents from Northern Appalachia (*n* 104), Southern Appalachia (*n* 114), and the non-Appalachian South (*n* 115) with twenty-nine features associated with Appalachian Englishes (see companion website for the complete list) cutting across all levels of the grammar (lexical, phonological, and morphosyntactic). We asked the respondents to report both their usage of and their familiarity with hearing these features.

Appalachian Englishes and Southern English

Grouping both subregions of Appalachia together to compare with the Southern respondents, there is an indication that Appalachian Englishes are something unique from Southern English. Lexically, some traditional words like *bald* (a mountain above the tree line) and *poke* (a sack) are primarily used only in Appalachian Englishes, yet more distinctions are seen in the phonological features. While both Appalachian and Southern respondents report high usage of the Southern Vowel Shift (see Reed chapter 2), the Appalachian respondents lead the South for hearing /aɪ/ ungliding and back vowel fronting (e.g., pronouncing the vowel in *goat* [got] more in the front of the mouth closer to the vowel in *but* [bət] or *face* [fes]). These responses indicate that Appalachian respondents seem to be paying more attention to the first and last stages of the Southern Vowel Shift compared to their general Southern counterparts, perhaps an indication of the Southern Vowel Shift's continued importance in Appalachian identity construction (Irons 2007b; Greene 2010; Reed 2014; Hazen 2018).

Additionally, two morphosyntactic items are led by the combined Appalachian groups: positive *anymore* (*anymore* used in a non-negative sentence, e.g., *It seems to rain a lot here, anymore*) and zero plural measurement (lack of the plural morpheme *–s* on measurement terms, e.g., *That road is five mile_ long*). So, overall, there appears to be an indication of subtle differences between Appalachian Englishes and Southern English, giving some credence to Wolfram and Christian's (1976) belief that there may be some set of combined features that can be uniquely identified as Appalachian.

Southern Appalachia, Northern Appalachia, and Southern English

Yet, the relationship between the Appalachian subregions and the general South is rather complex. Though the Appalachian subregions pattern together for some features, often we see Southern Appalachia behaving more like the South, while Northern Appalachia patterns differently from both of these regions. For example, Southern Appalachia patterns with the South for greater use of several traditional words like *y'all*, *carry* (for *take*, e.g., *Can you carry me to the store?*), *tote* (for *transport*, e.g., *Tote this to the barn for me*), and *yonder* (as a measure of distance, e.g., *It is over yonder*). Additionally, Southern Appalachia speakers pattern closely with the South for greater use of morphosyntactic features like the use of the double modal (two modal auxiliary verbs in the same sentence, e.g., *I might could take you*) and *fixin to* (for *about to*, e.g., *It looks like it's fixin to rain*), while Northern Appalachia again lags behind. In fact, the only individual feature that is led by the Northern Appalachian respondents is usage of positive *anymore*. This finding may be expected given this feature's early attestations in areas of Northern Appalachia and some northern Midwestern states (Murray 1993).

Southern Appalachia and Northern Appalachia

The differences between Southern and Northern Appalachia become clearer when comparing the subregions directly to each other. For the lexical items, Southern Appalachia leads Northern Appalachia in using many traditional lexical items including *y'uns*, *y'all*, *poke*, and *bald*. Phonologically, as stated above, Southern Appalachia and Northern Appalachia pattern together for the first and last stages of the Southern Vowel Shift, yet for other stages of this shift, Southern Appalachian respondents show greater usage of lax and tense vowel merging before /l/ (e.g., *feel* and *fill* pronounced the same). Additionally, Southern Appalachia leads Northern Appalachia in the usage of the *pin/pen* merger (e.g., *pen* and *pin* pronounced the same).

The differences between Southern and Northern Appalachia are most distinct when looking at the morphosyntactic features. Southern Appalachia leads Northern Appalachia in use of several features: double modals, *fixin to*, and *a*-prefixing (e.g., *I was* a-running *down the road*). The well-known Appalachian *a*-prefixing being maintained in Southern Appalachia is especially interesting when compared to previous work showing it to be dying out in Northern Appalachia (Hazen, Butcher, and King 2010).

As indicated in previous studies (e.g., Hazen 2006), it seems that Northern Appalachia is losing many of the traditional features previously associated with Appalachia, yet in Southern Appalachia many of these features are being retained (e.g., Childs and Mallinson 2004; Irons 2007b; Hasty 2011; Reed 2014). We can perhaps make more sense of the variation between Northern and Southern Appalachia by looking at some social differences between these subregions.

REGIONAL PROXIMITY AND URBANITY

One important social difference between the subregions is their proximity to other regions, especially the South. For Northern Appalachia, Pennsylvania is located completely outside what linguists agree to be the South (Labov, Ash, and Boberg 2006), and while West Virginia is often included with the South, it is quite far removed from the rest of the South (not to mention its unique social history, becoming a state by seceding from Virginia at the onset of the Civil War). West Virginia is a border state between the South and the Midwest and even the North, and because of its proximity to these other regions, West Virginians often have to negotiate an identity between one of these other regions (Hazen 2005). In contrast, the Southern Appalachian state of Kentucky is also a border state with a complicated identity, torn between the Midwest and the South, yet the Appalachian areas of southeast Kentucky are much closer to Southern states like Tennessee and Virginia than to Ohio (see Cramer 2016 and Cramer chapter 5). The other states I have labeled as Southern Appalachia are all unequivocally located in the South and thus have proximities to subregions inside the South rather than other speech regions. Proximity is important given that linguistic distinctions are often most notable when given a contrast. In Southern Appalachia, the closest contrast is Southern English, while in Northern Appalachia it is a Midwestern or Northern variety.

It is also important to consider Appalachia's connection to urban areas. As Wolfram (1984) points out, the urban/rural distinction should be taken into consideration for language variation in Appalachia, and Cramer (2016) discusses the importance of urbanity in Kentucky for a perceived allegiance to regions other than Appalachia, like the Midwest. Technically speaking, few places in Appalachia, if any, could truly be considered urban other than Pittsburgh, Pennsylvania (population greater than two million[3]). The US Census Bureau primarily uses population density to identify urban areas with a threshold of at least 1,000 people per square mile (Ratcliffe et al. 2016). With this measure, the majority of Appalachia is decidedly rural, with population densities lower than many other regions of the United States. Based on the 2000 census data, the only county in Appalachia that could officially be considered an urbanized area is Allegheny County in Northern Appalachian Pennsylvania (population density 1,756/square mile) anchored by Pittsburgh, while the only other counties that even come close are Knox County, Tennessee, (population density 752/square mile) centered around Knoxville and Hamilton County, Tennessee, (population density 568/square mile) centered around Chattanooga. All other counties within Appalachia contain fewer than 500 people per square mile (ARC 2000). With Appalachia being so rural, perceptions of urbanity and proximity to perceived urban areas are important to consider and further highlight subregional differences.

In a region that is decidedly rural, perceptions of urbanity and what constitutes "the big city" are certainly different from other, more populated regions. In much of Northern Appalachia, there is a rather close proximity to true urban areas, all of which are clearly outside of the South: Pittsburgh, PA; Philadelphia, PA; Columbus, OH; and Washington, DC.[4] That is, Northern Appalachia is closer to Northern and Midwestern urban centers than to urban areas in the South. For example, from the center of West Virginia, the closest urban areas (within 300–400 miles) are Washington, DC, Columbus, OH, and Pittsburgh, PA. However, in Southern Appalachia the closest urban areas are either the much smaller Appalachian cities of Knoxville, TN (population 186,239 within city limits and 303,625 in metro), and Asheville, NC (population 89,121 within city limits and 424,858 in metro), or larger urban areas in the general South like Charlotte, NC; Raleigh, NC; and Atlanta, GA.

These urban differences, then, help to explain why in Northern Appalachia many canonical, vernacular features of Appalachia are dying out and why in our survey Northern Appalachia is often not patterning with Southern Appalachia or the South. Many Northern Appalachian speakers are apparently beginning to align more with non-Southern varieties, perhaps targeting urban varieties from outside the region. However, in Southern Appalachia with its proximity to the South and to urban areas either within Appalachia or the South, many younger speakers have been instead revitalizing some of the older Appalachian features (see Hasty and Childs 2013).

CONCLUSION

So, while we have seen that Appalachia is a unique region historically associated with the larger South, we have also seen that there are subregional differences within Appalachia. While there are certainly still features (or perhaps a certain constellation of features) that may unify Appalachia as a whole, there is also good evidence to propose the plural Appalachian Englishes view of this speech region. I have sketched out this variation here in terms of a Northern and Southern divide, and many of these subregional differences seem to stem from proximities to other regions (i.e., the Midwest, the North, or the South). There is also an indication that urbanity and perceptions of the closest "big city" may be at work in subregional variation, especially as areas of Appalachia become increasingly less isolated. More research on variation within Appalachia is needed, particularly research directly comparing different subregions and different constructions of urbanity. Additionally, social identity is keenly important to the variation seen throughout Appalachia, and any true understanding of Appalachian variation must take individuals' attitudes about who they are into account, as these have a direct bearing on both the uniqueness and the variation of Appalachian Englishes.

Notes

1. The nearby city of Kingsport, Tennessee, was the second-most self-identified Appalachian city in Cooper, Knotts, and Elders (2011).
2. For access to the survey, see http://snap.coastal.edu/snapwebhost/s.asp?k=1564157 40879.
3. Including the greater metro area. Population estimates given are according to the 2016 US Census unless otherwise noted.

4. Preston (1997) shows Washington, DC, associated with northeastern cities and thus not a part of the South.

References

Appalachian Regional Commission. 2000. *Census Population Change, 1990–2000.* Accessed 19 January 2018. https://www.arc.gov/reports/custom_report.asp?report_id=16.

Appalachian Regional Commission. 2009. *Subregions in Appalachia.* Accessed 19 January 2018. https://www.arc.gov/research/mapsofappalachia.asp?map_id=31.

Appalachian Regional Commission. 2018. "The Appalachian Region." Accessed 19 January 2018. https://www.arc.gov/appalachian_region/theappalachianregion.asp.

Appalachian Regional Development Act. 1965. Title 40. Subtitle IV. Accessed 19 January 2018. https://www.arc.gov/images/newsroom/publications/arda/unitedstatescode title40subtitleiv.pdf.

Appalachian Trail Conservancy. 2018. Appalachian Trail Conservancy home page. Accessed 9 February 2018. http://www.appalachiantrail.org/home/explore-the-trail.

Batteau, Allen. 1990. *The Invention of Appalachia.* Tucson: University of Arizona Press.

Carver, Craig. 1987. *American Regional Dialects: A Word Geography.* Ann Arbor: University of Michigan Press.

Childs, Becky, and Christine Mallinson. 2004. "African American English in Appalachia: Dialect Accommodation and Substrate Influence." *English World-Wide* 25, no. 1: 27–50.

Cooper, Christopher, H. Gibbs Knotts, and Kathy Elders. 2011. "A Geography of Appalachian Identity." *Southeastern Geographer* 51, no. 3: 457–72.

Cramer, Jennifer. 2016. *Contested Southernness: The Linguistic Production and Perception of Identities in the Borderlands.* Publication of the American Dialect Society 100. Durham, NC: Duke University Press.

Feagin, Crawford. 1987. "A Closer Look at the Southern Drawl: Variation Taken to Extremes." In *Variation in Language: NWAV-XV at Stanford*, 137–50. Stanford, CA: Stanford University Department of Linguistics.

Fenneman, Neven. 1917. "Physiographic Divisions of the United States." *Annals of the Association of American Geographers* 6: 46–59.

Goddard Earth Sciences Data. 2009. "Appalachian Mountains." National Aeronautics and Space Administration. Accessed 19 January 2018. https://web.archive.org/web/20161201090927/http://daac.gsfc.nasa.gov/geomorphology/geo_2/geo_plate_t-11.shtml.

Greene, Rebecca. 2010. "Language, Ideology, and Identity in Rural Eastern Kentucky." PhD diss., Stanford University. https://purl.stanford.edu/fh361zh5489.

Hartman, James W. 1985. "Guide to Pronunciation." In *Dictionary of American Regional English* 1: xli–lxi.

Hasty, J. Daniel. 2011. "I Might Not Would Say That: A Sociolinguistic Investigation of Double Modal Acceptance." *University of Pennsylvania Working Papers in Linguistics* 17, no. 2: 91–98.

Hasty, J. Daniel. 2018. "They Sound Better Than We Do: Language Attitudes in Alabama." In *Speaking of Alabama: The History, Diversity, Function, and Change of Language*, edited by Thomas Nunnally, 192–200. Tuscaloosa: University of Alabama Press.

Hasty, J. Daniel, and Becky Childs. 2013. "The Old Is New Again: Curvilinear Patterns of Linguistic Change in Appalachia." Paper presented at New Ways of Analyzing Variation 42, Pittsburgh, PA, October 2013.

Hasty, J. Daniel, and Becky Childs. 2016. "Language Change and Identity in the New Appalachia." Paper presented at the American Dialect Society Annual Meeting, Washington, DC, January 2016.

Hazen, Kirk. 2005. "Mergers in the Mountains: West Virginia Division and Unification." *English World-Wide* 26, no. 2: 199–221.
Hazen, Kirk. 2006. "The Final Days of Appalachian Heritage Language." In *Language Variation and Change in the American Midland*, edited by Beth Simon and Thomas Murray, 129–50. Philadelphia: John Benjamins.
Hazen, Kirk. 2018. "The Contested Southernness of Appalachia." *American Speech* 93, no. 3-4: 374–408.
Hazen, Kirk, and Ellen Fluharty. 2004. "Defining Appalachian English." In *Linguistic Diversity in the South: Changing Codes, Practices, and Ideology*, edited by Margaret Bender, 50–65. Athens: University of Georgia Press.
Hazen, Kirk, Paige Butcher, and Ashley King. 2010. "Unvernacular Appalachia: An Empirical Perspective on West Virginia Dialect Variation." *English Today* 26, no. 4: 13–22.
Irons, Terry. 2007a. "On the Status of Low Back Vowels in Kentucky English: More Evidence of Merger." *Language Variation and Change* 19, no. 2: 137–80.
Irons, Terry. 2007b. "On the Southern Shift in Appalachian English." *Penn Working Papers in Linguistics* 13, no. 2: 121–34.
Labov, William, Sharon Ash, and Charles Boberg. 2006. *The Atlas of North America English: Phonetics, Phonology, and Sound Change*. New York: Mouton de Gruyter.
Murray, Thomas E. 1993. "Positive *Anymore* in the Midwest." In *Heartland English: Variation and Transition in the American Midwest*, edited by Timothy C. Frazer, 173–86. Tuscaloosa: University of Alabama Press.
Pederson, Lee. 2001. "Dialects." In *English in North America*, edited by John Algeo, 253–90. Vol. 6 of *The Cambridge History of the English Language*. Cambridge: Cambridge University Press.
Preston, Dennis. 1997. "The South: The Touchstone." In *Language Variety in the South Revisited*, edited by Cynthia Bernstein, Thomas Nunnally, and Robin Sabino, 311–51. Tuscaloosa: University of Alabama Press.
Ratcliffe, Michael, Charlynn Burd, Kelly Holder, and Alison Fields. 2016. *Defining Rural at the U.S. Census Bureau: American Community Survey and Geography Brief*. US Department of Commerce, Economics, and Statistics Administration.
Reed, Paul. 2014. "Inter- and Intra-generational Monophthongization and Appalachian Identity." *Southern Journal of Linguistics* 38, no. 1: 159–94.
Roosevelt, Franklin D. Jr. 1964. *Appalachia: A Report by the President's Appalachian Regional Commission*. Washington: Government Printing Office. https://www.arc.gov/noindex/aboutarc/history/parc/PARCReport.pdf.
Thomas, Erik. 2001. *An Acoustic Analysis of Vowel Variation in New World English*. Publication of the American Dialect Society 85. Durham, NC: Duke University Press.
Ulack, Richard, and Karl Raitz. 1981. "Appalachia: A Comparison of the Cognitive and Appalachian Regional Commission Regions." *Southeastern Geographer* 21, no. 1: 40–53.
Watts, Ann DeWitt. 1978. "Does the Appalachian Regional Commission Really Represent a Region?" *Southeastern Geographer* 18: 19–36.
Wolfram, Walt. 1984. "Is There an 'Appalachian English?'" *Appalachian Journal* 11, no. 3: 215–24.
Wolfram, Walt, and Donna Christian. 1975. *Sociolinguistic Variables in Appalachian Dialects*. Report for National Institute of Education of the Department of Health, Education, and Welfare, NIE-G-74–0026.M. Arlington, VA: Center for Applied Linguistics. https://files.eric.ed.gov/fulltext/ED112687.pdf.
Wolfram, Walt, and Donna Christian. 1976. *Appalachian Speech*. Arlington, VA: Center for Applied Linguistics.

CHAPTER 2

Phonological Possibilities in Appalachian Englishes

Paul E. Reed

SUMMARY

This chapter summarizes and reviews the literature on phonological and phonetic variation in Appalachian Englishes. The focus falls on the features and variation that are current and thriving in the twenty-first century among consonants, vowels, and other features, such as intonation. Many of these features have received quite a bit of scholarly attention but have often been described in categorical terms while the reality is much more nuanced. A good example is /aɪ/ ungliding, which has highly variable usage but is stereotypically cast as a common trait for speakers of Appalachian Englishes. This chapter examines such common features but also considers the diversity and variability of their use.

INTRODUCTION

Humans are a noisy species. We make lots of sounds. We yell when we are at stadiums cheering on sports teams; we whistle for pets; we react in pain when we stub our toe; and we also talk, a lot! We can make many different sounds, but we only use a small subset of those when we talk. We are quite chatty creatures, first making coos and cries as an infant but very quickly moving on to syllables and words within the first year or so of life. However, when we look at spoken language, we can start to classify and describe the sounds that we use for speech. We use these sounds in contrasting combinations to create meaning. For example, if we swap the vowel sound in the word *cat* /kæt/ with the vowel sound from the word *but* /bət/, we get a new word with a new meaning,

/kət/, the word *cut*. When the change in sounds results in different meanings, the contrasting sounds are considered *phonemes*. This distinction is a fundamental use of sounds in language, to contrast different meanings. Languages can differ in how many phonemes they have (or how many sound contrasts they maintain) (Clark, Yallop, and Fletcher 2007). Varieties of English have around forty phonemes, depending on the dialect (Ladefoged and Disner 2012). Phonemes are mental sounds, the patterns we use for perception and contrast to tell words apart. This system means that speakers of English tend to interpret the pronunciations of /t/ in the word *top* and the word *stop* as the "same" even though they are not. Since we English speakers think of these sounds as the same, /t/ is a phoneme, a contrast unit, of English.

However, if you say these two words, you will notice that when you say *top*, there is a big puff of air that comes out during the /t/. When you say *stop*, however, there is no big puff of air during the /t/. The actual way that we articulate the two versions of /t/ is different. In *top*, we use aspiration and represent it like [tʰ] (note the square brackets are for the actual pronunciation). In *stop*, we use a plain version of the phoneme, and we represent it as [t]. We English speakers do not interpret these as being different sounds, even though we articulate them differently. In English, these two sounds, [tʰ] and [t], are *allophones* or variations on a phoneme. We mentally interpret these two as the same sound even though the actual phonetics (how we physically produce the sounds) are different.

The English varieties of Appalachia have been described as some of the most "divergent" varieties of American English (Wolfram and Christian 1976, 1). In particular, the ways that Appalachians articulate and pronounce syllables and words are quite different from many other non-Southern varieties. Sometimes, Appalachian speakers use completely different patterns of sounds than other North American English varieties. Linguists describe these differences in two ways. First, the *phonetics* of Appalachia is different in that some sounds are pronounced differently, and second, sometimes the *phonology* is different in that the overall patterns of which sounds occur is somewhat distinct (either different phonemes, allophones, or sound patterns). What these distinctions mean is that sometimes Appalachians have the same system as other US English speakers, but the way they pronounce the sound will be a little different (phonetics), and other times, the patterns and predictable occurrence of sounds are different (phonology). The differences from standard American varieties are not haphazard or random. Standard American varieties is an umbrella term for the types of English that we learn about in school, that appear on news broadcasts, and that do not have stigmatized, recognizable regional features. In contrast, English varieties in Appalachia have systematic differences from standard American varieties, and the differences can be accurately described. Importantly, the differences do not come from errors or incorrectness. The current chapter will describe these differences from standard American varieties but will also discuss the variation within Appalachian Englishes as well.

A NOTE ABOUT APPALACHIAN VARIETIES

There is a persistent myth about Appalachian English varieties: namely that they are often described as "Elizabethan" or "Chaucerian," preserving very old features of English. This mistaken belief leads many people to think that these varieties are some type of antiquated versions of English, little changed from when immigrants began arriving to the region in the seventeenth and eighteenth centuries. Such a belief is false (Montgomery 1999; Cramer 2014), but it is telling. Often, when people (and sometimes linguists) write about Appalachia, they overlook the ways that Appalachian varieties are similar to other varieties.

Appalachia is a dynamic region with language varieties that are equally dynamic. Some of the features in the region are not any different from those sounds in other regions, particularly southern US regions. This similarity is a point that needs to be highlighted, particularly as we discuss ways in which Appalachian varieties are different. Many times, the differences are matters of quantity, where something occurs more often in Appalachia, and not a matter of quality, where something is unique to Appalachia. And, like all places, there is considerable variation within the communities and subregions that comprise Appalachia. This fact means that some Appalachian varieties will have every feature that I describe in this chapter, while others may have only a handful. There also may be speakers who have none of these features.

Since Appalachia is stigmatized in the broader American society, most Appalachians are keenly aware of their speech (Greene 2010; Reed 2014, 2016). Some of the features described below are closely associated with the region, with home. Thus, when the feature is present in speech, the speaker is potentially using the feature as a kind of signal of belonging, to show that Appalachia is important to their sense of self. In my research, I call this sense of belonging rootedness (Reed 2016), and it impacts many of the features described below. Some Appalachian speakers have a strong sense of rootedness and, as a result, use many of the features or a greater percentage of the features. Other speakers may not have the same sense of belonging, or perhaps do not want to face the social stigma that using the features might bring, and as a result, they avoid the features or use relatively fewer of them.

I make these last points to underscore that the features described below should be considered possibilities in the varieties of Appalachia. Not every Appalachian will use them all, or they may only use them in certain contexts. Other speakers may use them all quite frequently in all contexts. This complexity is one of the beautiful aspects of language—speakers get to express different parts of their identities. Now, on to the sounds!

APPALACHIAN SOUNDS

The following sections outline some of the phonological features of Appalachian Englishes. When linguists look at the sounds of a region, there are two main divisions in the types of sounds: vowels and consonants. Consonants are sounds that are made with some kind of constriction (narrowing) in the vocal tract (basically, the "tube" that runs from your larynx to your lips) (Ladefoged and Disner 2012). I discuss the consonantal variation first, as there is not as much contrast with other varieties for consonants. Then, I discuss the differences in vowels. Vowels are sounds made with a fairly open vocal tract, with some differences in where your tongue is. Much of the variation in Appalachia is found in the vowel system.

Consonants

In Appalachian Englishes, the consonant systems as a whole are fairly similar to many other varieties of American English. While there are undoubtedly individual differences in the precise location of the lips and tongue for particular sounds, in general many of the consonants sound like and pattern like other regions. However, there are some consonants and consonant processes that can be different in the region's varieties (Hall 1942). I will address each in turn below.

Which Witch? /ʍ/ and /w/

This sound occurs in some words with spellings that begin with <wh>, like *what*, *which*, or *whale*. In many varieties of American English, this sound is a voiced labiovelar approximant, /w/. With this sound, a speaker purses their lips and also raises the back of their tongue toward their soft palate while their vocal folds are vibrating. However, in some Appalachian varieties, this sound is not voiced; it is a voiceless labiovelar fricative /ʍ/ (the vocal folds are not vibrating). With this sound, some Appalachian speakers differentiate between *which* and *witch* or *whale* and *wail* or between *whine* and *wine*, a distinction that reflects the original history of these two sounds. As will be a common theme in this chapter, there is much variation at the individual level.

Some speakers will have a robust difference between these two, while others may have the two sounds merged like speakers of other varieties. Hazen, Lovejoy, Daugherty, and Vandevender (2016) found that speakers in West Virginia were losing the distinction between the two sounds and that they were merging. However, speakers with college education seem to be maintaining the difference at a higher rate than those without any college education.

Leaping Fall Lizards /l/
In all varieties of English, there are at least two types of L sounds, a clear [l] and a dark [ɫ]. Historically, the clear variant [l] (voiced alveolar lateral approximant) occurred in syllable-initial positions, while the dark variant [ɫ] (voiced velarized lateral approximant) occurred in other positions. You can probably feel and hear this difference by saying the words "lab" and "ball." Notice how you make the first [l] sound by raising your tongue tip upward. However, in "ball," you raise the back of your tongue toward your soft palate and shift your tongue back a bit to make [ɫ]. The tongue position is the difference in these two L sounds. In many varieties of American English, this distinction between initial sound and final sound is not clear cut, as the two sounds can show up in the same places. Many speakers are using darker [ɫ] variants in syllable-initial positions. However, many Appalachian speakers maintain a very clear /l/ variant in syllable-initial position, particularly when the /l/ occurs between vowels, like in the words *belly*, *valley*, or *Tellico*.

Also, many Appalachians will tend to use a very dark [ɫ] in syllable-final position as in *coal* or in syllable-final clusters as in *belt*. In fact, often the [ɫ] will almost sound like a back vowel. So, words like *school* are actually pronounced [skuw] or [skuʊ] (the actual vowel sound can vary). This process is called L-vocalization and occurs in many varieties of English. In Appalachia, this feature can be quite common and found across social groups, but there is much variation (see Hamilton and Hazen 2009). What is interesting is that L-vocalization may be receding across time, as younger speakers (particularly younger females) are vocalizing less (Dodsworth and Hazen 2011).

Minding Your "Bidness" /z/
The next consonantal processes occur with the sound /z/, a voiced alveolar fricative. The first of these processes happens word-medially. When this sound occurs in the middle of a word and before a nasal sound,[1] it is often realized in Appalachia as /d/. When this change happens, the word *business* will sound like *bidness*, or the contracted word *wasn't* will sound like *wadn't*. As with some of the other processes discussed here, this variation happens in

other varieties of American English as well. However, it can be more common among speakers of Appalachian Englishes.

The second process that can occur with /z/ in Appalachia happens word-finally. Appalachian speakers can make the /z/ sound more like an [s]; this change means that the word *cheese* can sound like *cheess*. This variation is a very subtle difference, but if you pay close attention, you can hear it from the mouths of Appalachian speakers more than Southern English speakers (Walker, Southall, and Hargrave 2017). This devoicing process involves many acoustic parameters, and there is much individual variation (Hazen, Lovejoy, et al. 2015).

Consonant Additions

In some Appalachian varieties, particularly from older natives in more rural communities, there are occasions when speakers will pronounce consonants that are absent in other varieties. Words like *once, twice, cliff,* and *across* are spoken with a final [t] sound, and sound like *oncet, twicet, clifft,* and *acrosst*. This addition is rarely heard in younger speakers or speakers from more urban areas.

Another process of consonant addition is pronouncing *it* or *ain't* with an initial /h/ sound, realizing them as *hit* and *hain't*. This variation primarily occurs at the beginning of a phrase, as in *Hit's gonna rain today* or *Hain't you going?* The forms with initial /h/ can be traced far back into the history of English. However, this dialect feature is fading among younger speakers as well. Related to this process, Hazen et al. (2016) found that West Virginia had little /h/ in words that historically began with /h/ like *help*. More research is needed for this process!

Consonant Deletions

Many Appalachian varieties allow for some consonants to be deleted where other varieties maintain them. This process can occur at the beginning, the middle, or the end of words. Each of the following paragraphs outlines these positions, respectively.

Words like *this, these, that, those, there, than,* and *then* (all begin with initial /ð/, the voiced (inter)dental fricative) can be pronounced without the initial /ð/, especially in running or rapid speech. While this process occurs in many varieties of American English, it appears to occur more frequently and in more contexts in Appalachia. For example, the sentence *There's a big storm coming* can sound like this one: *'Ere's a big storm coming*.

Initial /w/ in the words *was* and *would* is often lost after the pronouns.

While contraction occurs in all English varieties, this particular contraction is common in many Appalachian varieties and does not appear to be socially stigmatized. Such a process renders *I was* to *I'z/I'uz* or the contraction of *he would* to *he'd/he'ud*. This contraction of past tense *be* is intriguing because it rarely happens in English. Research has shown that this feature has been part of Appalachia at least from the start of the twentieth century and has increased in some areas of Appalachia by the end of the twentieth century (Hazen 2014).

In other positions, medially and finally, there is a process of consonant cluster reduction. This process occurs when sequences of consonants that are in the same syllable are simplified. Reduction happens primarily at the ends of words and particularly with the alveolar stops, /t/ and /d/. Words like *first* or *mind* might be pronounced without their final consonant, rendering *firs'* or *min'*. However, consonant cluster reduction is a complex process. If the cluster occurs before another consonant, like in the phrase *first thing*, there is a greater chance of deletion. But, if the cluster occurs before a vowel, like in the phrase *first order*, the consonant is much less likely to delete. Hazen (2011) found 30 percent deletion before vowels yet 90 percent before nonalveolar consonants. Another factor in consonant cluster reduction is that it can be affected by morphology in some dialects: a word with only one morpheme (like *first*) may have a reduced consonant cluster more often than a word with two morphemes (like *trapped*, where you have the verb *trap* and the past tense marker *–ed*). However, this result does not seem to have as much of an effect in Appalachia. Varieties of English differ on which of these factors is most important (following sound or morphology). In Appalachia, the following sound is most important. When compared to other varieties of English, ethnicity was also a factor contributing to the presence of consonant cluster reduction (in line with other varieties), whereas social class was not.

In medial position, many Appalachian varieties reduce clusters of two or three consonants, and again, /t/ and /d/ are subject to this deletion, along with /l/. In words like *directly* or *chestnut*, the medial /t/ is often deleted, rendering *direckly* and *chesnut*. In words with a medial /d/, particularly after /n/ or /l/, the /d/ can be deleted; this means *Caldwell* sounds like *Callwell* and *hundred* sounds like *hunred*. When /l/ occurs in clusters, but is not the final sound, the /l/ is subject to being vocalized (as described above) or deleted outright—where *bulb* sounds like *bub*.

Vowels

As a person who was educated in English in the United States, I learned early on that English had five or maybe six vowels, "*a, e, i, o, u,* and sometimes *y*."

However, this idea refers to the vowels that we write orthographically (regular spelling). In speech, we have between thirteen to fifteen vowels. We can see this difference in observing that *heed, hid, hayed, head, had, hod, hawed, hood, hoed, who'd, Hud, heard, hide, how'd,* and *Hoyd* are words that are distinguished only by vowel sounds. So, depending on the variety, English has rather many vowels! Our issue is that many of these vowels use some of the same written letters for different sounds. English orthography has not kept up with pronunciation.

Since American English as a whole has so many vowels, it is natural that there is a lot of variation in how speakers actually pronounce these vowels. Most people are aware of regional dialects because of the vowel sounds, and Appalachian Englishes are no exception. There is actually a series of vowel differences that form some of the characteristic sounds found in several varieties of English spoken in Appalachia.

The Southern Vowel Shift

Across large portions of the southern United States, including parts of central and all of southern Appalachia, there are several particular vowel pronunciations that are characteristic of many of the English varieties spoken. These pronunciations are called the Southern Vowel Shift (Labov, Yaeger, and Steiner 1972; Fridland 2001; Thomas 2001, 2003), and this shift can be described in general terms as /aɪ/ ungliding, a rotation of the front vowel sounds, and fronting of the back vowels. Figure 2.1 shows a graphical representation of the shift, and I elaborate upon each part below.

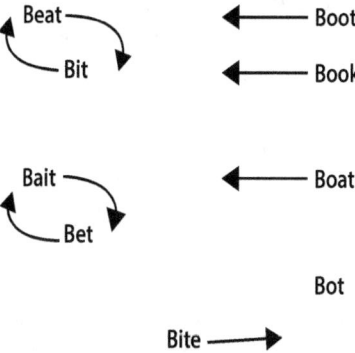

Figure 2.1. The Southern Vowel Shift. Illustration by Paul E. Reed.

/aɪ/ Ungliding

In many parts of the South, and especially in southern Appalachia (see chapter 1), the vowel sound in words like *bite*, *buy*, and *time*, /aɪ/, is not realized as two vowel sounds but as one vowel sound (the actual quality varies by person). This sound is one of the hallmarks of Southern speech and is a prominent part of the Southern Vowel Shift (Thomas 2003). In many varieties of English, this sound /aɪ/ is a complex vowel that begins with the first vowel in *father* and ends sounding almost like the vowel in *kit*. This type of complex vowel is called a *diphthong*. The first part is called the *nucleus* or *onglide*, and the second part is called the *glide* or *offglide*. Thus, when the vowel sounds more like one sound than two, it is called *unglided*. This process is common across the South and southern Appalachia. Where some Appalachian varieties distinguish themselves from other Southern varieties is that the ungliding happens in all contexts. In other parts of the South, the ungliding happens in open syllables (like in *buy*) and before voiced sounds (like in *prize* or *time*). Voiced means that the vocal folds are vibrating when a speaker makes the sound, like /d/ or /m/. However, in some Appalachian varieties, you can find unglided /aɪ/ before voiceless sounds (like in *bite* or *price*). Voiceless refers to consonants that are made without vibrating the vocal folds, like /t/ or /s/. Typically, ungliding before voiceless consonants is more stigmatized than the other contexts (Bernstein 2006). Speakers who use prevoiceless /aɪ/ ungliding are seen as more "country" or "mountain" and perhaps less educated or less sophisticated than other speakers. Many Appalachians are aware of what this sound can mean socially, and they will not use it. Others, however, may know its social meaning and actively use it (Greene 2010; Reed 2014, 2016).

In many studies, speakers are quite aware of this /aɪ/ vowel and its social meanings, particularly the ungliding in prevoiceless contexts. However, many speakers still use this unglided production in spite of the negative social connotations. To these speakers, especially those that are more rooted to the local area, this unglided vowel signals "home" and the positive connotations of Appalachia. Thus, they tend to have more of the unglided production of /aɪ/ overall and especially those of the prevoiceless unglided variety.

Rotation of the Front Vowels

Another feature of the Southern Vowel Shift that is found in some Appalachian varieties is the rotation of the front vowels. Sometimes this variation is described as the vowels "swapping places." While not technically correct, it does help to explain what is going on. With this shift, the first part of the vowel in words like *bit* sounds more like the first part of the vowel in *beet* and vice versa.

So, *bit* sounds something like *bee-ih-t* [biɪt]. *Beet*, in contrast, sounds something like *bih-ee-t* [bɪit]. A similar rotation happens in the vowels of *bait* and *bet*. The first part of the vowel sound in *bet* sounds like *bait*, and then the second half sounds like *bet*, sounding something like *bay-eh-t* [beɛt]. Relatedly, the first part of the vowel sound of *bait* sounds like the first part of *bet*, and the second half rises to sound like the last half of *bait*, rendering [bɛet].

For both of these rotations, the fully articulated versions can even have three vowel sounds, depending on the speaker, and, as mentioned earlier, some speakers may shift both sets of vowels (particularly older speakers). Other speakers, however, may only shift one of the sets, and other speakers may not shift either. Reed (2018) found that speakers who were more rooted tended to have more rotation in the *bait/bet* set and not the *beet/bit* set. Many of these changes depend on how a speaker views themselves and the region. There is a lot of individual variation in Appalachia!

Fronting of the Back Vowels
Across much of Appalachia, many speakers will *front* the articulation of the back vowels /u/, /ʊ/, and /o/ (particularly the sounds in *boot*, /u/, and *boat*, /o/), another aspect of the Southern Vowel Shift. In parts of Appalachia, this process seems to have been completed by the 1920s (Hazen 2018). During the vowel pronunciation, the tongue is pushed slightly forward, and thus the sound /u/ in *boot* sounds like a cross between *boot* and *beet*, something like *biewt*. Similarly, the /o/ sound in *boat* is realized like a cross between *boat* and *bait*, something like *beowt*.

Many varieties of American English have a somewhat similar process happening for the back vowels. What sets both the Southern and Appalachian versions apart is that the fronted vowels each sound like two or three vowels, whereas in other varieties there is not as much change across the production of the same vowel sound.

Vowel Breaking
Another common vowel process in southern Appalachian varieties is what is known as vowel breaking (see Labov, Ash, and Boberg 2006, particularly map 11.1). This term refers to a process where one vowel sound "breaks" into two sounds (Feagin 1996, 2008). Many Appalachian speakers will break the /æ/ sound in *bat* into two sounds, although some speakers may break others. So, the word *bad* will sound almost like it has two syllables with two or three vowel sounds and will be pronounced almost like *bae-id* or *bae-ed*, [bæɪd] or [bæɛd]. Many times, people refer to this process as "drawling," as in the

"Southern Drawl" or the "Mountain Drawl." This feature occasionally gives the perception of a slower speech rate, even though the speakers are not talking any slower. There is some evidence that such breaking might be decreasing across apparent time (Jacewicz, Fox, and Salmons 2011).

Pin/Pen Merger

Across much of the South, and across a good portion of central and southern Appalachia, the words *pen/pin* and *ten/tin* are homophones—that is, they sound the same (Hazen 2005). Specifically, the vowel sounds in these words are the same, meaning that they have merged (i.e., the *pin/pen* merger). In this particular case, the merger only happens before nasals in the United States, or sounds made with air coming out of the nose: /n/, /m/, and /ŋ/. These are the final sounds in *seen, seem,* and *sing,* respectively. When a mid-front vowel occurs before a nasal, the production of the vowels /ɪ/ as in *pit* and /ɛ/ as in *pet* merge. In some areas, the vowels merge toward the *pit* vowel; in others, toward the *pet* vowel. Typically, in southern Appalachia, it goes toward *pit*. Thus, words like *temperature* begin with /tɪm/, like the name *Tim*. Brown (1991) showed that, in Tennessee, there was little social or ethnic variation and that most people born after 1900 had the merger. Growing up in East Tennessee, we were aware of this merger at some level, and we would talk about an "ink pen" and a "stick pin" to disambiguate. Mergers can trigger some crafty language use!

Cot/Caught Merger

In parts of northern Appalachia, akin to many parts of North America, the vowel sounds in words like *cot* and *caught* are the same (Hazen 2005). This pattern is another merger and is usually termed the *cot/caught* merger or low-back merger (because it takes place in the low-back part of the mouth). Specifically, where some US varieties make a distinction between the /a/ in *cot* and the /ɔ/ in *caught*, in parts of Appalachia (particularly younger speakers), speakers pronounce these words the same. Unlike the *pin/pen* merger, the *cot/caught* merger happens in every word these vowels occur. So, words like *bot/bought* and *hock/hawk* sound quite similar if not the same.

The fact that the *cot/caught* merger is present in Appalachian varieties is quite interesting, in that it shows that Appalachian Englishes are not as isolated as usually described in some scholarly literature. Since this merger is spreading across large parts of the English-speaking world, its presence in Appalachia counters the notion that the region is radically isolated from other parts of the country and underscores that Appalachian varieties are dynamic, just like all living language varieties. Appalachia and its dialects are a vibrant part of change, and this aspect deserves more attention.

In other parts of Appalachia, particularly in southern Appalachia and more rural parts of the central Appalachian region, however, a different sound is sometimes used in words with the *caught* vowel. Rather than a merger, speakers tend to use a different vowel. Here, speakers use a diphthong /aʊ/ (Hall 1942), which starts with the vowel sound in *father* and ends with a vowel sound a bit like the vowel in *foot*. These speakers have different vowels in *cot* and *caught* like some US English varieties. The difference is that, rather than distinguishing /a/ and /ɔ/, these varieties contrast /a/ and /aʊ/. However, this particular usage might be less common among younger speakers, as they tend to be those that have the *cot/caught* merger described above.

INTONATION

One of the features of Appalachian Englishes that is quite characteristic, but less mentioned and studied, is the use of intonation. This aspect is quite salient to listeners but has been less often described in the linguistics literature. Intonation describes the melody of speech, how some syllables have higher or lower pitch. We use intonation for all sorts of purposes. Some are related to semantics: the meanings of the sentences.

All English speakers use it to mark the difference in a question or a statement, even when the words and word order are the same. For example, *You went to the store*, with falling pitch at the end, is a statement. However, *You went to the store?* with rising pitch at the end may signal a question. We are not using the syntax (word order) of the sentence to get the different meanings, as the order is the same. It is the way we are saying the sentence that gives the different interpretations. The falling pitch signals statement, and the rising pitch signals question.

Yet, intonation is not just used for the difference in questions and statements. We use intonation to contrast some meanings. For example, if your friend said that Mark left early, but it was actually Mike, you might say, "No, MIKE left early," with a higher pitch on *Mike*. This higher pitch has a contrastive interpretation. You can also emphasize the other words, and the interpretation is also contrast. For example, if you say, "No, Mike LEFT early," you are perhaps contrasting leaving versus arriving. You could say, "No, Mike left EARLY," where the emphasis on *early* contrasts with leaving on time or late. These uses of intonation are shared widely across many varieties of English.

Some of the variation in intonation is common to many varieties of

English. There are sometimes differences in how high the pitch may need to go to signal a question, or whether the final rise signals question or statement. There are some varieties of English, particularly among younger speakers, that use lots of final rises on both statements and questions. This change is happening in Australia, Great Britain, Canada, and the United States. However, these types of intonation are not what sets certain Appalachian Englishes apart.

The use of intonation that is more characteristic of Appalachian varieties is a bit different than what I have described thus far. In parts of Appalachia, some of the varieties appear to emphasize many more words in sentences (Greene 2006; Reed 2016). Speakers place a pitch accent, a rise in pitch that makes the word stand out, on many more words that are not contrastive, which is different from the examples I used above. These pitch accents give the impression of a lot of emphasized words, or a lot of pitch rises and falls across a sentence. So, some Appalachian speakers will have many of these prominent words in lots of utterances. For example, an Appalachian speaker may say, "MIKE left EARLY," in a situation where there is no reason to signal contrast with some other person or whether they are early, on time, or late. Some have described this pattern as a "musical" quality to Appalachian speech. Others interpret this pattern as emphatic or a storytelling quality.

Another aspect of Appalachian intonation is not only numerous prominent words in sentences but also large pitch changes in those prominent words. The difference in an unemphasized word and an emphasized word can be relatively large. This distinction adds to the impression of emphasis and prominence. At the same time, because the change in pitch is rather large, the pitch change has to occur quite rapidly (because it is a big change happening across a relatively short syllable or word). This rapid change adds to the storytelling quality of Appalachian Englishes, as most other varieties only utilize these types of changes when narrating a story or during dramatic tellings.

One thing to note about this pattern of intonation is who uses it. I have referenced the importance of rootedness above when discussing vowels, but the same importance is at play with intonation as well. Since many of the vowel productions described above are caricatured or stigmatized, speakers may be aware of them and can sometimes change them. However, with the intonational features, many times speakers are not consciously aware of them, and they are present in their speech even when some of the other vernacular features (like the Southern vowel patterns) are absent. Reed (2016) showed that the presence of many rising pitch accents (i.e., lots of prominent words) set that Appalachian community apart from non-mountain Southern varieties. However, within the Appalachian community studied in Reed (2016), the speakers who were more attached to the local community (more rooted) had more rising pitch accents than the speakers who were less rooted to the local community. Additionally, the more rooted Appalachian speakers had quicker rises in pitch than the less rooted Appalachian speakers. So, the intonation is not just a distinguishing feature of some Appalachian Englishes, it is also variable within Appalachian communities themselves.

With these findings, it seems that intonation has two social meanings. One is that it is a feature of some Appalachian varieties. Overall, the varieties have more rising pitches than other varieties. The second meaning, related to the first, is that speakers might be subconsciously aware that using lots of rising pitches and having quick rises in pitch signal rootedness to the local community (because they signal Appalachia). Furthermore, Appalachian speakers who are more rooted will use more of the rising pitches and have faster rises than speakers who are less rooted. Both groups would be considered Appalachian speakers, but one group has a different relationship to place and to the region than others.

CONCLUSION

One of the clearest expressions of Appalachia is the speech used by those native to the region. The way one speaks represents a part of the identity of that speaker. Human languages are constantly changing and evolving, and Appalachian speech is no different. The particular sound features described above represent a part of that dynamic system. Like all varieties, Appalachian Englishes are living and changing, because the speakers of these varieties are changing as the world around them changes and evolves. Variation is present at many levels. Older Appalachians do not use the exact same sounds as younger Appalachians, nor do urban Appalachians use the same as rural folk. Some speakers will use many if not all of these features, while others will use very few. Certain speakers may not use any of these features and could be somewhat indistinguishable from speakers from the Midwest. However, these differences are woven together to form the beautiful tapestry of Appalachian Englishes.

Notes

1. A nasal is a sound produced with a closure in the mouth and air escaping out the nose. In English, we have three nasal sounds, /m/, /n/, and /ŋ/. These are the bilabial nasal, the alveolar nasal, and the velar nasal, respectively.

References

Bernstein, Cynthia. 2006. "Drawing Out the /aɪ/: Dialect Boundaries and /aɪ/ Variation." In *Language Variation and Change in the American Midland: A New Look at 'Heartland'*

English, edited by Thomas E. Murray and Beth Lee Simon, 209–32. Philadelphia: John Benjamins.
Brown, Vivian R. 1991. "Evolution of the Mergers of /ɪ/ and /ɛ/ before Nasals in Tennessee." *American Speech* 66, no. 3: 303–15.
Clark, John, Colin Yallop, and Janet Fletcher. 2007. *An Introduction to Phonetics and Phonology*. Malden, MA: Blackwell.
Cramer, Jennifer. 2014. "Is Shakespeare Still in the Holler? The Death of a Language Myth." *Southern Journal of Linguistics* 38, no. 1: 195–207.
Dodsworth, Robin, and Kirk Hazen. 2011. "Following *L* over Hill and Dale: Changes in L-Vocalization through Space, Time, and Methods." Paper presented at New Ways of Analyzing Variation 40, Georgetown University, Washington, DC, October 2011.
Feagin, Crawford. 1996. "Peaks and Glides in Southern States Short-A." In *Variation and Change in Language and Society*, edited by Gregory Guy, Crawford Feagin, Deborah Schiffrin, and John Baugh, 135–60. Vol. 1 of *Towards a Social Science of Language*. Amsterdam: Benjamins.
Feagin, Crawford. 2008. "Just What Is the Southern Drawl?" In *Tributaries 10: Journal of the Alabama Folklife Association*, edited by T. Nunnally, J. Brackner, A. Kimzey, and D. Boykin, 91–115. Montgomery, AL: Alabama Folklife Association.
Fridland, Valerie. 2001. "The Social Dimension of the Southern Vowel Shift: Gender, Age, and Class." *Journal of Sociolinguistics* 5: 233–53.
Greene, Rebecca. 2006. "Pitch Accents in Appalachian English." Unpublished qualifying paper, Stanford University.
Greene, Rebecca. 2010. "Language, Ideology, and Identity in Rural Eastern Kentucky." PhD diss., Stanford University. https://purl.stanford.edu/fh361zh5489.
Hall, Joseph S. 1942. "The Phonetics of Great Smoky Mountain Speech." *American Speech* 17, no. 2: 1–110.
Hamilton, Sarah, and Kirk Hazen. 2009. "Dialect Research in Appalachia: A Family Case Study." *West Virginia History* 3, no. 1: 81–107.
Hazen, Kirk. 2005. "Mergers in the Mountains." *English World-Wide* 26, no. 2: 199–221.
Hazen, Kirk. 2011. "Flying High above the Social Radar: Coronal Stop Deletion in Modern Appalachia." *Language Variation and Change* 23, no. 1: 105–37.
Hazen, Kirk. 2014. "A New Role for an Ancient Variable in Appalachia: Paradigm Leveling and Standardization in West Virginia." *Language Variation and Change* 26, no. 1: 77–102.
Hazen, Kirk. 2018. "The Contested Southernness of Appalachia." *American Speech* 93, no. 3-4: 374–408.
Hazen, Kirk, Jordan Lovejoy, Emily Vandevender, Margery Webb, and Kiersten Woods. 2015. "The Sociophonetics of Z Devoicing." Paper presented at the Southeastern Conference on Linguistics 82, Raleigh, NC.
Hazen, Kirk, Jordan Lovejoy, Jaclyn Daugherty, and Madeline Vandevender. 2016. "Continuity and Change of English Consonants in Appalachia." In *Appalachia Revisited: New Perspectives on Place, Tradition, and Progress*, edited by William Schumann and Rebecca Adkins Fletcher, 119–38. Lexington: University Press of Kentucky.
Jacewicz, Ewa, Robert Fox, and Joseph Salmons. 2011. "Cross-generational Vowel Change in American English." *Language Variation and Change* 23, no. 1: 45–86.
Labov, William, Malcah Yaeger, and Richard Steiner. 1972. *A Quantitative Study of Sound Change in Progress: Volumes 1 and 2*. Report on National Science Foundation Contract NSF-GS-3287. Philadelphia: University of Pennsylvania.
Labov, William, Sherry Ash, and Charles Boberg. 2006. *Atlas of North American English*. New York: Mouton de Gruyter.
Ladefoged, Peter, and Sandra F. Disner. 2012. *Vowels and Consonants*. 3rd ed. Malden, MA: Wiley.

Montgomery, Michael. 1999. "In the Appalachians They Talk like Shakespeare." In *Language Myths*, edited by Laurie Bauer and Peter Trudgill, 66–76. London: Penguin.

Thomas, Erik R. 2001. *An Acoustic Analysis of Vowel Variation in New World English*. Publication of the American Dialect Society 85. Durham, NC: Duke University Press.

Thomas, Erik R. 2003. "Secrets Revealed by Southern Vowel Shifting." *American Speech* 78: 150–70.

Reed, Paul E. 2014. "Inter- and Intra-generational Monophthongization and Southern Appalachia Identity." *Southern Journal of Linguistics* 38, no. 1: 159–93.

Reed, Paul E. 2016. "Sounding Appalachian: /aɪ/ Monophthongization, Rising Pitch Accents, and Rootedness." PhD diss., University of South Carolina.

Reed, Paul E. 2018. "Rootedness and the Southern Vowel Shift in Appalachia." Paper presented at the American Dialect Society Annual Meeting, Salt Lake City, UT, January 4–7, 2018.

Walker, Abby, Rebecca Southall, and Rachel Hargrave. 2017. "An Acoustic and Phonological Description of /z/-devoicing in Southern American English." *The Journal of the Acoustical Society of America* 142, no. 4: 2678.

Wolfram, Walt, and Donna Christian. 1976. *Appalachian Speech*. Arlington, VA: Center for Applied Linguistics.

CHAPTER 3

Grammar across Appalachia

Kirk Hazen

SUMMARY

This chapter reviews the scholarship on grammar variation in Appalachia with an eye to which dialect features have persisted in the twenty-first century. Traditional scholarship on grammar patterns describes the types of morphological and syntactic variation, yet both diachronic and synchronic trends provide insights into grammar's uneven patterns. Stereotypical portrayals of Appalachia use the most vernacular, and thereby "showy," types of grammar, such as the *a*-prefix in *She's* a-fishing. These grammatical patterns vary widely in how often they are actually used. Despite the increased attention Appalachian Englishes have received in the last two decades, many of the traditional forms in the literature on grammatical variation have not been well-studied lately, and these areas of research are ripe for future study. For example, variation in irregular past tense verb forms such as *come/came*, *seen/saw*, and *sneak/snuck* have not had any kind of quantitative assessment but are often a topic of public interest. For language change, a grammatical feature's stigma has guided who maintains which forms. Developments in grammar patterns at the end of the twentieth century and future trends are also discussed.

INTRODUCTION

Many people see grammar as one of the real problems in Appalachia. They might describe the vowels of *hill* and *mine* as lilting or the innovative consonant of *warsh* as quaint, but a sentence like *Them squirrels wasn't no good* is out of line for most folk. They feel it requires correction. Linguists study sentences like these to find patterns in the words and their ordering. In those patterns, we find regular human language, just like all other varieties on earth. When biologists study sea creatures, they do not find whales to be faulty swimmers because they do not swish their tails like fish. There are different ways to get the job done. Humans speak around seven thousand languages and many more dialects of those languages. All of them work according to the brain's design, and because of their patterns, they are all grammatical. Linguists do recognize that some patterns are more socially stigmatized than others. The difference between *grammatical* and *stigmatized* is discussed in the next section.

This chapter contains an explanation of linguists' ideas about grammar and subsections with explanations about some of the grammar patterns across Appalachia. There is not enough room to detail all the grammar patterns that linguists have studied over the last hundred years; for an extensive list, consult Michael Montgomery's *Dictionary of Smoky Mountain English* (Montgomery and Hall 2004).

GRAMMAR IS AS GRAMMAR DOES

Beer can be considered an ancient beverage. It was first brewed six thousand years ago in modern-day Iran. However, when you crack open a cold one today, you are not drinking an ancient beer. The beer is hopefully fresh. Beer is not wine, and nobody wants to drink an old beer. Yet, the process to make the beer is ancient.

Some processes of English grammar can be considered ancient: the three suffixes of English spelled with <s> all come from Old English and do different grammar jobs. Consider this sentence: *The cat's toy car races over the leaves*. The first suffix is the possessive *'s* on *cat*: it shows that the cat owns the toy. In Old English, possessive *'s* was spelled *-es* on words like *scipes*, "ship's," and this suffix took over the marking of possession for all nouns as time went on. The second one is the verbal *-s* on *races*: it marks the verb as singular and third person to align with the subject. In Old English, the job of verbal *-s* was taken care of by a *-th* suffix on verbs like *sitteth*, but along with destruction, the Vikings brought in the verbal *-s* suffix, even though it was much later when verbal *-s* won the competition with *-th*.[1] The third one is the plural *-s* on *leaves*. In Old English, the plural *-s* was spelled *-as* on words like *bātas*, "boats," and this plural form eventually pushed all others aside in a centuries-long game of king of the hill.[2] In modern English, all three of these suffixes have ancient roots. Still, if a child learns to say, "Look at his fingers," she is not speaking Old English, even though every word in that phrase existed in Old English as well as the plural *-s*. Speakers alive today speak modern English.

The English varieties spoken in Appalachia are also part of modern English.

One of the most persistent myths about Appalachian Englishes is that they are stuck in some ancient time (Montgomery 2001; Cramer 2014). Whether it is English from Chaucer's time period or even older forms, from at least 1900 on, people have believed that Appalachians have a culture and a language frozen in time. Accordingly, any variation different from an outside variety is popularly seen as an older form regardless of whether it is an innovation or a retention. Like making beer or pluralizing nouns, some grammar patterns in Appalachia have roots in earlier varieties, but modern speakers have only modern varieties. Importantly, people critique *vernacular* dialect features, and the distinction between vernacular and *standard* requires some special explanation.

With dialect differences in sound, there can be fine distinctions that people place on a social scale: a pronunciation of *mine* can be more or less Southern depending on small differences in the vowel. If it is socially relevant to us, we can hear less of the consonant *r* in words like *hard* and *bore* when listening to British or Southern speakers. With R-dropping, it is again a dialect difference in sound, and social judgments can be positive (with British speakers) or negative (with rural Southern speakers), depending on whether the listeners view those people as good or bad. With grammar patterns, there is often a different set of criteria for judging.

The difference between *We was walkin'* and *We were walking* is a sharp change, not gradient. Either the verb is *was* or *were*, and the suffix is *–in'* or *–ing*. These kinds of binary choices lend themselves to interpretations of right or wrong. Since grammar is more directly discussed in school, it is there that these interpretations force such choices. Traditional schooling makes students choose one form or the other, thus teaching them that one is inherently right and the other wrong. Everyone remembers grammar lessons, and few people remember them fondly. Instead of explaining how language works, most grammar lessons in schools focus on prescriptive notions of "right and wrong." These prescriptive notions are actually usage guidelines for the genre of formal, academic writing, and when applied to informal spoken language, many mismatches can be found. The judgment about whether any spoken language is good or bad depends on whether the social group that speaks it is stigmatized in a society. African American and Southern varieties are stigmatized because these groups have been viewed negatively throughout US history. Stigma of dialect features comes from prejudice against people, not from fault with the language itself.

The grammatical patterns discussed below are stigmatized to some extent, but all of them are part of a grammatical system. Within linguistics, grammar is made up of two overlapping areas: morphology and syntax. Morphology is the area of the mind that puts together parts of words into larger words: *un + happy + ness = unhappiness*. Syntax is the area of the mind that puts together words in certain orders to create phrases:

Nouns: ocean, floor, squid, itself
Verb: *propelled*
Determiner: *the*
Preposition: *across*

After syntax does its job: *The squid propelled itself across the ocean floor.*

The grammar patterns in this chapter involve both morphology and syntax. There is also some vocabulary variation with choices between words like *y'inz* and *y'all*. The modern patterns, both linguistic and social, are discussed for the grammatical features below.

THE GRAMMAR PATTERNS

A-Prefixing

The song "Christmas Time's A-Comin' " was first recorded by Bill Monroe in 1951 and has been covered many times since. As it is a bluegrass song, the vernacular grammar gives it a homey feel. If dialect features had a popularity contest, the most famous for Appalachia would be *a*-prefixing. In a sentence like *Fire was* a-flaming *everywhere* (Wolfram and Christian 1975), the *a*- prefix is attached to the progressive participle.

Scholars believe that *a*-prefixing historically comes from using prepositions like *on* or *at* in front of certain verb-like forms, like *a-fishing*. As Montgomery (2009, 7) notes, this grammatical pattern seems to have started in Early Modern English and was still going strong in the early 1600s when it was recorded in both Shakespeare and the King James Bible: "Simon Peter saith unto them, I go a fishing" (John 21:3). It is important to realize that *a*-prefixing was used in the writing of educated scribes and was not stigmatized at the time. It also came from southern England (Montgomery 2009). A few handbooks began to prescribe against *a*-prefixing in the 1700s, but it was not until the middle of the 1800s that it was put into the mouths of literary characters considered rural or rustic (Montgomery 2009, 7). From that point forward, it has been a stigmatized dialect feature associated with rural life and a lack of education.

There are three main grammatical trends with *a*-prefixing (Wolfram and Christian 1975), although there are exceptions to these trends (Montgomery

2009). The first trend is that the *a*-prefix usually attaches to verbs: *She was* a-building *a house* would work well, but the sentence A-building *is hard work* would not be grammatical for speakers with *a*-prefixing. The second trend is that the *a*-prefix does not get placed next to prepositions: the sentence *They make money* a-building *houses* is OK, but no speaker with this feature would produce a sentence like *They make money by* a-building *houses* with the preposition added. The third trend is that most often the *a*-prefix is attached to verbs with a stressed first syllable: the sentence *She was* a-fóllowing *a trail* would work fine, but *She was* a-discóvering *a trail* would not because the stress is on the second syllable of the verb. Despite its reputation as being uneducated, it has a complex system of linguistic rules.

For many of the stigmatized grammar patterns in this chapter, their use in day-to-day conversations dwindled as the twentieth century wore on. The number of people with a high school education increased steadily over the twentieth century, and Appalachia was part of this trend. The rate of adults with a high school degree in West Virginia was 84 percent in 2010, compared to the national rate of 83 percent. That rate is a big jump up for West Virginia from the 18 percent with a high school degree in 1940. With the increasing reach of educational norms, dialect features like *a*-prefixing became a greater shibboleth after World War II. In interviews done at the end of the twentieth century with native West Virginians, no speaker born after 1947 used this feature (Hazen, Butcher, and King 2010). Paul Reed does report (pers. comm.) that *a*-prefixing continues to be used in daily conversations in East Tennessee, so it is safe to say that *a*-prefixing is not yet dead in Appalachia. Its range and frequency, however, are more restricted than they were a hundred years ago.

Multiple Negation

One of the most common quips about grammar is "two negatives make a positive." It is cast to discredit sentences like *We did*n't *have no use for it noways* (Montgomery 2004). It was first written by one of the most prominent prescriptive writers of the 1700s, Robert Lowth. His intellectual climate was focused on crafting English to be a more logical language, yet Lowth errored in two ways with this quip, one minor and one major. On the minor front, only in multiplication and division do two negatives make a positive. For example, $(-3) \times (-3) = 9$; yet with addition, two negatives make a negative. For example, $(-3) + (-3) = -6$. On the major front, human language is not math. As Lowth was a bishop, his prescriptive preferences were more a moral decision and a judgment on the people who used multiple negation.

From the very start, English has had multiple negation. It was a common feature in Old English and Middle English. A similar system continues in modern English, but it became stigmatized starting in the 1500s. For example, from Chaucer's writing:

> "This world," quod I, "of so manye and diverse and contraryous parties, *ne* myghte *nevere* han ben assembled in o forme." (From Chaucer's translation of Boethius's *Consolation of Philosophy*)

> ("This world," said I, "of so many and diverse and adverse parts, not could never have been united in one form.")

Once multiple negation was associated with socially disfavored groups, teachers began chasing it down and chastising their students for it. It is a part of many vernacular varieties, including those in Appalachia, and the social stigma against it has not lessened (Labov 1972). In a survey of acceptability, researchers found that multiple negation in *He didn't have no common sense* rated the lowest possible score (one out of five) for being "normal" and that people were unified in this judgment (Hazen, Kinnaman, et al. 2015).

There are several patterns for multiple negation. The first is that two or more negatives can be used to add up to one negative meaning. As Montgomery (2004) writes, negative concord is where "all indefinite elements in a clause conform in being negative" as in "I have *not never* heard of that." Related to negative concord is a process called negative inversion, where the conjugated verb is placed before the subject of a phrase. Montgomery (2004) gives an example of "There's an old house up here, but *don't* nobody live in it" as a declarative sentence.

Despite the continued level of stigma that multiple negation receives, there is little chance it will disappear completely from Appalachia. It is a well-rooted part of English and is part of the home language for many people.

Leveled *Was*

One of the more common grammar variations in Appalachia is the use of *was* where *were* would be expected in more standard varieties. The variation is called leveled *was* because each slot in the verb paradigm is leveled smooth with *was*. The motto here for language change is "One form, one function" (see table 3.1).

The forms *were* and *was* have been fighting it out since at least 600 CE to see who will take over the past-tense realm of the verb *be*. Originally, *was* did the job with singular subjects, and *were* did the job with plural subjects: the *were* form comes from the *was* form plus a plural suffix. Over the last fifteen hundred years, different dialect varieties have chosen different paths. For example, on the Outer Banks of North Carolina, some varieties have made *was* the positive form in phrases like *We* was *there* and *weren't* the negative form in phrases like *I* weren't *home last night* (Wolfram, Hazen, and Schilling-Estes 1999). In Appalachia, the main form for both positive and negative is *was*: *The rumors* was *starting down there* and *They* wasn't *really into nothing* (Hazen 2014).

Across all of North America, the most common place to find leveled *was* is in sentences with "existential subjects." These subjects usually have *there* or *it* in the subject slot: There *was between eight hundred and a thousand people*. The *there was* construction is similar to the standard French form *Il y a*, "there is/are," in sentences like *Il y a trois voitures*, "There are three cars." The *there was* construction has become common enough in English that it has lost much of its vernacular status (Nevalainen 2009).

Leveled *was* with other plural subjects has also been common in Appalachia, but its use has declined over recent decades. In part, this decline is because leveled *was* is associated with lower social classes. With this association and the spread of mandatory high school at the end of the twentieth century, leveled *was* has seen a decline. Researchers in the 1970s found that speakers in Kentucky and West Virginia used leveled *was* between 45 and 80 percent of the time. In a more recent study, speakers born between 1919 and 1947 used leveled *was* 57 percent of the time. In contrast, speakers born in the 1980s only used it 8 percent of the time. There was a dramatic drop for speakers born after World War II, and leveled *was* never recovered its previous frequency (Hazen 2014).

One of the ways that leveled *was* survived into the twenty-first century has been with the help of a sound sleight of hand. The contracted form of *was* has been noted in Appalachia for some time, and one of its qualities is that it can camouflage leveled *was* (Hazen 2014) in sentences like *I's starting kindergarten*. Contracted *was* is unstressed, and this less prominent display allows it to flow more freely in regular conversation. Some studies have found contraction on the decline in the Smoky Mountains but on the rise in West Virginia (Hazen 2014).

Overall, although leveled *was* is no longer as common as it used to be, it is still a part of Appalachia and will not fully fade from this region.

Demonstrative *Them*

In the first season of the *Dukes of Hazzard* (episode 8), one of the more vernacular grammar features is used: "As long as you keep wearing *them* boots, I'd let sleeping dogs lie." In the United States over the last century, saying *them boots* would sound "country" for most people. The English language has a system

Table 3.1. Leveled *Was* Paradigm

	Singular	Plural
First	I was	we was
Second	you was	you was
Third	she was, he was, it was	they was

for pointing out things: *this squid, that kitten, these cookies, those cocktails*. This system uses demonstrative pronouns because they demonstrate nouns. Old English had several of these demonstrative pronouns, including the ancestors of *that* and *this*, but modern-day *these* and *those* developed irregularly. Because *those* as a form did not become stable until the 1500s, several varieties of English innovated with *them* as a demonstrative pronoun. Since that time, *them* and *those* have been competing to see who will be the final piece in the demonstrative pronoun puzzle.

In the United States, the social tides turned against demonstrative *them* by at least the close of the 1800s. It became tied to rural speech as urban areas grew increasingly cosmopolitan, and whether it was connected to older farmers or unrefined frontiersmen, demonstrative *them* ended up on the vernacular side of the social spectrum. As a well-known vernacular feature, it is regularly used in characterizations of Appalachian speech, from comics to TV shows. From the sociolinguistic patterns over the twentieth century, West Virginians appear to have reacted to this stigma. Hazen, Hamilton, and Vacovsky (2011) found a sharp drop in the percent of the time that people used demonstrative *them*, with the oldest speakers using demonstrative *them* 22 percent of the time but following generations using it only 3 percent of the time. As with other vernacular dialect features, it did not completely disappear, but it did gain a country profile. For the oldest speakers, there was also a stark split between females and males, with the oldest females using demonstrative *them* only 13 percent of the time while the oldest males used it 36 percent of the time. In the twenty-first century, it is one grammar pattern that Appalachians all know about but few use in regular conversations.

Reflexive Regularization

In Appalachia, some grammar patterns stand out more than others. With showcase patterns like demonstrative *them* or *a*-prefixing, people notice them in conversations and do a double take when they hear them. With other grammar patterns, they are not as strongly associated with any social meaning. Consider this sentence: *After three hours at Ikea, they finally bought theirselves some chairs for their new patio.* Here, this particular grammar pattern is less tightly associated with any one community, but it is certainly a part of Appalachia. The use of *hisself* or *theirselves* is part of many vernacular varieties around the world, but these forms are not socially standard in any region even if they are common.

The use of *hisself* dates back to at least the 1300s. Here is an example from 1450: "Mekely he clothys *hys selfe* as he hade bene þe lawest man in kynderyd" (OED), which can be read as "Meekly he clothes *hisself* as if he had been the lowest man in lineage." The use of *theirselves* was common in England and not openly chastised until 1760 (OED). It was first written in the 1500s in sentences like *They had gret desyre to prove* their selfes. For centuries these forms were used without prescriptive guilt, and they continue to persist today. This grammar pattern involves pronouns called *reflexives*. Pronouns are words that refer back to a noun, something like a placeholder. They come in several different shapes and sizes, with three *persons* along with singular and plural. Table 3.2 shows personal pronouns.

Table 3.2. Personal Pronouns

	Singular	Plural
First	I	we
Second	you	you
Third	she, he, it	they

The reflexive pronouns are used to emphasize the personal pronouns: for example, We *bought* ourselves *ice cream*; I *got* myself *a sports car*. The reflexives themselves have some irregular patterns in their socially standard forms (see table 3.3). These reflexives are built out of a few different forms. The pronouns *my*, *your*, *her*, and *our* all show possession, as in the following sentence: Her *book fell off the shelf*. The exceptions are with *himself* and *themselves*. These two use the object forms *him* and *them*: *The squid liked* him; and *She sold* them. With these different forms, there is an imbalance in the method of making reflexives.

Table 3.3. Reflexive Pronouns

	Singular	Plural
First	myself	ourselves
Second	yourselves	yourselves
Third	herself, *him*self, itself	*them*selves

Human language does not like imbalances of this type. As with leveled *was*, one of the more consistent themes in language change is the motto "One form, one function." Appalachians, with *hisself* and *theirselves*, have fixed this imbalance by using possessive pronouns as the base for all their reflexives. The natural rhythms of language change have been trying to clean up this pattern for centuries.

Second-Person Plural

A popular slogan in the fight for LGBTQ rights across the US South has been "Y'all means all." The slogan conveys that the quintessential Southern pronoun includes all people. It also shows how certain pronouns become badges for some regions.

Before the mid-1600s, English speakers had a more diverse repertoire of personal pronouns. For a little over a thousand years in English, the pronouns for second-person singular were different from those of second-person plural. People could say, "Thou wast right," and everyone knew that sentence referred to one person. All kinds of changes happened between Old English and Early Modern English, but the personal pronouns looked like table 3.4 by the time Shakespeare wrote around 1600. By 1700, *thou*, *thee*, and *thine* had been voted off the island by *you*, and they mostly only showed up in Christian writings cast in a more conservative style. People began to use *you* as both singular and plural. This kind of confusion in pronouns had not happened before, and people in many different varieties of English began to innovate to fix this problem.

Different varieties have developed different solutions. Most of them have moved towards leaving *you* as a singular form and creating new plural pronouns. In the northern United States, *you guys* is the standard second-person plural form. Despite the *guy* part, it freely refers to people of any gender. In

Pittsburgh, *y'inz* is the famous plural form that can be found on merchandise all over the city. The natives of Pittsburgh can even call themselves *y'inzers*. Some areas of the upper South have two forms, either *you all* or the shorter *y'all* for second-person plural. In the Smoky Mountains, the plural *you'uns* was the dominant form for decades, but it has given way recently to *y'all* in many spots (Montgomery 2004). When headed to the lowland South, by the time you get to any area that has a choice of different kinds of grits in the grocery store, you have most likely entered full *y'all* territory. If we want to know what form they use in Appalachia, the answer is all of them. The counties of the Appalachian Regional Commission stretch from New York to Mississippi, and all of these plural forms are in Appalachian Englishes.

-ing Variation

People in Appalachia produce variation with *-ing* in the same ways as do English speakers in almost all parts of the world. They alternate between the alveolar nasal [n] in words like *no* and *not* and the velar nasal [ŋ] in words like *ring* and *ingot*.

The history of *-ing* shows its modern variation to be echoes of the past. The form *-inde* was a suffix used on verbs and eventually became the progressive form: *I was walking*. The form *-inge* was a suffix used to make verbs into nouns as in *Walking is fun*. These are often called *gerunds* today. These forms were two different suffixes with their own pronunciation and spelling. Eventually in spelling, these two suffixes became more similar. Early printers in the 1500s opted for the *-ing* spelling for each suffix rather than maintaining separate spellings. This spelling cover-up was so effective that, by the turn of the 1900s, people were writing letters to the editor complaining about corruption of the English language from the *-in* [n] pronunciation.

The modern linguistic pattern for this alternation is connected to its history. The alveolar nasal [n] shows up more often on progressive verbs, following in the footsteps of *-inde*, which had an alveolar nasal [n]. The velar nasal [ŋ] shows up more often on gerunds, following the pattern of *-inge*, which had a velar nasal [ŋ]. The influence of the previously separate suffixes persists today in the patterns of *-ing* variation for Appalachian speakers, as they do for English speakers around the world (Labov 1989).

Socially, people follow two patterns for *-ing* variation. On the one hand, how often people use [n] is connected to their social class. The lower the social class, the more often they will use [n] for *-ing*. Early on after the printing press, the alveolar nasal [n] got connected to lower social classes, and the association

Table 3.4. Personal Pronouns in Early Modern English

	Singular	Plural
First	I, me, mine	we, us, our
Second	thou, thee, thine	you, you, your
Third	she, her, her he, him, his it, it, its	they, them, their

has stuck in every community that has *-ing* variation. On the other hand, everyone uses the velar nasal [ŋ] more in formal situations and the alveolar nasal [n] more in informal situations. We know from studies of children that they can learn this social pattern as early as six years old (Labov 1989).

In the West Virginia area of Appalachia, people use the alveolar nasal [n] three times as often with progressive verbs as they do with gerunds. In situations where they are less focused on how they talk, people use the alveolar nasal [n] slightly more than four times as often as more formal situations. Social class also lined up with the rate of the alveolar nasal in the expected way, with working-class speakers having a rate of 73 percent, lower-middle-class speakers having a rate of 50 percent, and upper-middle-class speakers having a rate of 38 percent. In support of that finding, the extent of people's college experience also correlated with their rates of alveolar [n]: those with no college experience had a rate of 67 percent, while those with even some college experience had a rate of 45 percent. In the United States, researchers have observed that people from the South use the alveolar nasal [n] more in *-ing* variation. This pattern is also true for West Virginia, where people from the southern half of the state have the alveolar nasal 59 percent of the time, whereas people from the northern half have it 46 percent of the time (Hazen 2008).

Quotative *Be Like*

In Frank Zappa's 1982 unintentional hit song "Valley Girl," Moon Zappa utters the grammatical phrase that would be tagged to Valley girls from there on out: *She's like, "Oh my god."* Around that time, the use of *be like* to introduce quotes spread like wildfire from California.

This change in the grammar patterns of English swept around the world at the end of the twentieth century, and as far as sociolinguists are concerned, it was the fastest global language change in the history of English. Appalachia was fully part of this change. The pattern involves quotatives, those words people use to introduce quotes: *We said, "No chance."* There are actually plenty of ways to introduce direct quotes—including *tell, shout, exclaim*—but historically people have used just a few. The verb *say* was the leader for a long time, with the verb *go* doubling sometimes as a quotative in phrases like *And then she goes, "Yeah I want ice cream."* Starting at the end of the 1970s, a new quotative emerged, quotative *be like*. Over the next two decades, this quotative would spread around the world and become king of the quotative hill, even in Appalachia (Buchstaller and D'Arcy 2009).

It may seem odd for *like* to partner with the verb *be* and start this new adventure, but *like* has had a complicated history. There are at least two different *like* words that happen to be homonyms, with both spelling and pronunciation identical. The verb *lician* was part of Old English from the beginning and went through several changes before it reached its modern usage as a verb: *I like chocolate*. A different word, Old English *gelic*, was used as an adjective, sometimes a noun, but eventually developed into a modern preposition: *The cabbage is like a paperweight* (D'Arcy 2017).

In Appalachia, the quotative *be like* era came in at the same time that it developed elsewhere across the United States. In a study of West Virginia, only speakers born after 1960 had quotative *be like*, but those speakers had this new variant 29 percent of the time (Hazen forthcoming). In contrast with vernacular patterns like leveled *was* and demonstrative *them*, which were both on the decline in the twentieth century, quotative *be like* is on the rise and is used more often by females. In addition, the upper-middle-class speakers use it more than any other social class. It might be noted at times, but quotative *be like* is an Appalachian grammar pattern that is not vernacular. In several ways, it shows the connection between Appalachia and other varieties of US English.

OTHER GRAMMAR PATTERNS

There are numerous other grammar patterns not discussed in this chapter. This section mentions a few of them, but a full account, especially of older patterns, is given in Montgomery and Hall (2004). One of the more researched patterns involves a verb suffix that is also found on the Outer Banks of North Carolina (Wolfram et al. 1999). It involves the addition of an *–s* suffix on verbs with a plural subject that is not a pronoun. In this sentence from Johnson J. Hooper, "But I'm told the yankees always sing*s* a psalm before they go_ into battle," the verb *sing* gets an –*s* but the verb *go* does not because of the pronoun *they* (Ellis 2013). This pattern has been around for centuries but has dropped quickly since the 1950s.

Another well-noted pattern related to verbs is variation with past-tense forms. It is not uncommon in Appalachia to have the past-tense verbs of *We knowed*, *I seen him*, or *She come home yesterday*. These variations may be true for younger speakers as well as older speakers. This area of variation is one Appalachia shares with many vernacular varieties around the world.

One innovation that Appalachians have developed is the occasional use of *a* before words starting with a vowel, as in *I bought a apple* (Hazen, Woods, et al. 2015). This usage is the end stage of a thousand-year process: originally the word *one* was used before nouns, as in *one book*, and after a long while, the form *an* developed from it to become an actual indefinite determiner, as in *an book*. After a few centuries more, a second form developed before consonants where the *n* was dropped: *a book* versus *an ape*. Some in Appalachia are bringing the process to its logical conclusion where the indefinite determiner is fully reduced, as in *Need* a *oil change*?

One of the grammar patterns that some Appalachians and outsiders most enjoy are phrases like *I might could do that* and *They're saying we may shall get some rain*. These constructions are called *double modals* (Hasty 2012; Montgomery and Reed, n.d.). This feature is a pattern found throughout the South, and it generally does not extend into the northern half of Appalachia. Other forms shared with the southern United States include the verbs *liketa* in *I liketa died* and *fixin to* in *We are fixin to go to the mall*. Not to be left out of regional connections, the northern half of Appalachia shares a grammar pattern with the Midwest in using verb constructions like *The cats need fed*. Here the verb *need* takes a past participle rather than a verb phrase as in *The cats need to be fed*.

Other grammatical features in Appalachia include the absence of plural –*s* when numerals precede the noun as happens with *twenty mile* in *There wasn't a church to go to within* twenty mile *of where I lived* (Montgomery 2004). That particular feature is similar to the more widespread variation of dropping the –*s* when the plural noun does the job of an adjective: *It was a twenty-mile walk*.

How frequent any of these forms are varies from one Appalachian community to another. Some are divided by region, while others are only used by the oldest speakers and may not survive long into the twenty-first century.

CONCLUSION

People used many of the vernacular grammar patterns of Appalachia less and less often after World War II, yet their decline does not necessarily indicate their demise. When the King James Bible was published in 1611, the editors included grammar patterns like the verb suffix *-th* and the second-person singular pronouns *thou*, *thee*, and *thine*. For most English speakers at the time, these forms were already fading out of use. They were becoming old fashioned when it was published, and since that time, in the United States,[3] these forms only show up in verses like "The waters which *thou* sawest, where the whore sitt*eth*" (Revelation 17:15). Because these forms are normally experienced in hymns and Christian Bible verses, they are tightly associated with this genre. Grammar patterns like *a*-prefixing and demonstrative *them* are often experienced in representations of Appalachians and are connected to whatever social qualities people believe Appalachians have.

Throughout the twentieth century, especially after World War II, Appalachia felt the influence of increasingly ubiquitous external norms that were imported from people moving in and out of the region and implemented through formal education (Hazen 2018). With these forces working on successive generations, stigmatized variants became less widely used and thus more distinctive of social group divisions. Grammatical variation will continue in Appalachian Englishes because they are living varieties, but the varieties of the twenty-first century will not be the same as those from the previous century. Instead of seeing grammar as one of the problems with Appalachian Englishes, linguists see grammar as an opportunity to study the complex and beautiful patterns of language variation.

Notes

1. The *-th* suffix was last widely used in the King James Bible published in 1611, but all indications are that it was not widely spoken even at that time.
2. One of the few surviving plurals was the *-en* of *oxen* and *children*. This plural used to be more widely used, including in words like *eyen*, "eyes."
3. In some dialects of northern England, variations on *thou* still live on in modern usage.

References

Buchstaller, Isabelle, and Alexandra D'Arcy. 2009. "Localized Globalization: A Multi-Local, Multivariate Investigation of Quotative *Be Like*." *Journal of Sociolinguistics* 13, no. 3: 291–331.

Cramer, Jennifer. 2014. "Is Shakespeare Still in the Holler? The Death of a Language Myth." *The Southern Journal of Linguistics* 38, no. 1: 195–207.

D'Arcy, Alexandra. 2017. *Discourse-Pragmatic Variation in Context: Eight Hundred Years of LIKE*. Studies in Language Companion Series 187. New York: John Benjamins.

Ellis, Michael. 2013. "The Treatment of Dialect in Appalachian Literature." In *Talking Appalachian*, edited by Amy Clark and Nancy Hayward, 163–81. Lexington: University Press of Kentucky.

Hasty, J. Daniel. 2012. "We Might Should Oughta Take a Second Look at This: A Syntactic Re-analysis of Double Modals in Southern United States English." *Lingua* 122, no. 14: 1716–38.

Hazen, Kirk. 2008. "(ING): A Vernacular Baseline for English in Appalachia." *American Speech* 83, no. 2: 116–40.

Hazen, Kirk. 2014. "A New Role for an Ancient Variable in Appalachia: Paradigm Leveling and Standardization in West Virginia." *Language Variation and Change* 26, no. 1: 77–102.

Hazen, Kirk. 2018. "Listening to Rural Voices: Sociolinguistic Variation in West Virginia." In *Rural Voices: Language, Identity, and Social Change across Place*, edited by Christine Mallinson and Elizabeth Seale, 75–90. Lanham, MD: Lexington Books.

Hazen, Kirk. Forthcoming. "A Rapid Reconfiguration: Quotative Variation in Appalachia." Unpublished manuscript.

Hazen, Kirk, Paige Butcher, and Ashley King. 2010. "Unvernacular Appalachia: An Empirical Perspective on West Virginia Dialect Variation." *English Today* 26, no. 4: 13–22.

Hazen, Kirk, Sarah Hamilton, and Sarah Vacovsky. 2011. "The Fall of Demonstrative *Them*: Evidence from Appalachia." *English World-Wide* 32, no. 1: 74–103.

Hazen, Kirk, Jacqueline Kinnaman, Lily Holz, Madeline Vandevender, and Kevin Walden. 2015. "The Interplay of Morphological, Phonological, and Social Constraints: *Ain't* in Appalachia." In *Ain'thology: The History and Life of a Taboo Word*, edited by Patricia Donaher and Seth Katz, 178–94. Newcastle upon Tyne, UK: Cambridge Scholars.

Hazen, Kirk, Kiersten Woods, Jordan Lovejoy, Emily Vandevender, and Margery Webb. 2015. "An/A in Appalachia." Paper presented at the Southeastern Conference on Linguistics 82, Raleigh, NC.

Labov, William. 1972. "Negative Attraction and Negative Concord in English Grammar." *Language* 48, no. 4: 773–818.

Labov, W. 1989. "The Child as Linguistic Historian." *Language Variation and Change* 1, no. 1: 85–97.

Montgomery, Michael. 2001. "Myths: How a Hunger for Roots Shapes Our Notions about Appalachian English." *Now and Then: The Appalachian Magazine* 17, no. 2: 7–13.

Montgomery, Michael. 2004. "Appalachian English: Morphology and Syntax." In *Morphology and Syntax*, edited by Bernd Kortmann, Kate Burridge, Rajend Mesthrie, Edgar W. Schneider, and Clive Upton, 245–80. Vol. 2 of *A Handbook of Varieties of English*. New York: Mouton de Gruyter.

Montgomery, Michael. 2009. "Historical and Comparative Perspectives on *A*-Prefixing in the English of Appalachia." *American Speech* 84, no. 1: 5–26.

Montgomery, Michael, and Joseph S. Hall. 2004. *Dictionary of Smoky Mountain English*. Knoxville: University of Tennessee Press.

Montgomery, Michael, and Paul Reed. n.d. MULTIMO: A Database of Multiple Modals. Accessed 23 January 2018. https://artsandsciences.sc.edu/multimo/welcome.

Nevalainen, Terttu. 2009. "Number Agreement in Existential Constructions: A Sociolinguistic Study of Eighteenth-Century English." In *Vernacular Universals and Language Contact: Evidence from Varieties of English and Beyond*, edited by M. Filppula, J. Klemola, and H. Paulasto, 80–102. New York: Routledge.

OED. 2007. Oxford English Dictionary Online. https://www.oed.com/.

Wolfram, Walt, and Donna Christian. 1975. *Sociolinguistic Variables in Appalachian Dialects*. Report for National Institute of Education of the Department of Health, Education, and Welfare, NIE-G-74-0026.M. Arlington, VA: Center for Applied Linguistics. https://files.eric.ed.gov/fulltext/ED112687.pdf.

Wolfram, Walt, Kirk Hazen, and Natalie Schilling-Estes. 1999. *Dialect Change and Maintenance on the Outer Banks*. Publication of the American Dialect Society 81. Tuscaloosa: University of Alabama Press.

PART II

Language in Society

CHAPTER 4

Discourse in Appalachia

Allison Burkette

SUMMARY

This chapter begins with a brief definition of discourse by addressing the following questions: What is discourse? How do we study discourse? How does discourse create social meaning? In answering these questions, this chapter addresses topics such as conversational narrative, language as a social practice, and the relationship between grammatical features of Appalachian Englishes and speaker stance, all of which comes back to the point of affirming the connection between discourse and the construction of social meaning. Finally, this chapter addresses the future of the study of discourse and how nonlinguistic elements can be included in our discussions of discourse. In order to demonstrate how all of these concepts apply to Appalachian Englishes, this chapter contains a series of specific examples from Western North Carolina.

INTRODUCTION

What is discourse? The term *discourse* carries with it an everyday definition that has to do with people talking and is often used interchangeably with the words *discussion* or *conversation*. However, when linguists talk about discourse, they are usually referring to the way that larger ideas and identities are reflected within individual interactions between speakers. For instance, you can talk about how ideas associated with being from a particular place can surface within a conversation between two people from the same hometown. In linguistics, discourse is considered to be a social practice, which means that it can be thought of as a bundle of repeated activities, behaviors, and beliefs that, because they are repeated, make up a socially recognized way of doing something.

From this perspective, language is something that speakers *do* (not something that speakers simply *use*), and through language, speakers can perform different identities and styles, as well as create different kinds of social meaning. All of these things—identity, style, meaning—are discursive in nature, which means that they are continually created, recreated, and reflected by the language we use in our daily interactions (see Cramer chapter 5). Because this process is ongoing, discourse is always connected to social, historical, and political contexts; to physical and cultural environments; to the speakers engaged in interactions; to the topics being discussed; and to other discourses. It might seem like a complicated web of concepts and contexts, but as speakers of a language and as members of various communities, we participate in this web largely without giving it a second thought.

HOW DO WE STUDY DISCOURSE?

In some senses, the study of discourse entails treating spoken language as a text. Linguists who do discourse analysis approach their texts in much the same way literary scholars approach prose or poetry: by engaging in a close reading of the language, context, and assumed intentions of authors and readers. Instead of looking at literature and talking about writers and readers, however, linguists study speech as it is used and understood by speakers and hearers. Speech is not "authored" in the same way that a published book has been, but speaker intention is still a part of language in use, whether that language occurs as part of a conversation, a classroom discussion, or an audio-recorded interview. Discourse analysts often gather their data through ethnography (i.e., by observing a community from the inside as a participant of that community) and then study transcripts of language as it was used in various contexts, using specific points from transcript texts to support their analyses.

Discourse analysts will often focus on the use of specific words, pronunciations, or grammatical features in order to assess what kinds of speaker identities, styles, and attitudes are at play in a given exchange. In studying the discourses of Appalachian speakers, one avenue of investigation is to look closely at features associated with Appalachian Englishes and the contexts in which they occur. For example, within interviews I conducted in Western North Carolina in the early 2000s, the four most common Appalachian grammatical features encountered were *a*-prefixing, nonstandard past tense, leveled *was*, and multiple negation (see Hazen chapter 3). It has often been these features that have been the focus of my analyses of Appalachian interview texts:

- *a*-prefixing (e.g., *I didn't know she was* a-watching *me*)
- nonstandard past tense, five main categories:
  - same form for present and past tense (e.g., *A black cat* run *across the road*)
  - regularized (e.g., *She* throwed *that just as far as she could*)
  - same form for perfect participle and past tense (e.g., *Everybody* seen *a haint every time they turned around*; *They've* tore *that down*)
  - different past-tense form (e.g., *He* clum *that tree all the time when he was little*)
  - double-past form (e.g., *That was the only thing I ever* stoled)
- leveled *was* (e.g., *They* was *all crying*)
- multiple negation (e.g., Ain't nothing *wrong with that*)

In order to get an idea of how the study of discourse works, consider an example from an eighty-five-year-old Appalachian woman named Ruth. I interviewed Ruth some years ago, and she told the following story while we were sitting on the floor in her living room, going through a box of cards and pictures. This particular story is about going into labor with her second child, and it starts with a neighbor stopping by to let her know that the child of a mutual friend is seriously ill.

> She *come* by here and she said that somebody had come by and told her that young-un they *knowed* was *a-dying*. And would I care to walk out there with her, we never thought about having a car which you could go in, you walked if you, without the *menfolks was* at home, and uh we walked out there and I didn't feel good but when I got home I *knowed* truthfully I'd done the wrong thing and the next morning bright and early I knew I had. And I was *a-fixing* a bunch of flowers, back then our kitchen was right here where the dining room is and where the window is I was *setting* in the door, had the door open and was *setting* there *a-fixing* that bunch of flowers and I waited as long as I could and I, Luke didn't work that day, naturally, on account of that child, he died while *we was* out there that evening. Course I went out of the room and uh don't know but I can remember the doctor coming to the kitchen porch and saying that he *done* all he could do but he was gone. So she was, she was uh born the day that they had his funeral. Now wasn't that something?

There are a number of Appalachian features in this excerpt: nonstandard past tense (e.g., *come, knowed, setting, done*), *a*-prefixing (e.g., *a-dying, a-fixing*) and leveled *was* (e.g., *menfolks was, we was*). But, now that we have identified some dialect features, what do we do to analyze the discourse? The short answer is that we think about what these features are *doing*.

Sometimes, when analyzing discourse, it helps to take a step back and look at the bigger linguistic picture; in this case, it was helpful to look at the entire interview in terms of how many times Ruth used each of these vernacular features mentioned above. In terms of this particular passage, what interests me is Ruth's use of nonstandard past tense. Below is a list of the five most frequent nonstandard past-tense forms that appear in Ruth's speech and the number of times each one occurred, along with the corresponding standard form and the number of times it occurred.

knowed (14)	knew (5)
come (13)	came (0)
set (13)	sat (1)
give (10)	gave (0)
seen (6)	saw (0)

For four out of these five verbs, the standard past-tense form occurs either once or not at all, which suggests that the so-called nonstandard forms are part and parcel of Ruth's language use; for the past tense of *to know*, however, there is something else going on. Over the course of the entire interview, Ruth used *knowed* as the past-tense form of *to know* fourteen times and *knew* only five times. And, when we look closely at Ruth's story, we see that she shifts from *knowed* to *knew* at its climax:

> I didn't feel good but when I got home I *knowed* truthfully I'd done the wrong thing and the next morning bright and early I *knew* I had.

The shift in past-tense form—which in this case is a shift away from Ruth's more frequently used Appalachian form and into a so-called standard form—works to communicate emphasis. She might have had an inkling that the day's walking had triggered labor that evening, but she knew for sure that labor had started early the next morning. Ruth's shift in past-tense forms is a good example of how "additional" meaning can be communicated (in this case by a verb) within a specific interactional context. Extricating meaning from a single instance of a verb form (or other linguistic feature) is only possible against the backdrop of an entire interview (or set of interviews); consideration of larger patterns is often what reveals the potential interpretations of linguistic occurrences that differ in some way from what is expected.

HOW DOES DISCOURSE CREATE SOCIAL MEANING?

Language is a form of social action, one facet of a larger set of cultural practices, which is bound up in the "particular social contexts in which it is used" (Ahearn 2012, 8). Because of the active and ongoing social life of language, linguists talk about the capacity of speech to produce social meaning, meaning that arises from the interactions between speakers.

Sometimes it is hard to pinpoint what the social meaning of a linguistic feature might be. Take the *a*-prefix for example. One of the questions that surfaces when looking at discourse in Appalachia in particular has to do with the function or meaning of the *a*-prefix. Earlier thinking on this feature suggested that the *a*-prefix has some sort of meaningful content, perhaps as a signal of a habitual or ongoing action (Stewart 1967) or of intermittent action (Hackenberg 1972). Feagin (1979, 115) connected the *a*-prefix with narrative speech, stating that the prefixes were used as intensifiers that indicate that a speaker was using "older, more rural forms." Wolfram (1988, 248) agreed, stating that the *a*-prefix seems to "favor intensity," though he cautioned that this feature is by no means restricted to stylistically intense situations. Wolfram also suggested a connection between "narration of stories with dramatic vividness" and the use of "older, rural vernacular forms" as part of a speaker's storytelling style (1988, 249). Frazer (1990, 90–1), using data from Midwestern speakers, concludes that the *a*-prefix acts as an indicator of a "shift into vernacular style," though for speakers born after 1950, the feature tended to occur alongside specific topics, such as those associated with crises, children, and humor. Frazer observed that the younger speakers thus differed in their use of the *a*-prefix from the older speakers, whose use of the feature was not connected to any particular topic or situation.

I found a similar situation in my Appalachian interview data. After I divided up each interviewee's speech into narrative and nonnarrative passages (see Burkette 2007 for details), I looked at how many times speakers of different generations used the *a*-prefix in each context, counting the instances of when a speaker *did* use the feature as well as when each speaker *could have* used it, and then I used those numbers to come up with a percentage, or frequency distribution. The actual and potential counts were used to run a quick statistical test (the chi-square) to see if the differences between the appearance of the *a*-prefix in narrative and nonnarrative speech were statistically significant. Table 4.1 contains a list of the speakers, their ages, all the numbers, and the

Table 4.1. Speakers' Use of A-Prefixing in Narrative and Nonnarrative Contexts

speaker	age	a-prefixing did/could have				chi-square
		narrative		nonnarrative		
Ellen	97	18/36	50%	2/4	50%	0
Opal	96	19/57	33%	4/9	44%	.3329
Ruth	84	18/38	47%	15/35	43%	.1538
Roy	67	15/18	83%	3/8	38%	3.361[a]
Jeff	39	16/32	50%	0/8	0%	5.332[b]

[a] significant at p < .10
[b] significant at p < .05

chi-square test results (see Holmes and Hazen 2014 for a description of these sociolinguistic methods).

For the three oldest speakers (Ellen, Opal, and Ruth), there was not a statistically significant difference in the way that they used the *a*-prefix; the feature appeared at basically the same rate in both narrative and nonnarrative speech. For Roy, the speaker in the middle age-wise, there was a slight preference for the *a*-prefix within narrative passages, but for the youngest speaker, Jeff, there was a significant correlation between narration and the *a*-prefix. In fact, every instance of the *a*-prefix in Jeff's speech was found within a story.

This brief comparison hints at the changing role of the *a*-prefix, an issue addressed by Wolfram (1988, 252), who explained that the use of this feature is "a way of reconciling the linguistic past with the present, as speakers grapple with the meaning and significance of changing forms. As forms become less frequent, they may take on specialized significance as stylistic and/or vernacular indicators."

Taken as a whole, the data that I collected in Appalachia indicates that the *a*-prefix is less frequent only in the *nonnarrative speech of younger speakers*, which supports Wolfram's suggestion concerning the "reconciliatory" nature of this feature. Let's look for a moment at one of Jeff's stories to see how this might work. I asked Jeff if he knew any "community stories," and what follows is one of the stories he shared, a story told to him by his mother about hearing ghost horses pull up to the house of a relative who was dying:

> So they stepped through the gate at the edge of the little old gravel road and, uh, they heard a team of horses *a-coming* and it was coming down Ashe Road, and they said that uh, mom said the *horses was* just like a run-away wagon; she said you could hear the horses, I mean their hooves just *a-pounding* the ground and the wagon, you know how they'll bounce and all the racket *they's a-making* and uh she told her they'd better jump back through the gate you know and so they did. And they heard it, and it *come* right up to the house and then no wagon, no nothing, just the noise, and it just stopped.

What makes this story "Appalachian?" Not a whole lot in terms of the story itself; the "phantom carriage" motif is found throughout many cultures' folklore. What I would argue makes Jeff's story Appalachian in the sense that it is *local* is the use of a road name and the repetition of the *a*-prefix. Again taking a step back, it appears to be not just the *a*-prefix by itself that is creating social meaning here, but the cluster of grammatical features from Appalachia that appear together in this story. The phenomenon of feature clustering is found throughout my Appalachian data, especially in the narrative passages of younger speakers. Because features such as the *a*-prefix are strongly associated with Appalachia, younger speakers like Jeff can use them to perform their Appalachianness, even though the story being told is a generic ghost story.

The study of discourse is clearly informed by the research conducted by sociolinguists in order to build a case for a connection between specific linguistic features and identification with the communities that use them. It is because of the work of sociolinguists such as Walt Wolfram that someone studying Appalachian discourse would know what kinds of linguistic features to look for. As someone whose work has been informed by both sociolinguistics and by discourse analysis, I look at these two approaches to the study of language not as competing perspectives, but as complementary ones. While sociolinguists look at large amounts of data (i.e., thousands of occurrences of one vowel within the speech of a community) in order to make statements about trends and tendencies (e.g., the use of /aɪ/ in words like *nice* and *night* by natives who identify strongly as being from Appalachia), discourse analysts are more apt to look at the creation, reproduction, and manipulation of social meaning within individual interactions. But, as stated earlier, these two perspectives on language use are complementary since sociolinguistics provides invaluable information about which features and which community identities might be called on to perform the social practice of meaning-making.

HOW DOES DISCOURSE ALLOW SPEAKERS TO CREATE SOCIAL MEANING?

One way to describe the creation of social meaning is to talk about speaker stance-taking. Johnstone (2009, 30–31) defines stance as "the methods, linguistic and other, by which interactants create and signal relationships," specifically, relationships between what speakers are saying and who they are saying it to. Stance can thus be used to signal alignment (or lack of alignment) between speakers and between speakers and their topics and/or environments. In order to enact a stance, people draw on already-existing generalizations about language and style. For example, speakers can use the words *y'all* or *yonder* to signal their participation in a Southern identity, and they can make this move because these are words that are recognized broadly as being used by Southerners. The creation of social meaning is a process that plays out over and over as people simultaneously speak a certain way and identify themselves as having a certain identity (or as belonging to a certain group or community).

Kiesling (2009, 172) echoes this idea, explaining that stance becomes "associated with a social group meaning in a community over time and repeated use," which again brings us back to the idea that language is a practice, an activity, and that people are agentive in their use of it. In many ways, then, when we talk about dialects or varieties of a language, we are actually referring to "sets of stance-taking choices associated with places and/or associated social identities" (Johnstone 2009, 32). Because of the social meanings attached to specific linguistic forms, speakers can use those forms to indicate who they are and where they are from.

Perhaps most keenly, we see the performance of different aspects of self through narrative (Bauman and Briggs 1990). The study of narrative is not just about characters, story plots, or action resolution; it is about what speakers are *doing* as they tell stories in conversation. Coates (2003, 7) describes the links between conversational storytelling and identity, noting that speakers are always making choices about the language they use: "Every aspect of story-telling contributes to our presentation of self.... The characters we construct in our story-telling and their relationships with each other, our attitudes as narrators to the characters in our stories and their actions, the voices we use to animate characters in chunks of direct speech, all combine to express who we are." Storytelling, then, is a piece of the discourse puzzle, and taking a close look at conversational narratives and the choices that speakers make in bringing those narratives to life is one way to talk about the creation of social meaning.

DISCOURSE IN APPALACHIA

Much of the previous research on discourse in Appalachia has focused on topics such as the rhetoric of resistance (e.g., Fisher 1993), requesting practices (Puckett 2000), and the way that particular topics resonate richly within Appalachian conversations. For example, Puckett (2001, 136) talks about "kinship talk" as a well-developed type of interaction within Appalachian communities, which functions to "place individuals both within a network of relatives and at a specific geographical locale." So, Appalachian discourse has a lot to do with family and place. Let's take a look at an example from another Appalachian speaker from Western North Carolina, looking closely at the interplay of Appalachian grammatical features and the way that discourse performs family and place.

Linda is the sixty-two-year-old daughter of Ruth (whose narrative was discussed above). The two have (at times) a somewhat contentious relationship, which I discuss in detail elsewhere (Burkette 2013). Ruth uses many of the traditional grammatical features of Appalachian Englishes liberally, while Linda uses features such as *a*-prefixing, nonstandard past tense, and multiple negation at statistically lower rates than her mother. Neither woman's speech demonstrates a correlation between the use of Appalachian features and narrative speech. So when *does* Linda use these features?

Table 4.2 contains the ages, numbers, and the (not significant) chi-square test results for Linda's and Ruth's use of *a*-prefixing. As we have already established, the use of the *a*-prefix is characteristic of Ruth's speech; the feature appears thirty-three times within her recorded interview. In contrast, Linda uses the *a*-prefix only six times during her interview conversation, a circumstance that begs for further investigation. Of Linda's six uses of the *a*-prefix, two occur within a single narrative where they carry out the classic *a*-prefix function of creating dramatic effect, one occurs in a narrative about getting into trouble because of her brother, two occur as Linda reports her mother's speech, and one occurs as she's talking about her mother. This final example is included here:

She wasn't mean to us, but she was very strict and she meant—I mean, she meant what she said. For instance, if we went out on a date, she said eleven o'clock. If we was five minutes late, she's *a-standing* at the door waiting on us.

This example, in addition to the narrative instances in which Linda voices an admonishment from her mother with an *a*-prefix, demonstrates the way that a vernacular dialect feature can be used to enact a series of complex stances. Given that Linda rarely uses the *a*-prefix and that two of its six appearances occur in speech attributed to Ruth, it seems possible that Linda is using this feature to position her mother as being old-fashioned. This claim is supported by Linda's nonnarrative uses of the *a*-prefix, both of which occur within utterances that specifically describe Ruth as being "strict," as seen in the curfew enforcement example above. For Linda, Appalachian features function as part of a larger rhetorical strategy aimed at differentiating herself from her mother while still expressing solidarity with the larger community.

It is not only language that can accomplish stance-taking work; objects can also be used to create this kind of social meaning. Though one can apply this idea more broadly within the study of discourse, the relationship between stance-taking and objects seems a good avenue for Appalachian discourse in particular. Puckett (2001, 136) comments that Appalachian discourse serves to situate an individual "in a matrix of material objects that signify complex personal and family histories and identities." Material objects can signal complex relationships and identities. In my own research, I take Puckett's idea and put a slight spin on it, arguing that language and material objects can work together to situate and signify a speaker's stance in relation to a place and a family.

NEW DIRECTIONS IN THE STUDY OF DISCOURSE

Linguistic anthropologists have for a while asserted that physical objects play an important role in discourse practices—and not simply because objects are part of a physical context. They see meaning as a *process* that includes nonlinguistic elements as well as linguistic ones. The idea, then, is that objects and artifacts—be they graphic artifacts (Hull 2003), text artifacts (Silverstein 2003), houses (Stasch 2003), drink (Manning 2012), or design (Murphy 2014)—can be mediators of meaning-making processes in much the same manner as language. Objects have meaning in the sense that they act as physical touchstones that both represent and create socially significant relationships between people and between people and their physical surroundings.

Table 4.2. Linda's and Ruth's Use of A-Prefixing

speaker	age	a-prefixing did/could have				chi-square
		narrative		nonnarrative		
Ruth	84	18/38	47%	15/35	43%	.1538
Linda	62	4/27	15%	2/7	29%	.6670

Further, texts (both spoken and written) and objects can work together, each creating a context for the other. An artifact may be important because it is mentioned in a historical document; likewise, interpretations of that historical document may be contingent upon the presence of that artifact. Paying attention to objects as they are used in meaning-making, and to the interaction between objects and texts, helps us to better understand the multifaceted ways in which language makes meaning.

Among the Appalachian speakers that I interviewed in Western North Carolina, one stood out due to his noticeable lack of Appalachian grammatical features. JD was sixty-five when I spoke with him, and his interview resonated with me for the intertwining of stories and physical objects. For instance, JD tells a story about his great-grandfather, a Confederate soldier in the Civil War who had a "fanatical" dislike of dark blue. JD explained that this ancestor "was so fanatical that if he bought a new pair of overalls, great-grandmother Amanda would have to bleach those with lye soap because he couldn't stand the color blue; it had to be gray." This explicit mention of the Civil War and JD's common ancestor's participation in the Confederate Army is clearly a stance-taking strategy, one that JD uses to align himself with his regional and family history as well as his authoritative knowledge of that history.

Shortly after he spoke of his great-grandfather's behavior, JD stood up, walked to another room, and returned with something in his hands. With a solemn two-word statement, he presented me with "his sword." The audio recording captured the fact that I sat there, trying to unsheathe the sword, while JD said to me, "you see the scabbard has been, been bent a little bit, makes it difficult to pull out but you can get it." As I pulled the sword from its scabbard, JD told the following story, one closely associated with the object in question.

Now there are two stories about the killing of the Yankee soldier who was coming back North and it supposedly, supposedly occurred, one of the stories is that the, that the killing occurred in the springhouse over there where my grandfather and my grandmother lived, where I was born, and that granddad, great-granddaddy Chris had brought this sword home with him and had hanged it in the springhouse to keep the children away from it for fear they'd be hurt with it, and that he was drinking water when he saw the guy coming at him from behind and he grabbed that sword and he killed him with it. As I grew up this sword was always painted silver, just had silver paint on it and the reason they said was to hide the bloodstains that went into the metal.

When JD placed the sword in my hands, he tied a narrative to a physical object and thus anchored a hypothetical story to something tangible. The joint presentation of narrative and object allowed JD to enact a dual stance that has to do with both authority and affiliation; his possession of the sword affirmed his ties to his ancestor and to his community as well as the authority to tell that ancestor's story.

Coupland (2007, 24) notes that "social meaning doesn't exclusively reside in linguistic forms," and we have seen now how social meaning can be accomplished by other means as well. Language and material objects are involved in a two-way exchange. The stories that we attach to material artifacts evidence the meaning that objects create for us, while those same objects offer concrete support for the stories in which they appear.

CONCLUSION

What does the future hold for the study of discourse in Appalachia? Stance and stance-taking offer a great deal of potential for the continued discussion of the use of Appalachian features and the attitudes, assumptions, and beliefs of its speakers. One way to move forward in looking at stance-taking in Appalachia, specifically, is to narrow a stance-based analysis to attitudes toward Appalachian language itself, which would also take advantage of work being done in language perception and identity (see Cramer chapter 5). Another potential avenue of extended inquiry is further consideration of the interplay between language and material culture. Pushing forward with this kind of investigation might entail conducting interviews that directly address material aspects of everyday life, such as pantry contents, family letters, photographs, collections, and mementos.

There is precedent for this kind of investigation. Recent discussions within discourse analysis stress the importance of considering the multimodality of discourse, a concept that addresses the many modes with which we communicate, to include text, sound, image, and movement. Multimodal analysis provides a potential framework for understanding how people talk about their homes, their homelife, habits, and belongings. Analysis of supplementary materials, such as notes about and pictures of relevant physical structures and objects, could be combined with linguistic analysis to see how the discourses about Appalachian material culture differ from generation to generation or subregion to subregion. Finally, interviews with craftspeople about the tools and materials employed in their trade would serve to address the connections between language and the creation of material artifacts, with the additional benefit of documenting the present-day production of traditional Appalachian crafts. Just as multimodal analysis can be used to address communication beyond the linguistic, our conception of "artifact" can be expanded to encompass more than physical objects.

Clark and Hayward (2013, 19) discuss Appalachian language features as "linguistic artifacts" that are linked to ancestry in the same way as "a 150-year-old letter, a lock of hair, or a uniform that we hold in awe as we consider history." And though these authors might be using the term "artifact" to connote aspects of language that seem older, or perhaps even rare, the word works in the context of the present discussion in that it provides a link between the linguistic and the material. In archaeology, they talk about "artifacts" as objects that have been (in one way or another) manipulated, used, kept, or created by humans. This concept applies to language just as well as it does to items such as letters, swords, and locks of hair. But artifacts in the archaeological field also serve as *evidence* of human habitation and culture. Artifacts are used to build arguments about the shape and structure of human habitation and culture, especially about communities for which the artifacts are all that is left. Much like the sword handed to me by JD, artifacts are evidence of the truth in the stories that we tell. Viewed from this perspective, linguistic artifacts are evidence, too. Of belonging. Of the past. Of being connected to a tradition. Of being a part of something greater than one's self.

References

Ahearn, Laura M. 2012. *Living Language: An Introduction to Linguistic Anthropology*. Oxford: Blackwell Publishing.

Bauman, Richard, and Charles Briggs. 1990. "Poetics and Performance as Critical Perspectives on Language and Social Life." *Annual Review of Anthropology* 19: 59–88.

Burkette, Allison. 2007. "Constructing Identity: Grammatical Variables and the Creation of a Community Voice." *The Journal of Sociolinguistics* 11, no. 2: 286–96.

Burkette, Allison. 2013. "Constructing the (M)other: A-Prefixing, Stance and the Lessons of Motherhood." *Language in Society* 42, no. 2: 239–58.

Clark, Amy D., and Nancy M. Hayward, ed. 2013. "Introduction." In *Talking Appalachian: Voice, Identity, and Community*, 1–22. Lexington: University Press of Kentucky.

Coates, Jennifer. 2003. *Men Talk*. Oxford: Blackwell Publishing.

Coupland, Nikolas. 2007. *Style: Language Variation and Identity*. New York: Cambridge University Press.

Hackenberg, Robert G. 1972. "Appalachian English: A Sociolinguistic Study." PhD diss., Georgetown University.

Holmes, Janet, and Kirk Hazen, ed. 2014. *Research Methods in Sociolinguistics: A Practical Guide*. Malden, MA: Wiley-Blackwell.

Hull, Matthew. 2003. "The File: Agency, Authenticity and Autobiography in an Islamabad Bureaucracy." *Language and Communication* 23, no. 3–4: 287–314.

Feagin, Crawford. 1979. *Variation and Change in Alabama English*. Washington, DC: Georgetown Press.

Fisher, Stephen L., ed. 1993. *Fighting Back in Appalachia: Traditions of Resistance and Change*. Philadelphia: Temple University Press.

Frazer, Timothy. 1990. "More on the Semantics of A-Prefixing." *American Speech* 65, no. 1: 89–93.

Johnstone, Barbara. 2009. "Stance, Style, and the Linguistic Individual." In *Stance: Sociolinguistic Perspectives*, edited by Alexandra Jaffe, 29–52. New York: Oxford University Press.

Kiesling, Scott. 2009. "Style as Stance: Stance as the Explanation for Patterns of Sociolinguistic Variation." In *Stance: Sociolinguistic Perspectives*, edited by Alexandra Jaffe, 171–94. New York: Oxford University Press.

Manning, Paul. 2012. *Semiotics of Drink and Drinking*. London: Continuum.

Murphy, Keith. 2014. *Swedish Design: An Ethnography*. Ithaca, NY: Cornell University Press.

Puckett, Anita. 2000. *Seldom Ask, Never Tell: Labor and Discourse in Appalachia*. Oxford: Oxford University Press.

Puckett, Anita. 2001. "The Melungeon Identity Movement and the Construction of Appalachian Whiteness." *Journal of Linguistic Anthropology* 11, no. 1: 131–46.

Silverstein, Michael. 2003. "Indexical Order and the Dialectics of Sociolinguistic Life." *Language and Communication* 23, no. 3–4: 193–229.

Stasch, Rupert. 2003. "The Semiotics of World-Making in Korowai Feast Longhouses." *Language and Communication* 23, no. 3–4: 359–83.

Stewart, William A. 1967. "Language and Communication in Southern Appalachia." In *Contemporary English: Change and Variation*, edited by David Shores, 107–22. Philadelphia: Lippincott.

Wolfram, Walt. 1988. "Reconsidering the Semantics of A-Prefixing." *American Speech* 63, no. 3: 247–53.

CHAPTER 5

Identity and Representation in Appalachia: Perceptions in and of Appalachia, Its People, and Its Languages

Jennifer Cramer

SUMMARY

Perceptions play a large role in determining how individuals understand their social worlds through a linguistic lens. The study of linguistic perceptions is crucial to more fully understand the identity distinctions speakers possess and express. Perceptual dialectology provides a set of tools for examining how these perceptions reveal and reflect the local understandings of perceived varieties within the broader speech community. With these tools, we can explore the nuances of identity by asking participants where linguistic variation exists in their communities and what they think of the speakers of those varieties. I present research conducted within a perceptual dialectology framework in Kentucky, a place where the prestige of the variety plays an important role for those located at the margins both socially and geographically. In particular, many Appalachian Kentuckians, whose speech has been ridiculed by outsiders, believe that their place in the American linguistic hierarchy is near the bottom and that urban varieties within the state are "better" than their own. They also express pride in their local speech norms, which sets them apart from other varieties.

INTRODUCTION

Barefoot and pregnant. Married to a cousin. Missing teeth. If you asked the average American to describe someone from Appalachia, assuming they knew what and where that was, these might be among some of the descriptors. If you asked them about how Appalachians talk, the sentiments will be similarly negative (Cramer 2018). People do have *some* positive things to say about Appalachia, but for the most part, Appalachia exists in the American consciousness simply as home to the mythical hillbilly personalities depicted in movies like *Deliverance* (Cramer 2014). That consciousness often extends to Appalachians themselves, many of whom fully believe the stereotypes about Appalachian people and their language (cf. Billings 1999).

Such beliefs have real and detrimental implications for how Appalachians view their own linguistic identities, which, like any other kind of identity, has everything to do with belonging. Linguistic identities are "produced through contextually situated and ideologically informed configurations of self and other" (Bucholtz and Hall 2005, 605). Therefore, linguistic identities have been called "double-edged swords" (Joseph 2006) because people must understand their linguistic selves both through personal experience and the "us versus them" dichotomy created in the dialogic construction of these selves. For example, African Americans who, like all speakers of any language, style-shift between varieties, sometimes sounding like speakers of African American English and other times not, have their linguistic behaviors mapped onto various social distinctions by members of the African American community as well as nonmembers. Their conceptions of self are tied in with those distinctions, which include preconceptions about what it means to "sound Black," and individuals' authenticity can be challenged (e.g., Rahman 2008; Lippi-Green 2012). Perceptions of the identity distinctions speakers possess and express become important in understanding linguistic identities. Perceptual dialectology (e.g., Preston 1989) provides a set of tools for examining how these perceptions reveal and reflect the local understandings of perceived varieties within the broader speech community. With these tools, we can explore the nuances of identity by asking participants where linguistic variation exists in their communities and what they think of the speakers of those varieties.

This chapter presents the case of linguistic identities in Kentucky, a place where rural, urban, and mountain-rural varieties coexist (Cramer 2016a) and the prestige of the variety spoken is salient, especially for speakers of those varieties perceived to be less prestigious (Cramer 2016b). This salience is the case regardless of whether that prestige comes from perceived urbanity, education, or some other factor. In particular, Appalachian Englishes have been ridiculed by outsiders (including non-Appalachian Kentuckians) to the point that many speakers of those varieties believe that their place in the American linguistic hierarchy is near the bottom. Yet, through their own eyes, their speech is seen as pleasant, beautiful, and part of what it means to be Appalachian.[1] Using a perceptual dialectology framework, this chapter explores the nuances of linguistic identity enactment and representation among Appalachian and non-Appalachian Kentuckians, with an emphasis on how perceptions of prestige and marginality work together to produce a particular dialect landscape for Kentuckians.

PRESTIGE AND MARGINALITY IN APPALACHIA

The notion of linguistic prestige, whether overt or covert (Labov 2006), comes from the level of respect accorded to a specific language variety *relative to* other varieties that members of a speech community could potentially be expected to have access to. Standard American varieties, for example, carry overt prestige, which means that they are socially acknowledged as a "good" way of speaking and thus typically highly valued by members of the speech community. Americans are expected to have access to a standard variety of English through media and education in the United States, but they likely also have access to other linguistic varieties that carry various levels of (usually covert) prestige relative to their region's standard. In exploring overt prestige in the American context, we see things like lower classes feeling pressure from upper classes to produce certain linguistic features because the varieties spoken by higher-level classes are considered to be standard; they are seen as overtly prestigious simply by virtue of the speaker's class. An example of the effect of overt prestige can be seen in Labov's (1966) work with lower-class production of R-dropping (e.g., *card* → *cahd*) associated with upper-class speech in New York City. Lower-class speakers used many more R sounds when doing more formal tasks, like reading a story, than they did in their conversational interviews. Covert prestige, on the other hand, is about finding value in nonstandard speech forms, such as Trudgill's (1974) finding that men in Norwich often overreport nonstandard usage, as doing so indicates higher levels of manliness and lower levels of care for speech, attributes that must be seen as attractive for these speakers.

Related to the notion of prestige is social marginality, which relates to how a person or social group is situated in society. Those experiencing marginality are positioned at the margins of society, excluded from full participation. From a linguistic standpoint, a common way in which this distinction is discussed has to do with standardness. Those who use and have access to a variety of standard English are considered to be core members of American society, while those who speak nonstandard varieties are located at the margins (e.g.,

Lippi-Green 2012). So, just as with prestige, the notion of marginality is relational; marginality is about creating dichotomies based on certain social characteristics. This definition means, of course, margins exist for many other distinctions beyond language, such as rich and poor or Black and White. In every case, one group is positioned as the dominant or preferred group, while the other is left in the margins.

For Appalachians, it is clear that these two factors, prestige and marginality, go hand in hand. In terms of culture, education, wealth, language, and numerous other features, the practices of people who live in Appalachia are often seen as peripheral to mainstream American values. The picture of Appalachia painted in the national imagination is divided. On the one hand, Americans have constructed a romantic myth of Appalachia as isolated, frozen in time, untouched by outside influences, and existing as an idyllic mountain paradise of a time gone by (Montgomery 1999). On the other hand, media representations of Appalachia, like those found in countless movies and television shows, depict characters here as dangerous, vengeful, ignorant, and lawless. These contradictory images, both of which can be considered peripheral to mainstream American cultural tropes, position Appalachians as distinct and, therefore, marginal.

In eastern Kentucky specifically, this marginal status is quite visible, as the educational system is described as being much worse than non-Appalachian areas of the state (e.g., Elam 2002), with Kentucky already ranking rather low in the country in terms of education.[2] Additionally, some of the poorest counties in the United States are located in Appalachian Kentucky (e.g., Lowrey 2014), which is used as justification for considering the people, culture, and language of eastern Kentucky to be of lower prestige. Anecdotally, I have noted that linguistic marginality seems to be experienced most critically by students from these rural counties who move to larger urban areas for university. These students relate stories about being laughed at by roommates and being asked to "perform" when the linguistic features under scrutiny were previously just how people talked in their experience. Faced with this otherness, Appalachian Kentuckians cite the need to walk a linguistic tightrope. They discover that their home variety lacks overt prestige in this new setting, yet the covert prestige associated with it is necessary for acceptance when they return home for school breaks. They know they must maintain their home varieties or face ridicule by their families for getting "above their raising."

The comparative nature of both prestige and marginality presented here is directly connected to the notion of relationally constructed identities in Bucholtz and Hall (2005). Identities are produced, constructed in interaction, and always considered in relation to the self and the other. Identities gain their social meaning through interactions with other people. Thus, identities are subjected to the same impacts of perception as prestige and marginality. For example, the linguistic tightrope phenomenon is about balancing (at least) two distinct identities: one at school and one at home, where the linguistic identity associated with the former is devalued among the latter and vice versa. The individual must perceive this distinction and speak accordingly.

Ultimately, prestige, marginality, and identity are all about perception. To understand this importance, one must take the view from both the core and the periphery. How does the linguistic minority view linguistic variation? How does that differ from the view of those not in the minority? How do those on the margins and those not on the margins understand their positions with respect to each other? How do they perceive one another? In what follows, I explore how perceptual dialectology can help us answer these questions.

PERCEPTUAL DIALECTOLOGY

Given the importance of perceptions, it seems crucial to explore the metalinguistic awareness of marginal and core speech communities to more fully understand perceived distinctions in prestige. Metalinguistic awareness refers to the ways in which speakers (explicitly or implicitly) perceive, notice, and understand "what linguistic differences exist and what their social meanings are" (Squires 2016, 80). For example, when speakers of Southern American English are asked to take part in job interviews, knowing that many people perceive Southern features like *y'all* and *fixin to* as being uneducated, those speakers may attempt to conceal their Southernness by removing such words from their interview speech. Perceptual dialectology is a field of study that focuses on how nonlinguists define and understand the dialect landscapes they live in. It allows for in-depth analysis of the linguistic attitudes that individuals use in interpreting their social worlds. These attitudes reveal notions of prestige and marginality within a community and provide a glimpse into the ways in which speakers construct their linguistic identities vis-à-vis the other dialect varieties they perceive. Research in perceptual dialectology showcases how aware speakers are of language variation in their communities and considers language perception data to be a necessary correlate to the production data prominently featured in traditional dialectological studies. That is, understanding how speakers perceive language can help us understand how they produce it.

There are many tools used in perceptual dialectology to extract these ideas about language. One of the most common methods is the draw-a-map task, in which, given some geographic space, respondents draw and label the dialect boundaries they perceive (e.g., Preston 1989). Typically such research also involves understanding not just where the varieties are spoken but also how "good" the respondent believes the varieties to be (e.g., Preston 1996). In such tasks, respondents are given a list of social characteristics, like education, correctness, and pleasantness, and are asked to rate varieties on a scale from good to bad (e.g., educated–uneducated; correct–incorrect).

In these kinds of studies, what has typically been found is that respondents draw the most stigmatized areas first, which is followed by adding more nuanced detail to their home regions (Preston 1999). In much of the research conducted in the United States, the most commonly delimited area, regardless of the origin of the respondent, is some kind of representation of the American South, which is typically perceived in a negative light, as evidenced by the common usage of negative labels like *hick* and *redneck* (cf. Lovejoy chapter 8). Furthermore, when asked to rate varieties, Preston (1999) generalized that respondents who have high levels of linguistic insecurity (Labov 1966) will rate their home regions as rather pleasant while selecting other areas as being more correct; those who are linguistically secure will rate their own varieties as correct and pleasant. As one might expect, Southerners (and speakers of other nonstandard varieties) tend to be less linguistically secure than those who perceived themselves to be speakers of standard varieties.

This kind of approach is interesting and appropriate for Appalachian respondents (and those living in close proximity to the Appalachian region) because as a cultural region we know Appalachia to be highly stigmatized. Americans' language ideologies about Appalachia are primarily negative (e.g., the varieties spoken there are thought to be uneducated, incorrect, backwards). A perceptual dialectology approach can highlight the perceptions in and of Appalachia, and in a state like Kentucky, with both an Appalachian and a non-Appalachian contingent, the impact of those larger, national language ideologies can be discovered.

BROADER PERCEPTIONS

Little work in perceptual dialectology (aside from the work reported here) has focused on the Appalachian region specifically. Certainly research that aims to discover impressions of the entire American dialect landscape using the draw-a-map task would include references to Appalachia, yet those that exist seem few and far between. Often the Appalachian area is either subsumed under a broader Southern label or left undefined altogether. More can be found in the smaller studies that examine partially Appalachian areas. Benson (2003), for example, showed that Ohioans perceive a three-way distinction that essentially aligns with production maps, showing Northern, Midland, and South Midland/Appalachian areas. This work, however, does not delve into the language attitudes held with respect to Appalachia.

Other tasks in perceptual dialectology, like the more qualitative sociolinguistic interviews, have revealed different contexts for understanding perceptions of Appalachia. A good deal of Preston's research in Michigan involved interviews with second-generation Appalachians (typically from Ypsilanti, Michigan) who fully believe they have acquired local (Michigan) speech patterns and cannot hear the Appalachianness of their own speech. Thus, they are using elements of "a variety which is strongly (generally negatively) caricatured" (Preston 1996, 341) while at the same time disparaging that very same variety.

Another project (Hayes 2013), which was not explicitly couched in perceptual dialectology framework, used semistructured sociolinguistic interviews with people from Tennessee and various non-Southern locales to gauge perceptions of Southern/Appalachian Englishes.[3] He found that Southerners made more distinctions in the South than non-Southerners, including a precise distinction between having a "Southern accent" and using "bad English." This distinction meant Southerners could describe (positive) social functions for the Southern accent, like politeness and solidarity. The non-Southerners, however, "perceived the entire variety as it differed from Standard American English to denote lack of education, along with expectations of the speaker being ultra-conservative, religiously fundamentalist, and xenophobic" (Hayes 2013, 62). Such an understanding of how Southerners and non-Southerners describe Southern speech begins to paint a clearer picture of the metalinguistic awareness held by nonlinguists, in that while Southerners can find positive attributes of their own speech, non-Southerners prefer to link Southern speech with the typically negatively evaluated social behaviors of ignorance and prejudice.

In other parts of the country, even as far as Washington State, the notion of Appalachia (and general Southernness) can be evoked in perceptions of rurality. Evans (2013) found a significant rural/urban divide among her Washingtonian participants' perceptions. One participant from Seattle, to indicate rurality, claimed that rural Washington dialects "can take on an embraced Appalachian or Texas sound" (72). But, despite Evans's claim that such a statement was considered neutral by her respondents, it is important to realize that evoking "Appalachian" here has the potential to bring with it more than just the rural connotation. Indeed, I would argue that the choice of "Appalachian" indicates an even stronger statement, with the respondent likely intending other readings as well.

My own research has centered on how people from Louisville, Kentucky—the largest urban area in a predominantly rural and partially Appalachian state—perceive their own dialect landscapes, with a focus on whether Louisvillians see themselves as Southern. At Louisville, the Ohio River forms the northern border between Kentucky and Indiana, and it is often seen as the northern border of the South. Cramer (2016b) showed that Louisville's location on the border between Southern and non-Southern locales causes regional identity alignments to be neither simple nor straightforward. In exploring this question of Southernness, I discovered that Louisvillians not only feel a need to distance themselves from larger stereotypes associated with the South but also from the rural and mountain rural communities within their own state (Cramer 2016a), as seen in figure 5.1. This Louisvillian used the word "normal" to refer to speech in and around Louisville while using derogatory labels like "hick" and "country bumpkin" as a way to distance himself from those ways of speaking. Specifically, with respect to Appalachia, Louisvillians tend to ignore any positive attributes of the region, favoring the more negative stereotypes, calling the speech of the region incorrect, nonstandard, and informal (Cramer 2018). Indeed, from the perspective of all Kentuckians, the Appalachian portion of the state was rated "lowest in each of the social categories given on the language attitudes survey (i.e., correctness, pleasantness, standardness, formality, beauty, and education), while the more urban areas of central and northern Kentucky were rated highest" (Cramer 2016b, 73).

It seems that the view of Appalachian speech from outsiders is rather homogenous. Despite potential connections to the region, both in terms of proximity (Kentucky and Ohio) and heritage (Ypsilanti), outsiders view Appalachian Englishes in fairly negative terms, suggesting that the linguistic identities of those who use these varieties are not held in high esteem. But what do these identities look like from the other side? Appalachians certainly experience this othering, but do they return the favor? Do they express an Appalachian identity that differs from this negative portrayal?

A VIEW FROM THE MARGINS

If we ask people from Appalachia to complete the exact same tasks, the picture begins to look a little brighter. Cramer (2019) showed how, despite the

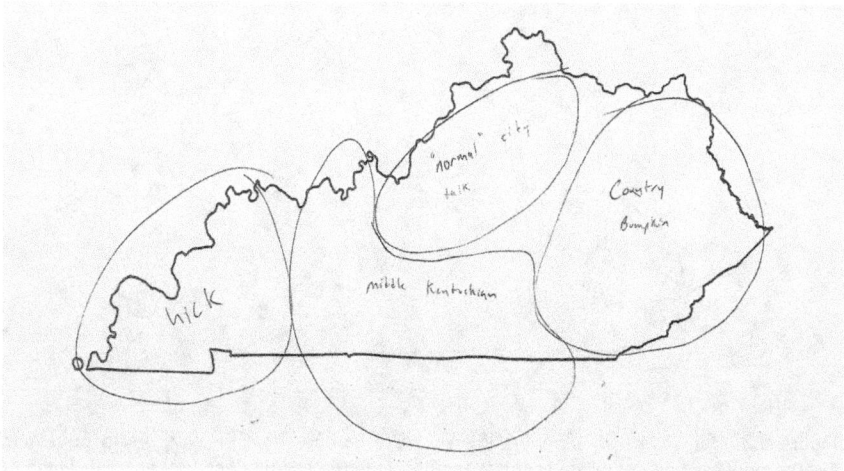

Figure 5.1. Map Drawn by Nineteen-Year-Old Male from Louisville. From *Contested Southernness: The Linguistic Production and Perception of Identities in the Borderlands* by Jennifer Cramer, © Duke University Press, 2016.

---

fact that characteristics like education and standardness get connected to the urban regions of Kentucky, Appalachians can "strike back" against the stereotypes leveled against them to showcase how their own ways of speaking are homey, pleasant, beautiful, and representative of their heritage and culture. For example, the map in figure 5.2 was drawn by a resident of Pike County, the easternmost county in the state. For her, the entire state is made up of "country" accents, but the level and type of "country" varies. In describing the "more urban accent/still country" region, she maintains that urban areas are more standard, but her inclusion of "still country" in the label expresses at least some level of doubt. But what is most interesting about her representation of Kentucky's dialect landscape is that the label she chooses for her home region contains the word "hillbilly." This is a word that has been shown to circulate in national narratives of power that serve to place mountain folk at the bottom of the social hierarchy (Ferrence 2012), but her inclusion of a heart and her description of the label as something that makes her "proud not angry" suggests that the term has been "redemptively claimed" (Hartigan 2005, 123) for self-identification. This designation is similar to how words like *queer* have been reappropriated (Chen 1998), such that the previously inherent negative connotations are stripped away, and

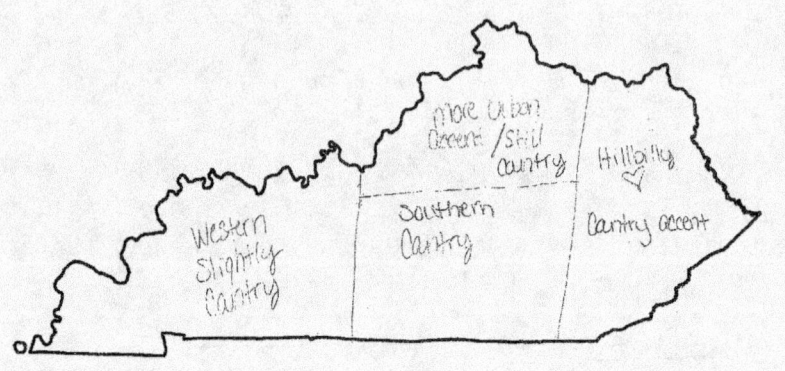

Figure 5.2. Map Drawn by Twenty-One-Year-Old Female from Pike Co. From *Contested Southernness: The Linguistic Production and Perception of Identities in the Borderlands* by Jennifer Cramer, © Duke University Press, 2016.

new, proud connotations are attached by the people previously disparaged by such words.

This phenomenon is not unexpected. There is a sense in which regional pride has always been evident among Appalachians, but new forms of communication, like blogs and social media, are becoming platforms for the expression of this pride. That pride includes language, where some commentators (e.g., Drye 2005; McCarroll 2018) are beginning to regret having sought to lose their accents earlier in life.

Another individual map that showcases the resistance to urban norms can be seen in figure 5.3. In circling the northern portion of the state and indicating that they "talk more like people from Ohio," this respondent is doing the same kind of othering that is often done to Appalachians. With the comments of "talk like me" in the "Appalachian Region," she is insinuating that not only is their variety different from her own but also that it is so different that she actually considers it to be non-Kentuckian as well. Again, the notion of "proper"[4] or standard speech gets connected to another area of the state, this time the area in which one can find the two major state universities, so as to further link standard speech and education (and, in the case of Kentucky, also urbanity, as these two universities are in the first- and second-largest cities in the state).

In terms of how eastern Kentucky respondents rate the varieties they perceive in the state, we find that they do not place the Appalachian region at the bottom in every social category. As you can see in table 5.1, eastern

IDENTITY AND REPRESENTATION IN APPALACHIA / 79

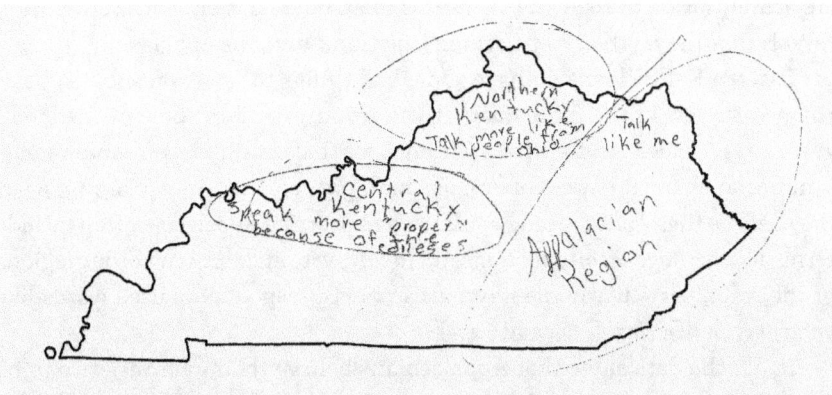

Figure 5.3. Map Drawn by Twenty-One-Year-Old Female from Rowan Co. From *Contested Southernness: The Linguistic Production and Perception of Identities in the Borderlands* by Jennifer Cramer, © Duke University Press, 2016.

Kentuckians perceive the eastern Kentucky region to be most similar to their own way of speaking (an expected result) and second most pleasant and beautiful. Yet, in all other categories, they place their own way of speaking at the bottom, thus categorizing it as incorrect, nonstandard, informal, and uneducated. These rankings reveal a low level of linguistic security for Appalachian participants; they are willing to call their own speech pleasant and beautiful, which likely serve as markers of solidarity in the community, but they cannot conceive of their varieties as having those markers of power that are often connected to urbanity. It shows that, even within their own communities, they

Table 5.1. Eastern Kentuckians' Rankings of Perceived Varieties by Social Category

	Similar	Correct	Pleasant	Standard	Formal	Education	Beauty
1: MOST	Eastern	Northern	Central	Central	Northern	Northern	Southern
2	Central	Central	Eastern	Northern	Central	Central	Eastern
3	Southern	Western	Western	Western	Western	Western	Central
4	Western	Southern	Southern	Southern	Southern	Southern	Western
5: LEAST	Northern	Eastern	Northern	Eastern	Eastern	Eastern	Northern

are acutely aware of the external norms of standardization. Such recognition reveals that the myth of Appalachian isolation cannot be upheld.

Eastern Kentuckians do have some bad things to say about non-Appalachian varieties. In the more qualitative responses and in some of the labels given to the dialect regions they perceive, we find that there are more important social characteristics for Appalachian participants. In explaining what they believe their labels mean, words used to describe Appalachia often include terms like *heritage*, *home*, *inviting*, and *family*; yet, in describing other regions of the state, particularly the more urban areas, respondents used words like *annoying*, *snobby*, *insulting*, and *Yankee*.

In all, the data show that Appalachians believe their own varieties to be connected to important social characteristics like family and home while also often denigrating the varieties associated with overt prestige for lacking these important qualities. Yet, while these Appalachians are more likely than non-Appalachians to attribute covert prestige to their own varieties, they seem to at least partially accept the negative stereotypes attributed to their language varieties.

CONCLUSION

Linguistic identities are complicated. We cannot boil them down by simply asking speakers who they are. In grappling with social perceptions, which are intensified by notions of linguistic prestige and marginality, speakers must find a balance. The contexts within which identities emerge and the ideologies that surround those contexts figure prominently in the construction of self and other. Individuals must interpolate those contexts and ideologies in the formation of their linguistic selves. How they perceive those contexts and ideologies is important, and their perception has been the focus of this chapter.

While these Kentuckians perceive certain characteristics like education, formality, and standardness to belong to the varieties spoken in the urban areas in the state, Appalachians find ways of expressing their linguistic identity in a way that, through covert prestige, allows them to identify with people and places that are often derided by outsiders. In terms of identity relations, in making these distinctions, Appalachian Kentuckians situate themselves as opposed to Kentucky urbanites. They set up this contrast to actively express their awareness of the rural/mountain/urban trichotomy present in the state. Appalachians recognize that their speech reveals an attachment to culture, heritage, home, and family, and they perceive their speech to be pleasant and beautiful. Therefore, while it might seem that Appalachians have accepted some of the negative stereotypes that circulate in the wider discourse about their varieties, in some ways, the notion of prestige has been flipped. There is more work to be done to understand how people in linguistic minority communities experience prestige within the dialect landscape, but this first look exposes a real challenge to the notion of linguistic hegemony. Covert and overt prestige work together in complex ways in this speech community, and through the lens of perceptual dialectology, we can begin to appreciate what role each plays for speakers of Appalachian Englishes.

More work can be done to better understand the perceptions of Appalachians. An Appalachian-focused perceptual dialectology study could present an even more nuanced picture of how people across the entire region understand their place and the place of other varieties in the dialect landscape of the United States. Perceptual dialectology tools like the draw-a-map task and language attitudes surveys, in combination with sociolinguistic interviews, can reveal how these perceptions operate both for defining Appalachian linguistic identities and defining the identities of speakers of other varieties. When we understand where speakers believe linguistic variation exists, we can better understand how they value or devalue that variation and the identities that get connected to the various ways of speaking that they perceive.

Notes

1. As noted elsewhere in this book, *Appalachian* is not a label typically used by people from the Appalachian Mountains to refer to themselves; indeed, in the minds of many Appalachians, the label is best used to describe some other place (e.g., Montgomery 1999). It is used here as shorthand.
2. Kentucky is ranked forty-seventh in bachelor's degree attainment at only 22 percent of the population, according to the ACS 2009–2013 (US Census Bureau 2017).
3. His participants were from Tennessee, some of whom were from Appalachian Tennessee, and he claimed that respondents did not make a distinction between Appalachia and the South.
4. Though I would argue, as I have elsewhere (Cramer 2015), that the use of quotation marks around the word *proper* serves to either distance herself from claiming the thought herself or to indicate doubt that such language is actually proper.

References

Benson, Erica J. 2003. "Folk Linguistic Perceptions and the Mapping of Dialect Boundaries." *American Speech* 78, no. 3: 307–30.

Billings, Dwight. 1999. "Introduction." In *Confronting Appalachian Stereotypes: Back Talk from an American Region*, edited by Dwight Billings, Gurney Norman, and Katherine Ledford, 3–20. Lexington: University Press of Kentucky.

Bucholtz, Mary, and Kira Hall. 2005. "Identity and Interaction: A Sociocultural Linguistic Approach." *Discourse Studies* 7, no. 4–5: 585–614.

Chen, Melinda Yuen-Ching. 1998. " 'I am an Animal!': Lexical Reappropriation, Performativity, and Queer." In *Engendering Communication: Proceedings from the Fifth Berkeley Women and Language Conference*, 128–40. Berkeley: University of California.

Cramer, Jennifer. 2014. "Is Shakespeare Still in the Holler? The Death of a Language Myth." *Southern Journal of Linguistics* 38, no. 1: 195–207.

Cramer, Jennifer. 2015. "Country vs. 'Country': Using Punctuation to Mediate Negative Perceptions in Labeling Appalachian Speech." Paper presented at the Southeastern Conference on Linguistics 82, Raleigh, NC.

Cramer, Jennifer. 2016a. "Rural vs. Urban: Perception and Production of Identity in a Border City." In *Cityscapes and Perceptual Dialectology: Global Perspectives on Non-linguists' Knowledge of the Dialect Landscape*, edited by Jennifer Cramer and Chris Montgomery, 27–53. Language and Social Life 5. Berlin: Mouton de Gruyter.

Cramer, Jennifer. 2016b. *Contested Southernness: The Linguistic Production and Perception of Identities in the Borderlands*. Publication of the American Dialect Society 100. Durham, NC: Duke University Press.

Cramer, Jennifer. 2018. "Perceptions of Appalachian English in Kentucky." *Journal of Appalachian Studies* 24, no. 1: 45–71.

Cramer, Jennifer. 2019. "Dialect Variation in Kentucky: Eastern Kentuckian Perceptions." In *Changing World Language Map*, edited by S. D. Brunn and R. Kehrein. Dordrecht, NL: Springer, Cham. https://doi.org/10.1007/978-3-030-02438-3_22.

Drye, Willie. 2005. "Appalachians Are Finding Pride in Mountain Twang." *National Geographic News*. Accessed 22 September 2016. https://web.archive.org/web/20170329214802/http://news.nationalgeographic.com/news/2005/05/0502_050502_twang.html.

Elam, Constance. 2002. "Culture, Poverty, and Education in Appalachian Kentucky." *Education and Culture* 18, no. 1: 10–13.

Evans, Betsy E. 2013. " 'Everybody Sounds the Same': Otherwise Overlooked Ideology in Perceptual Dialectology." *American Speech* 88, no. 1: 63–80.

Ferrence, Matthew J. 2012. "You Are and You Ain't: Story and Literature as Redneck Resistance." *Journal of Appalachian Studies* 18, no. 1–2: 113–30.

Hartigan, John. 2005. *Odd Tribes: Toward a Cultural Analysis of White People*. Durham, NC: Duke University Press.

Hayes, Dean. 2013. "The Southern Accent and 'Bad English': A Comparative Perceptual Study of the Conceptual Network between Southern Linguistic Features and Identity." MA thesis, University of New Mexico.

Joseph, John E. 2006. "Linguistic Identities: Double-Edged Swords." *Language Problems and Language Planning* 30, no. 3: 261–67.

Labov, William. 1966. *The Social Stratification of English in New York City*. Arlington VA: Center for Applied Linguistics.

Labov, William. 2006. *The Social Stratification of English in New York*. 2nd ed. Cambridge: Cambridge University Press.

Lippi-Green, Rosina. 2012. *English with an Accent: Language, Ideology, and Discrimination in the United States*. 2nd ed. New York: Routledge.

Lowrey, Annie. 2014. "What's the Matter with Eastern Kentucky?" *New York Times*, 29 June 2014. http://www.nytimes.com/2014/06/29/magazine/whats-the-matter-with-eastern-kentucky.html.

McCarroll, Meredith. 2018. "On and On: Appalachia Accent and Academic Power." *Southern Cultures*. Accessed 28 June 2018. http://www.southerncultures.org/article/on-and-on-appalachian-accent-and-academic-power/.

Montgomery, Michael. 1999. "In the Appalachians They Speak like Shakespeare." In *Language Myths*, edited by L. Bauer and P. Trudgill, 66–76. New York: Penguin.

Preston, Dennis R. 1989. *Perceptual Dialectology: Nonlinguists' Views of Areal Linguistics*. Dordrecht, NL: Foris.

Preston, Dennis R. 1996. "Where the Worst English Is Spoken." In *Varieties of English around the World: Focus on the USA*, edited by Edgar Schneider, 297–360. Amsterdam: John Benjamins.

Preston, Dennis R., ed. 1999. *Handbook of Perceptual Dialectology*. Vol. 1. Amsterdam: John Benjamins.
Rahman, Jacquelyn. 2008. "Middle-Class African Americans: Reactions and Attitudes toward African American English." *American Speech* 83, no. 2: 141–76.
Squires, Lauren. 2016. "Processing Grammatical Differences: Perceiving versus Noticing." In *Awareness and Control in Sociolinguistic Research*, edited by A. Babel, 80–103. Cambridge: Cambridge University Press.
Trudgill, Peter. 1974. *The Social Differentiation of English in Norwich*. Cambridge: Cambridge University Press.
US Census Bureau. 2017. American Consumer Survey (ACS). 2009–2013. Accessed 31 January 2018. https://www.census.gov/programs-surveys/acs/.

CHAPTER 6

Language, Gender, and Sexuality in Appalachia

Christine Mallinson and J. Inscoe

SUMMARY

Chapter 6 explores all available research on language and gender in Appalachia and provides a clear path forward for future work. The diversity of Appalachian speakers' gendered experiences provides an excellent area for intersectional scholarship. By incorporating interdisciplinary scholarship, this chapter incorporates ideas from fields outside linguistics including anthropology, sociology, education, and communications studies. The chapter also emphasizes the need for more research on language and gender among diverse communities in Appalachia.

INTRODUCTION

Language is a central mechanism through which key social structures—including gender and sexuality, as well as race/ethnicity, social class, and the like—are created, maintained, and reproduced (cf. Bourdieu 1977, 1986, 1991; Eckert and McConnell-Ginet 1999). In the 1980s, the subfield of language and gender exploded onto the sociolinguistic scene. As this body of literature has thoroughly demonstrated, gender is a primary factor in explaining language variation. At the same time, gender does not have universal effects on linguistic behavior; rather, gender interacts with other social factors to influence language in locally articulated ways (Nichols 1983; Eckert and McConnell-Ginet 1999). This perspective aligns with the work of scholars from sociology and related fields who take an intersectional approach to the study of social life (e.g., Crenshaw 1991; Collins 2000). In an intersectional perspective, scholars assert that social reality cannot be explained or understood one-dimensionally. Instead, we must examine how co-occurring factors give rise to various social locations by asking questions that center on context and variation and by exploring differences within as well as across social groups.

Today, sociolinguistic research that explores relationships between gender, sexuality, and language variation is robust, yet only scant attention has been paid to the relationship between language, gender, and sexuality for speakers of Appalachian Englishes. In studies in which gender is included as a variable in statistical studies of Appalachian Englishes, results generally show some correlation between speaker gender and the variable being studied, as will be discussed more fully below. But there is a dearth of sociolinguistic research on English in Appalachia that investigates gender specifically, and even fewer studies consider sexuality.

To give a fuller picture as to how language interacts with gender and sexuality for Appalachian speakers and within Appalachian communities, we broadly review scholarly work not only from linguistics but also from related fields, primarily education and cultural studies. Taking an intersectional perspective, we review how scholars have investigated the intersections of language, gender, and sexuality in the Appalachian region of the US. In doing so, we emphasize the heterogeneity of Appalachian speakers' lived experiences and the broad disciplinary range of studies that speak to this area of inquiry. Above all, this chapter highlights the need for much more research on language, gender, and sexuality among diverse speakers and communities in Appalachia.

LANGUAGE AS A MARKER OF APPALACHIAN IDENTITY

Research across disciplines highlights language, specifically accent, as a strong marker of identity and affiliation for Appalachians—across generations, across various ethnic groups, and regardless of whether speakers are located in the region or have migrated elsewhere (Wolfram and Christian 1976; Donehower 1997; Jones 1997; Mallinson and Wolfram 2002; Mallinson 2004; Mallinson and Childs 2007; Hazen and Hamilton 2008; Greene 2010; Reed 2012, 2014). Research on Appalachian Englishes generally has found that female speakers tend to align themselves more toward the norms of standard varieties. In a study of Appalachian West Virginia, Hazen (2014) found that, among younger speakers (born 1980–1989), female speakers showed notably lower rates of leveled *was*, the nonstandard form, than did cohort male speakers. In another study, Hazen, Flesher, and Simmons (2013) found that older female speakers also exhibit less frequent use of demonstrative *them* (e.g., *Look at* them *apples*) than older male speakers. Such findings are perhaps not surprising, since numerous sociolinguistic studies have found that female speakers tend to use more standard speech forms (and male speakers, more vernacular forms). But at the same time, female speakers also tended to use more pleonastic pronouns (e.g., *My baby brother, he was late*) and alveolar *-ing* (e.g., *walk*in')—which are vernacular variants (Hazen, Flesher, and Simmons 2013). These findings suggest the need for continued research to explore where and how Appalachian women are more standard and where and how they use vernacular forms.

For instance, Mallinson and Childs's (2007) mixed-methods study of middle-aged/upper-middle-aged African American women in a small, rural Appalachian community explored variability within women's language in Appalachia. Qualitative data collected over the course of ethnographic research in the community revealed two groups of women whose identity practices and language use reflected different adherences to ideologies about gender and femininity. One group, the "church ladies," who spent much of their time at church, projected a more conservative style, tended to hold higher-status jobs, were more invested in the institution of education, and engaged in gendered status displays, such as talking about manners and housekeeping and dressing more expensively. They were also more locally oriented and resistant to outsider and urban influence. The other group, the "porch sitters," whose time was largely spent in casual get-togethers on the porch of one of the women, projected a more casual style, did not attend church, and did not converse about topics such as housekeeping. They were less concerned about perceived threats to the community from outsiders, and they tended to hold jobs that afforded them less access to economic, cultural, and social capital. In their linguistic practice, these two groups of women differed significantly as well. The church ladies largely avoided using nonstandard linguistic features and features of African American English; they also rarely cursed. In contrast, the porch sitters were more likely to use nonstandard linguistic features and features of African American English. They were also much more likely to curse, to talk about racism and racial dynamics, and to share narratives that centered on topics related to sex or violence, which the church ladies avoided. This study demonstrates "the importance of social affiliations in language practices" (Mallinson and Childs 2007, 196–97) and points to the importance of examining the nuanced construction of identity for within-gender groups, which "allow[s] for variations within the categories 'men' and 'women'" (Mills 2003, 196).

Research has also found that degree of affiliation with the Appalachian region can also interact with gender to affect participants' speech. Reed (2016) conducted a study among Appalachians of /aɪ/ ungliding (*rahd* for <ride>) and rising pitch (moving from low to high pitch on a phrase). Reed (2016) describes /aɪ/ ungliding as a sign of Appalachian rootedness (i.e., local orientation). He found that participants who identified as male employed higher rates of /aɪ/ ungliding in word-list tasks as well as earlier pitch accent onset. Within the speech of female participants, however, only those who were more locally oriented employed more low–high tones and more strongly unglided /aɪ/. In a prestudy survey, Reed had found, however, that female speakers indicated greater feelings of rootedness. In sum, Reed's findings emphasize complex connections among gender, language, and sense of regional affiliation: women reported stronger orientation to Appalachia as a region, yet they exhibited lower usage of nonstandard Appalachian features (see Reed chapter 2).

Finally, a few studies have investigated how male and female Appalachian speakers are perceived. In a (1990) matched-guise study, Luhman found that listeners evaluated male speakers more positively on a solidarity scale than they rated female speakers. On the other hand, when speaking a standard English variety, those same male speakers were rated lower on the scale than standard-speaking female subjects were. In a more recent study of vowel identification, Jacewicz and Fox (2012) found that listeners more easily identified the vowels of female speakers from Jackson County, North Carolina, located within Appalachia. Further, Jacewicz, Fox, and Salmon's (2012) acoustic study also included gender as a variable in the examination of regionally distinctive vowels in children's speech. Female adults and female children from the same part of Appalachian North Carolina showed advanced sound change in comparison to their male counterparts, as did speakers from Ohio and Wisconsin.

Though findings from several sociolinguistic studies have suggested that gender often does play a role in differentiating language use for speakers in Appalachia, there is still much to be investigated in this area. In quantitative studies in which gender is included as one of several variables, such models may not reveal the nuances of identity and language use, particularly for within-gender groups. As Hill (2005, 11) points out, uniform populations rarely reside within categories that lump people together based on demographic variables, and broad categories—such as "gender"—may mask the diverse experiences of the people in each group. As a result, it will be important for future research on Appalachian varieties to further examine the complexities of language use among individuals and groups of different gender and sexual identities.

VOICE, IDENTITY, CULTURE, AND GENDER WITHIN DIVERSE APPALACHIAN COMMUNITIES

Scholars across disciplines have discussed the complicated and complex role of language as a marker of identity for Appalachian residents. Natives' attitudes toward Appalachian Englishes are often complex. On the one hand, many speakers appreciate their own dialect for its cultural significance in their lives; on the other hand, they may recognize (or even buy into) negative stereotypes about Appalachian linguistic and cultural deficiency that are often propagated by mainstream America (Luhman 1990).

In this section, we delve into how language plays a central role as an identity marker within the diverse experiences of women and men who live in Appalachia. Many of the scholars who are most vocal in expressing these tensions are Appalachian women. In an essay in *Southern Cultures*, McCarroll (2016) recounts her own experiences with language and regional identity, beginning with an anecdote from her first day attending an Appalachian college, in a class called "Experiencing Appalachia." As the students went around the room and said where they were from, she revealed herself (in both her answer and by way of her accent as she said it) as a local. In that moment, she writes, "I came to understand that I was Appalachian" (45). When she moved to Boston to attend graduate school, however, she came face to face with stereotypes about the Appalachian region and accent. As a result, she "actively tried to 'talk right' and hide [her] accent" by reattaching dropped *g*s and choosing different vocabulary items. She changed the way she pronounced her vowels—all in an effort to, as she writes, "[bleach] out the local color from [her] language" (46). Later, after hearing the writer and activist Silas House deliver an academic paper with an Appalachian accent, she reconsidered her own "repressed voice" and what aspects of her identity she had lost along with her accent. Now, she writes, "I consider the seemingly disparate layers of my own voice and identity—multi-generational Appalachian, first generation college graduate, economically privileged, queer, feminist, anti-racist, mother, writer, teacher. I am reminded of [my grandmother's] quilt when I look around and see the multiple ways to be Appalachian and to speak Appalachian" (48).

The winding nature of the discovery and development of one's voice and identity are also reflected in the poems included in a master of fine arts thesis by Erwin (2016). In her poems, she reflects on her experiences growing up in Appalachia, specifically the tension between her love of poetry (identified as "luxury") and the more practical and economically affirming education that her construction worker father wishes for her. Appalachian natives—particularly women—are often conscious of their voices, not only because one's language is integral to one's family, home, and community, but also because it can lead to exclusion from the mainstream.

In a recent study of Black women in Appalachia, Barbour-Payne (2014) further examines the connections among voice, identity, and memory as expressed through their oral histories as well as their creative works, primarily poetry. Recurring themes in these women's personal narratives and poems include language, home/homeplace, kinship, and terrain. As the author explains, dialect plays a strong role in signifying connectedness to the region and the meeting of identities, though this relationship is complicated for her speakers: "The poets embrace the language of Appalachia through their choice of dialect in their works. Transferred in performance and publication, these dialectical choices coupled with the Affrilachian accent, a mix of Black vernacular and Appalachian English, and Appalachian content illuminate an intertextual quality of Appalachian culture. By intertextual quality I mean the ways in which the works of Affrilachian writers work together with other Black and Appalachian forms" (37).

At the same time, participants recognized that language can also serve to demarcate identity boundaries. For example, the author recounts her own aunt's and mother's rejection of the label "Appalachian" as an index of social class. Their rejection of the Appalachian identity "translates into more important classed characteristics that work against the Appalachian stereotype: 'We are BLACK,' 'We are EDUCATED,' 'We are CIVILIZED' " (136). Appalachian stereotypes here serve as a specter against which participants define their racial identity. Indeed, studies find a great deal of variation in the degree to which individuals relate to the term *Appalachian*, with many residents preferring not to identify with this label, often in recognition of broader negative stereotypes held about the region and its people (Fisher 2010; Ludke et al. 2010).

Barbour-Payne's (2014) study not only highlights key themes of voice, identity, culture, and gender but also raises the issue that these topics are further complicated when experienced by non-White Appalachians. In 1991, the term *Affrilachian* was coined by poet Frank X Walker to refer to Appalachian African Americans, in part responding to a dictionary definition delimiting the Appalachian body as White. In his (2000) poem "Affrilachia," he writes, "yet still feeling complete and proud to say / that some of the bluegrass is black"—and, indeed, much of Walker's poetry delves into themes surrounding the intersection of voice, ethnic identity, and regional affiliation (92–93). Similarly, in an interview conducted by McCarroll (2014), Affrilachian contemporary poet Kelly Norman Ellis affirms the role of Black female storytellers in her life. Ellis reflects on the complexities of locating race in region: "[Appalachian] wasn't on my radar because in my mode of thinking, those were white people" (141). For Ellis, her identity foregrounds race and gender, while the role of place is more complicated. As she puts it, her thinking "about what Appalachia is" has shifted, as she highlights the all-too-common erasure of Black identity in the region (141).

Continuing these themes with a focus on Appalachian African American women, Troutman (2015) conducted a qualitative study using focus groups and observation with young women who transitioned from city environments to attend a private liberal arts college in rural Kentucky. Troutman describes a theoretical domain arising from discussions with these women: "Fabulachia," which considers "the cultural navigation and process-work that urban black females must undertake in order to succeed and survive as a new cultural minority" as they move into a rural Appalachian environment (2). Language use is shown to be deeply relevant in Fabulachia. Troutman's participants express their frustrations that arise from conversations with White locals, they engage in discourse strategies such as "checking" race-ignorant remarks made by White classmates, and they signal their solidarity with other Black students through body language, eye contact, and culturally specific humor (8). Participants also discussed how they negotiated the experience of encountering racial epithets and racialized insults used by White students both on and off campus. In response to these aggressions and microaggressions, Troutman explains that in some instances her participants "engaged (somewhat reluctantly) in forms of code-switching as an adaptive strategy, though none of them seemed willing to altogether abandon their native speech patterns, accents, and regional dialects" (10). Indeed, Troutman points out the irony of Black students feeling that they must change their speech patterns in Appalachia, a region frequently stigmatized for its own linguistic characteristics. She would have thought, she writes, "after the scrutiny that even white Appalachians have had to endure regarding their regional dialects and 'country' accents, that they would be more understanding of these speech and language criticisms leveled at blacks instead of replicating and perpetuating those very same (damaging) assertions" (10).

By the end of the study, Troutman notes that all of her participants graduated and left the rural area to return to more urban locations. As she concludes, "black female students thrive in spite of rather than because of interracial education at their college in rural Kentucky," an educational environment that "fail[ed] to address the specificity of the urban black females' experience/s, leaving them to access skills gained from 'home,' which become part of and/or make possible the necessary adaptations that black urban females use to survive the space of their educations" (10–11).

Whereas Troutman (2015) uses the term *Fabulachia* to highlight the intersection of racial, ethnic, and regional identity for her Black female participants, Garringer (2017) describes how Appalachian participants in her "Country Queers" oral history project used the term *Fabulachia* to speak to their experiences at the intersection of sexuality and place: "We're fabulous and we're Appalachians, so we're Fabulachians," one participant explained (82). Adding to the scant body of literature that examines language and identity use by members of queer/sexual minority communities in Appalachia, Garringer interviewed queer and transgender individuals in central Appalachia, focusing on the ties they feel to their region and home, even in the face of the bias and stigma they may face as a result of their gender/sexual identities. As one of her participants explained, the term *Fabulachian* captured these contradictions: "I identify as a Fabulachian, which—I love using that term . . . you know, putting the words *fabulous* and *Appalachian* together. . . . The term is Fabulachian and it is used to represent the queer community in the Appalachian region" (84).

As Hough (2017) points out in a presentation of their autoethnography, "Queerpalachia: Examining Rural Queerness through an Appalachian Lens," mainstream LGBTQ movements tend to gloss over queer individuals and queered relationships in rural areas. Growing up in West Virginia, the author found that LGBTQ communities harbored "disdain for . . . the people who lived there . . . [and] considered my home to be populated by 'those uneducated rednecks' or 'hillbillies' "—stereotypes that are commonly propagated in popular media and discourse about Appalachia. As a result, "poor, Appalachian queers are cut off from the rest of the pride movement," a division that can weaken the agency of sexual minority groups and undermine efforts for resistance.

Nevertheless, there is a tradition of community activism in Appalachia. Massek (2015) details a history (herstory) of Appalachian women as resisters, activists, and musicians. Drawing on traditional song and storytelling, she highlights the actions of and progress made by women in Appalachia and speaks to voices of Appalachia that have been marginalized or otherwise excluded from common characterizations of the region. As she writes, "Appalachian women artists from all disciplines bring light to the dark alleys of oppression. They educate us, inspire us, and give us the fortitude to continue working for our beloved mountains and for justice for all the mountain people. As has always been true, activism in the Appalachian Mountains rises in direct proportion to injustice" (294). As illustrated by Massek (2015), Hough (2017), and other studies on community activism in Appalachia, more research is clearly needed to examine how stereotypes and discourse can undermine and marginalize liminal gender and sexual identities in Appalachia—as well as how the Appalachian identity can also be mobilized for social progress.

LANGUAGE, LITERACY, AND EDUCATION

Education is a predominant theme at the intersection of gender and language for speakers of Appalachian Englishes and members of Appalachian communities. What is the relationship of dialect variation to student identity, agency, and bias in school settings? How do these factors affect students' literacy development, experience of learning, school belonging, and academic achievement in ways that shape and are shaped by gender?

Academic literature on these topics makes clear that the negotiation of one's regional and linguistic identity can often be a fraught experience within educational domains for all Appalachians. Students from Appalachia and the US South often report feeling that the culture and language of their home communities clash with that of their school (DeYoung 1995; Locklear 2011; Purcell-Gates 1997; see also Slocum chapter 10 and Dunstan and Jaeger chapter 11). These students may begin to feel disconnected from education, which can affect their ideas about achievement and the opportunities they seek out in life.

These issues can especially affect Appalachian women and girls, who may come face to face with regional and gender-based stereotypes and biases as they pursue their education. In a four-year ethnographic study, educational psychologist and Appalachian native Deborah Hicks (2005) followed a group of urban girls in an Appalachian diaspora community in Cincinnati, Ohio. These girls attended an after-school literacy program from second through sixth grade. Using discourse analysis as part of the ethnographic study, Hicks analyzed the girls' literacy and learning experiences against the backdrop of their everyday lives. By revealing how critical pedagogies could be used to validate these girls' linguistic and cultural experiences, Hicks calls for teachers to legitimize alternative modes of expression in schools and thereby become "more responsive to the distinctiveness" of the voices and experiences of their culturally and linguistically diverse students (213). Others have highlighted the important role that teachers and schools must play in making academic environments a safe and welcoming place for Appalachian students. Clark (2013) examined the literacy learning experience of twenty-one Appalachian women ranging in age from twenty-one to ninety-four. Drawing on her own memories of feeling embarrassed about her speech, she reflects on the connections between vernacular language and literacy in the face of standardized literacy education practices. Only with a more positive and progressive view of her dialect, Clark asserts, did she gain the courage to engage in traditional literacies; she advocates for this perspective in other school settings, where students from culturally and linguistically diverse communities are served.

Sohn (2013) explores these issues further through a study of nontraditional, working-class White college women at an Appalachian university. Through work that is part ethnography, part self-reflection, Sohn analyzes how her participants struggled to negotiate conflicting gender-based expectations about language use, just as Sohn did in her own educational journey. As Appalachian speakers, the women valued their language as a marker of their regional affiliation but at the same time recognized the prejudice they often faced as a result of their accents. As women, participants also reflected on general social expectations that they ought to restrain their language or remain silent. Taken together, these linguistic and social factors contributed directly to participants' feelings of being inarticulate and less intelligent—and hindered the women's confidence on their educational journeys (131).

In a similar vein, the Appalachian author Linda Scott DeRosier, who maintains her Appalachian accent and uses Appalachian linguistic features in her writing, reflects on how colleges and universities can be a particularly pernicious site for this linguistic and cultural oppression, where the voices of Appalachian women are often diminished and their opportunities limited. DeRosier recalled one instance when, after presenting a paper at a scholarly conference, a professor from the audience told her, "I don't think I have ever heard an intelligent person talk the way you do" (DeRosier 1999, 67). DeRosier also recounted her visit to the University of Kentucky, where one student from eastern Kentucky said "she was afraid to speak in her other classes, because she was worried that students would make fun of her accent" (Locklear 2011, 94).

Dunstan and Jaeger (2015) further reveal how accent stigmatization can hinder the academic achievement of Appalachian college students, yet the act of showing them that their dialects are valued can have positive benefits on their sense of belonging and academic persistence. Drawing upon qualitative interviews with twenty-six rural Appalachian students—twenty-five White, one African American—who were attending a large urban university in the South, the authors investigated how these students felt about their language and experiences on campus. In addition, quantitative sociolinguistic methods were used to analyze the participants' speech. Those students who exhibited the most vernacular patterns also stated that they participated less in class and felt anxiety when speaking in public settings, due to fears that they would be stereotyped and told their speech was unintelligible. Both men and women were included in this study, but the negative attitudes about language often were particularly salient for female participants—especially the one African American woman in the study, who believed that challenges surrounding her language use were compounded due to her regional background, race, and gender: "Asked how she feels about her belief that her variety of English is stereotyped as being 'country' and 'unprofessional,' she says: 'I think it's pretty dumb, and then me being Black, it's kind of a double whammy. And a female. That's a triple whammy' " (791). At the same time, the positive takeaway is that the opposite was also true for the students in this study who felt more comfortable around professors who also were from Appalachia or who were open-minded about language. These professional role models helped the student participants resolve the apparent disconnect between their own Appalachian language patterns and how "scholarly language" ought to sound.

Scrutiny of student language patterns was also a significant finding in Helton's (2010) qualitative study examining faculty perceptions about teaching rural Appalachian students in social work classrooms. Comparing the perceptions of social work faculty members at three Appalachian and three midwestern universities, the study found that faculty tended to view Appalachian students as being different from urban students along social as well as linguistic dimensions. For example, some faculty participants felt that "grammatical errors" related to regional dialect and spoken language style represented a major challenge for rural Appalachian students. As one faculty member asserted, these students "talk like they write and write like that talk," and their written expression tended to fall short of the richness of their verbal expression (70). Further, according to the faculty, "Urban African Americans were observed as having similar speech patterns to Appalachians and also experienced challenges in written expression" (70). Second-generation Appalachian students were noted as having better literacy skills and were, in one faculty member's words, "less colloquial in both their values and their speech" (69). Finally, faculty participants felt that male Appalachian students "tended to be more reticent and nonverbal, yet they were good with written work" (69). These findings demonstrate the clear need—in line with Clark (2013) and Dunstan and Jaeger (2015)—for faculty in college settings to develop pedagogical techniques for working with culturally and linguistically diverse student populations, as well as a need to reexamine faculty language ideologies, particularly in how they intersect with region of origin, gender, and race/ethnicity.

There are, however, messages of resistance to marginalizing ideologies about language and education. Fedukovich (2009) likewise locates her experience across various identity lines: woman, working class, Appalachian, and academic. Confronting the ideological divide between academia and the working-class Appalachian woman, she explores these identities in relation to her role as a composition teacher: "At those times when my southern mountain dialect emerges, I perform a different drag for my students: teachers of standard English must also be practitioners, they assume. My performance of Appalachian Academic intends to explode this notion while adding linguistic elements, such as code switching, to my pedagogical goals" (146). As her own experience indicates, Fedukovich maintains that scholars who locate themselves at the intersection of these identities inherently challenge the notion that "writing teachers cannot be both dialect and standard; they cannot be the voice of dominant culture . . . and simultaneously speak as a member of a disenfranchised culture" (148).

CONCLUSION

Although relatively few studies investigate the intersections of language, gender, and sexuality among speakers of Appalachian Englishes, existing research reveals some common themes. Proceeding from research in sociolinguistics, we find that gender does play a role in explaining language variation in Appalachia, though this relationship is underexplored. Further, gender effects on language use are not always straightforward. For instance, in some cases, men's and women's linguistic practices differ in expected ways, but in other cases, the patterns are unexpected. In addition, the potential for interesting findings about gender and language use in Appalachia is not limited to studying women versus men, as some sociolinguistic research has found considerable language variation for within-gender groups. However, the majority of this work has focused on women as opposed to men. There is a clear need for more research on masculinity and language within Appalachia, as well as for more research on language use by speakers whose identities lie outside the gender binary.

Expanding beyond the sociolinguistic literature, a good deal of research considers the cultural significance of dialect within Appalachia. As studies show, language can be a positive marker of regional identity and affiliation, but it can also serve as a negative marker that calls to mind, whether in outsiders' minds or in speakers' own minds, pervasive stereotypes about the supposed backwardness of the Appalachian region and its people—and Appalachian women may feel the tension of these competing expectations and cultural tropes most poignantly. Women are often celebrated as the bearers of cultural tradition and family life, and yet women's language is often policed and scrutinized. As a result, women who speak a vernacular Appalachian variety may face a double bind: even as their dialect may be valued for its role as a marker of local and regional identity, it may also be devalued for being nonstandard and non-mainstream. Stereotypes surrounding the linguistic deficiency of Appalachian Englishes and those who speak them can lead to bias and discrimination in educational settings. Women tend to face added pressure to assimilate their language to the mainstream and remain silent in classrooms. Such challenges, studies suggest, may be compounded for Appalachian women, Appalachians of color (particularly Appalachian women of color), and genderqueer individuals. Similar challenges are likely faced by Appalachian residents whose first language (or that of their family members) is not English; however, none of the research that we reviewed for this chapter touched on this issue, which remains an important one to explore.

Above all, as our chapter demonstrates, the use of vernacular Appalachian varieties cannot be generalized along the lines of gender and sexuality. To obtain a fuller picture of how language is used within this region, more attention must be paid not only to identifying the broader patterns of language use but also to subvariation within and across groups. Such research will illuminate the ways in which gender and sexuality influence language use for Appalachians in ways that are valuable to linguists as well as other scholars of the Appalachian region. At the same time, this research will add insight to the broader study of language, gender, and sexuality. We hope that it reveals how these factors interact with the dynamics of race, ethnicity, and social class for diverse speakers in diverse places and spaces.

Note

We gratefully acknowledge Walt Wolfram and Kirk Hazen for their feedback on earlier drafts of this chapter.

References

Barbour-Payne, Yunina Carol. 2014. "African American Women in Appalachia: Personal Expressions of Race, Place and Gender." PhD Diss., Texas A&M University.
Bourdieu, Pierre. 1977. *Outline of a Theory of Practice*. Translated by Richard Nice. Cambridge: Cambridge University Press.
Bourdieu, Pierre. 1986. "The Forms of Capital." In *Handbook of Theory and Research for the Sociology of Education*, edited by J. G. Richardson, 241–58. New York: Greenwood Press.
Bourdieu, Pierre. 1991. *Language and Symbolic Power*. Cambridge: Harvard University Press.
Clark, Amy D. 2013. "Letters from Home: The Literate Lives of Central Appalachian Women." *Appalachian Journal* 41, no. 1–2: 54–76.
Collins, Patricia Hill. 2000. *Black Feminist Thought*. 2nd edition. New York: Routledge.
Crenshaw, Kimberlé. 1991. "Mapping the Margins: Intersectionality, Identity Politics, and Violence against Women of Color." *Stanford Law Review* 43: 1241–99.
DeRosier, Linda Scott. 1999. *Creeker: A Woman's Journey*. Lexington: University Press of Kentucky.

DeYoung, Alan J. 1995. "Constructing and Staffing the Cultural Bridge: The School as Change Agent in Rural Appalachia." *Anthropology and Education Quarterly* 26, no. 2: 168–92.

Donehower, Kimberly. 1997. "Beliefs about Literacy in a Southern Appalachian Community." PhD diss., University of Michigan.

Dunstan, Stephany B., and Audrey Jaeger. 2015. "Dialect and Influences on the Academic Experiences of College Students." *Journal of Higher Education* 86, no. 5: 777–803.

Eckert, Penelope, and Sally McConnell-Ginet. 1999. "New Generalizations and Explanations in Language and Gender Research." *Language in Society* 2: 185–201.

Erwin, Thea. 2016. "You Pretty, You Bad." MA thesis, University of Miami.

Fedukovich, Casie. 2009. "Strange Imports: Working-Class Appalachian Women in the Composition Classroom." *Journal of Appalachian Studies* 15, no. 1–2: 140–54.

Fisher, Steve. 2010. "Claiming Appalachia and the Questions That Go with It." *Appalachian Journal* 38, no. 1: 58–61.

Garringer, Rachel. 2017. " 'Well, We're Fabulous and We're Appalachians, so We're Fabulachians': Country Queers in Central Appalachia." *Southern Cultures* 23, no. 1: 79–91.

Greene, Rebecca. 2010. "Language, Ideology, and Identity in Rural Eastern Kentucky." PhD diss., Stanford University. https://purl.stanford.edu/fh361zh5489.

Hazen, Kirk. 2014. "A New Role for an Ancient Variable in Appalachia: Paradigm Leveling and Standardization in West Virginia." *Language Variation and Change* 26: 77–102.

Hazen, Kirk, Jaime Flesher, and Erin Simmons. 2013. "The Appalachian Range: The Limits of Language Variation in West Virginia." In *Talking Appalachian*, edited by Amy Clark and Nancy Hayward, 54–59. Lexington: University Press of Kentucky.

Hazen, Kirk, and Sarah Hamilton. 2008. "A Dialect Turned Inside Out: Migration and the Appalachian Diaspora." *Journal of English Linguistics* 36: 105–28.

Helton, Lonnie R. 2010. "Faculty Perceptions of Differences between Teaching Rural Appalachian and Urban Social Work Students." *Contemporary Rural Social Work* 2: 66–74.

Hicks, Deborah. 2005. "Class Readings: Story and Discourse among Girls in Working-Poor America." *Anthropology and Education Quarterly* 36, no. 3: 212–29.

Hill, Shirley A. 2005. *Black Intimacies: A Gender Perspective on Families and Relationships.* Walnut Creek, CA: AltaMira Press.

Hough, Em. 2017. "Queerpalachia: Examining Rural Queerness through an Appalachian Lens." Paper presented at the Appalachian Studies Association Conference, Blacksburg, VA.

Jacewicz, Ewa, and Robert Allen Fox. 2012. "The Effects of Cross-Generational and Cross-Dialectal Variation on Vowel Identification and Classification." *Journal of the Acoustical Society of America* 131, no. 2: 1413–33.

Jacewicz, Ewa, Robert Allen Fox, and Joseph Salmons. 2012. "Regional Dialect Variation in the Vowel Systems of Typically Developing Children." *Journal of Speech, Language, and Hearing Research* 54: 448–70.

Jones, Patricia Smith. 1997. "Dialect as a Deterrent to Cultural Stripping: Why Appalachian Migrants Continue to Talk That Talk." *Journal of Appalachian Studies* 3, no. 2: 253–61.

Locklear, Erica A. 2011. *Negotiating a Perilous Empowerment: Appalachian Women's Literacies.* Athens: Ohio University Press.

Ludke, Robert L., Phillip J. Obermiller, Eric W. Rademacher, and Shiloh K. Turner. 2010. "Identifying Appalachian Adults: An Empirical Study." *Appalachian Journal* 38: 36–45.

Luhman, Reid. 1990. "Appalachian English Stereotypes: Language Attitudes in Kentucky." *Language in Society* 19: 331–48.

Mallinson, Christine. 2004. "The Construction of Ethnolinguistic Groups: A Sociolinguistic Case Study." In *Linguistic Diversity in the South: Changing Codes, Practices and Ideology*, edited by Margaret Bender, 66–79. Athens: University of Georgia Press.

Mallinson, Christine, and Walt Wolfram. 2002. "Dialect Accommodation in a Bi-ethnic Mountain Enclave Community: More Evidence on the Development of African American Vernacular English." *Language in Society* 31: 743–75.

Mallinson, Christine, and Becky Childs. 2007. "Communities of Practice in Sociolinguistic Description: Analyzing Language and Identity Practices among Black Women in Appalachia." *Gender and Language* 1: 173–206.

Massek, Sue. 2015. "Herstory of Appalachia: Three Centuries of Oppression and Resistance." *Appalachian Journal* 42, no. 3–4: 284–95.

McCarroll, Meredith. 2014. "Locating Affrilachia: A Conversation with Kelly Norman Ellis." *South Carolina Review*, 46, no. 2: 140–45.

McCarroll, Meredith. 2016. "On and On: Appalachian Accent and Academic Power." *Southern Cultures* 2: 45–48.

Mills, Sara. 2003. *Gender and Politeness*. Cambridge: Cambridge University Press.

Nichols, Patricia. 1983. "Linguistic Options and Choices for Black Women in the Rural South." In *Language, Gender, and Society*, edited by Barrie Thorne, Cheris Kramarae, and Nancy Henley, 54–68. Boston: Heinle and Heinle.

Purcell-Gates, Victoria. 1997. *Other People's Words: The Cycle of Low Literacy*. Cambridge, MA: Harvard University Press.

Reed, Paul. 2012. "Monophthongization and Southern Appalachian Identity: Change over a Lifetime." Poster presented at New Ways of Analyzing Variation (NWAV) 41, Bloomington, IN.

Reed, Paul. 2014. "Inter- and Intra-generational Monophthongization and Southern Appalachian Identity." *Southern Journal of Linguistics*, 38: 159–93.

Reed, Paul. 2016. "Sounding Appalachian: /ai/ Monophthongization, Rising Pitch Accents, and Rootedness." PhD diss., University of South Carolina.

Sohn, Katherine. 2013. "Silence, Voice, and Identity among Appalachian College Women." In *Talking Appalachian*, edited by Amy Clark and Nancy Hayward, 125–40. Lexington: University Press of Kentucky.

Troutman, Stephanie. 2015. "Fabulachia: Urban, Black Female Experiences and Higher Education in Appalachia." *Race Ethnicity and Education* 20, no. 2: 252–63.

Walker, Frank X. 2000. "Affrilachia." In *Affrilachia*. Lexington, KY: Old Cove Press.

Wolfram, Walt, and Donna Christian. 1976. *Appalachian Speech*. Washington, DC: Center for Applied Linguistics.

CHAPTER 7

Language and Ethnicity in Appalachia

Becky Childs

SUMMARY

This chapter reviews the linguistic literature on Appalachian ethnic language varieties across time, with sections covering each of the major ethnic varieties. While considering areas of linguistic overlap of the various ethnic groups through an examination of linguistic feature sets, the chapter also examines the diversity in the linguistic features between the groups. Additionally, the chapter examines the effect that donor dialects may have had on the development of these ethnic language varieties and the ways that contemporary social practices and migratory patterns continue to motivate language change in the ethnic language varieties of Appalachia.

INTRODUCTION

Despite myths that promote Appalachia as an ethnically homogeneous area of White residents, ethnic diversity has long been a part of the Appalachian region (Catte 2018). Indeed, before the arrival of the European settlers mythologized as "authentic" Appalachians, Native Americans inhabited the region. Although many Native Americans were forced out of the area in what has been popularly referred to as the Trail of Tears, a core group stayed in the region and formed what has come to be known as the Eastern Band of the Cherokee Nation. This group has now grown in size as well as social and political influence in the region and constitutes one of the many ethnic groups of Appalachia. In addition to a long-standing Native American presence in Appalachia, there has been a continuous and increasing population of

African American residents in the region. The influence of African American residents, often referred to as Affrilachians, and their language can be seen across a variety of iconic Appalachian social spaces such as bluegrass music, poetry, and art. In all, from its earliest days Appalachia has been an ethnically diverse area, and like other geographic regions across the United States, its ethnic diversity continues to grow and be reflected in the linguistic and social practices of the region.

NATIVE AMERICAN

Work on Native American English varieties in Appalachia has centered predominantly on the language of the Eastern Band of the Cherokee (Anderson 1999; Coggshall 2006, 2008). The history of the Cherokee in Appalachia is long: in fact, the Cherokee were the first inhabitants of southern Appalachia present when European explorers arrived during the late seventeenth century (Thorton 1990; Neely 1991). Despite a relatively large population during the late seventeenth century that spoke the Cherokee language exclusively, the forced removal of Cherokee peoples from the region by Andrew Jackson along the Trail of Tears tore apart the population and, as a result, their language. The current Eastern Band of Cherokee located in Western North Carolina are the descendants of those early Cherokee that escaped from the Trail of Tears and returned to their homelands. One of three federally recognized Cherokee tribes, many of the current members of the Eastern Band of Cherokee live in the Qualla Boundary, a land trust that spans five counties located in the Appalachian region of Western North Carolina.

With a well-known history of settlement, much linguistic work has focused on the ways in which the donor language varieties (Cherokee and English) are manifested in the English language variety spoken by current Cherokee residents. Specifically, linguists have been interested in the ways that Appalachian norms have been adopted into the speech of Cherokee residents. Additionally, it is important to know the ways that Cherokee language features have been maintained in the English variety spoken among Cherokee residents. One of the most ripe areas of investigation has been vowel sounds because of their salience to listeners and the differences in the vowels found in English and in Cherokee, with Cherokee having fewer vowel sounds than English. In fact, Cherokee has six vowel sounds as well as a nasalized schwa, while present-day American English has up to fifteen vowel sounds.

Diphthongs, which are vowel sounds that begin with one vowel sound and end in another, are one of these notable and salient areas of speech. In her work on the *bite* /aɪ/ and *boy* /ɔɪ/ vowel diphthongs among the Snowbird

Cherokee, Anderson (1999) finds that Cherokee English speakers maintain some distinctive pronunciations of these sounds from the White Appalachian community. Unlike the surrounding population that has unglided /aɪ/ in all sound environments (see Reed chapter 2 for further discussion), Cherokee English speakers maintain the /aɪ/ diphthong at the end of words like *bye*. They also keep their pronunciation as a diphthong at the end of a syllable when the next syllable begins with a vowel, as in *Hi everyone*. Interestingly, this pattern is also the same for the /ɔɪ/ diphthong in Cherokee English. Meanwhile, White speakers maintain a diphthong pronunciation for the *boy* vowel in all situations. The explanation for the differences in the pronunciation of the *bite* and *boy* vowels involves both the sound system of Cherokee and the sound patterns that it allows. The preferred sound structure of Cherokee is CV (consonant vowel), which means that when there are two vowel sounds together, as in a diphthong, the second vowel sound /ɪ/ is interpreted as the beginning of the next syllable rather than part of the previous vowel sound. The presence of a diphthong sound (which is longer in duration than a single vowel sound) at the end of a word or utterance among Cherokee English speakers is also unsurprising given their ancestral language sound patterning, which calls for lengthened vowel sounds at the end of an utterance.

Later linguistic work by Coggshall (2006) examined the *boot* /u/ and *bought* /ɔ/ vowel sounds. Unlike Anderson, Coggshall noted that the Cherokee English speakers pronounce a fronted *boot* vowel and have a back glide in the *bought* vowel quite similarly to that of the surrounding White community. In fact, differences in the pronunciation of these vowel sounds from that of the surrounding White dialect was found only among the oldest, nearly monolingual Cherokee speakers. In both of these studies, the differences in pronunciation among the oldest Cherokee residents points to the effect that the ancestral or source language (Cherokee) had on English speech patterns in the past. The nearly complete adoption of the Appalachian vowel pronunciations by younger generations who do not speak Cherokee as their first or primary language reflects the impact of local language norms on speech production.

Another area of interest for the Cherokee language in Appalachia is that of the rhythm or prosody in speech. This variation is of particular interest because Cherokee is a syllable-timed language, similar to that of Romance languages like French or Spanish, while English is a stress-timed language, like many other Germanic languages. The main difference in syllable-timed and stress-timed languages is the length or duration of the syllables. In syllable-timed languages, all syllables are the same length, while in stress-timed languages the syllable that gets the stress is held or pronounced for a longer time than the other syllables surrounding it. As a result of being a stress-timed language, English often sounds like it has a more irregular rhythm pattern. This pattern can be seen when we look at words of more than one syllable in English and Spanish. For example, the word *tomato* in English has great variation in pronunciation, so much so that whole songs have been written about its pronunciation. Despite debates about the pronunciation of the vowel sounds in the word, we can all agree that the middle syllable gets the stress. Therefore, we know that this syllable takes up more time in the pronunciation of the word. In contrast, the same word in Spanish—*tomate*—despite having three syllables, does not have one that occupies more time than the others.

Examination of the English spoken by Cherokee residents of Appalachia has shown that they have a distinctly different rhythm in their speech than that of the surrounding White community (Coggshall 2008). Cherokee speakers across all ages show a more syllable-timed language pattern, with syllables receiving the same amount of stress across a word, rather than having one syllable that receives primary stress (like the surrounding White varieties). This difference in the rhythm of speech points to the influence of the ancestral Cherokee language on the English spoken by current-day Cherokee.

Despite being different languages with different grammars, sounds, and writing systems, the assimilation of most younger Cherokee to an English-dominant language practice forced the Cherokee language to slip further away from the tribe. As a result, linguists, anthropologists, and educators have recently started a language revitalization program to bring the Cherokee language back into the Cherokee schools and community (Sauceman 2015). Currently in the Qualla Boundary in Western North Carolina at the Atse Kituwah Academy, children in kindergarten through eighth grade are taught a curriculum in the Cherokee language. In this school, students explore and learn about the history of the Cherokee, including the history of their language. Immersed in the Cherokee language during the school day, students come away from the classroom speaking and writing in Cherokee and understanding the linguistic and cultural importance of the Cherokee syllabary, the spelling system create by Sequoyah to write the Cherokee language. In addition to revitalization efforts in schools, the documentary *First Language: The Race to Save Cherokee* details the efforts of the Cherokee to save their ancestral language (Hutcheson 2014).

WHITE APPALACHIANS

White Appalachians are the most widely recognized ethnic group in the region. Mythologized as the "authentic" Appalachians since the Civil War, the White European settlers who arrived to the region in the seventeenth century have received the bulk of attention in language studies of Appalachia (Wolfram and Christian 1976; Montgomery 1991). As a result of the considerable attention, we have expansive descriptions of their sounds, grammar, and vocabulary and the changes that have occurred in their language over time. Likewise, as noted by Hasty in chapter 1, we have considerable information about language differences among White residents across the geographic subregions of Appalachia. Regardless of the subregion, White Appalachians share several salient core language characteristics. Although untrue, it is quite common to hear White Appalachian speech popularly referred to as being Elizabethan or even akin to the speech of Chaucer. It must be noted, though, that no matter how well-intentioned comparisons to Chaucer's English are, comments of this sort only stand to further frame Appalachian Englishes and the entire region as antiquated and unchanging (Montgomery 1999; Cramer 2014). As any resident can tell you, the region is one that is constantly in flux, and as this section will show, the region is full of linguistic retention, innovation, and change.

There are several notable features within the speech of White Appalachians that make it stand out from other surrounding English varieties spoken in North America and in the broader South. The differences from the surrounding English varieties are sometimes qualitative, meaning they can have different rules for when they occur. The differences are also sometimes quantitative in that they may occur more or less often than they do in surrounding Englishes. There is also the possibility that the differences are both qualitative and quantitative, with variability in both patterning and frequency. Below are some examples of the most salient features of White Appalachians with information about their patterning, frequency, and relationship to their donor dialects.

Sounds/Phonology

Some sounds that have been highly associated with White Appalachian speech are fading from use. As a result, we see these sound patterns remain primarily among older White speakers of the region. Two examples of this trend are the pronunciations of the /h/ and /t/ sounds in certain words. In some Appalachian varieties, /h/ can appear at the beginning of the words *it* and *ain't,* so that they are pronounced like *hit* and *haint.* This pronunciation is found most frequently among older speakers in more rural areas. What should be noted though is that this variation is not actually an addition to these words but rather a retention of the /h/ from the earlier forms of these words, when *it* and *ain't* in their standard English form began with an /h/ (Wolfram and Christian 1976). The addition of a /t/ sound at the end of a small set of words is another consonantal feature found primarily among older White residents in some rural locales. As Wolfram and Christian (1976) note, the words *once*, *twice*, *across*, and *cliff* can all be said with a /t/ sound at the end such that *once* sounds like *oncet* and *cliff* will be said like *clifft*.

The pronunciation of *extra* as *extry* can be heard among some older White speakers in Appalachia. This pronunciation occurs when a word ends in the unstressed vowel sound /ə/, like the second vowel in the word *sofa*. In those words, the unstressed final vowel is turned into the /i/ sound like in the word *bee*. In addition to *extra* this pattern can occur in words such as *soda* and *okra* among others.

Other sound characteristics are not fading from use but appear to be maintained or at least variable in their status over time. In general, the pronunciation of /r/ is a feature that shows this trend. White Appalachians tend to pronounce all /r/ sounds no matter where they are located in a word in contrast to some regions in the United States that do not always pronounce the /r/ sound. Among White Appalachians, there are additional instances where /r/ may emerge. Words that end in an /o/ sound may put an /r/ after it as long as that last syllable is not stressed. As a result, a word like *potato* can be pronounced as *potater* (Wolfram and Christian 1976; Williams 1992), though this pronunciation is highly stigmatized and most common among older speakers. One other notable characteristic of /r/ in parts of this region is the insertion of /r/ into words like *wash* such that it is pronounced as *warsh* (Montgomery and Hall 2004). This pronunciation variant is not as highly stigmatized as the previous example and can currently be found across northern Appalachia, especially in West Virginia, Pennsylvania, and southern Ohio.

Variation in vowel sounds is also quite robust in White Appalachian varieties. As a result, vowel sounds in Appalachia have received a great deal of attention. One of the most researched patterns lies with the vowel sound represented by the diphthong /aɪ/, as found in the words *bite* or *bide* (see Reed chapter 2 and Hasty chapter 1 for additional discussion). Within Appalachia, we see two patterns for the pronunciation of the sound based on subregion. The first pattern is found in southern Appalachia where White speakers pronounce the *bite* and *bide* diphthong similarly regardless of the voicing of the sound that follows. This pattern is quite different from the second pattern found among White speakers in northern Appalachia and the broader South that distinguishes the pronunciation of the /aɪ/ vowel based on the voicing of the consonant sound that follows it. For these groups, if the sound following the /aɪ/ vowel is voiced, then the second segment of the vowel is omitted or partially omitted. The word *bide* will sound something like *bahd*, but *bite* would be produced with the full diphthong. A similar rule and geographic distribution applies in words that have <ire>, <yer>, or <ier> letter sequences. In each of these cases, the diphthong sound completely omits the second part of the vowel before the /r/, and the result is the pronunciation of words like *fire* and *tire* as *far* and *tar*. While this pronunciation is characteristic of speech throughout the South, linguists have noted its occurrence at higher frequencies among residents of Appalachia.

Another notable feature of White Appalachian varieties is the fronting of back vowels. This pattern is most noted in the sounds /u/ and /o/ where the word *boot* will sound more like *beuwt* and the word *boat* will sound closer to *bowt*. What is notable about these pronunciations is that the vowels tend to sound longer to the listener because the tongue is moving from one place in the mouth to another during the articulation of the sound.

Like much of the speech of the broader South, White Appalachians pronounce the words *pin* and *pen* and *tin* and *ten* as homophones. This linguistic feature, called the *pin/pen* merger, is widespread in White varieties across southern and central Appalachia up through West Virginia (Hazen 2018). Any /ɪ/ (e.g., *bit*) or /ɛ/ (e.g., *bet*) vowel sound before /n/ or /m/ will merge and make the words sound the same. This merger of sounds and its prevalence in most of Appalachia is of little surprise as it is a long-standing feature of some English varieties (Montgomery and Eble 2004).

Grammar/Syntax

The grammar system of White Appalachian varieties displays several differences from mainstream and Southern English varieties just like the sound system (see Hazen chapter 3). Like the sounds, there are some grammatical features of White speakers that are fading from use. Perhaps the most well-known and salient grammatical feature of White Appalachian varieties that is on the decline is *a*-prefixing (Wolfram 1980, 1998; Montgomery 2009), which gives rise to sentences like *He went a-fishing in the stream*. This feature, which was present in Early Modern English, is still maintained in some areas of Appalachia today. Traditionally, there are three criteria for a word to be eligible for *a*-prefixing: (1) the word must be a verb, (2) the verb cannot come in a prepositional phrase, and (3) the verb must be stressed on the first syllable (Wolfram and Christian 1976). Despite its fairly complex rule structure and decrease in use in northern Appalachia, *a*-prefixing is still being used among White speakers in southern Appalachia.

Completive *done* and counterfactual *liketa* are two other highly salient features that have declined in use and presence in White Appalachian varieties.

Completive *done* shows up in sentences like *I done told you to stop making all that noise*. This grammatical feature occurs when *done* is substituted for *have* in the perfect aspect. It is used as an emphatic way to show that one has already completed an action. Although found in vernacular English dialects worldwide, the presence of this feature does draw considerable attention from listeners. Despite some presence in early studies of Appalachia, this feature has faded from use quite rapidly in northern Appalachia (Hazen, Butcher, and King 2010), and while still present, other subregions' use of the feature is becoming less common. Counterfactual *liketa* is used to express either an imagined or real possible outcome of an event, as in the sentence *I liketa tore the bottom of my car off going over that speed bump*. This feature is now present mainly among White speakers in southern Appalachia. Both of these are some of the more commented on features of White Appalachian speech, but their use is much more limited by geographic space and age in Appalachia today.

There are a few grammar features in Appalachia that find their roots in the Scots-Irish influence but have started to fade rather quickly over time, found nowadays primarily among the older, more rural speakers of the region. One example of a feature following this path can be seen in a sentence like *The kids plays there*. With this feature, a third-person plural verb takes an *–s* suffix (Mallinson et al. 2004).

Double modals like *might could* and *might should* are also following a path of decreased use and originate from Ulster-Scots English dialects. These are frequently cited features for identifying southern, central, and some northern Appalachian White varieties (see chapter 4). The combinations of two or sometimes even three modal auxiliary verbs in one phrase help to express a type of possibility not otherwise found in other varieties of English. While double modals are present to some extent in broader Southern English, they tend to be found more frequently and with wider variation in the Smoky Mountain region of Appalachia (Montgomery and Reed, n.d.). Yet today, the frequency and types of double modals you will hear in Appalachia are quite limited.

The pronunciation of the suffix *–ing* as *–in* is another long-standing grammatical feature of Appalachia. This feature can be seen in words such as *running*, which is often pronounced as *runnin'* when the word is a verb. While this pronunciation is found in English spoken around the world, the rate at which White Appalachian speakers use the *–in* ending in place of the *–ing* ending is less frequent than the lowland South but more frequent than non-Southern varieties of English (Hazen 2008).

The use of *y'all*, *you'uns*, or *y'inz* for the second-person plural pronoun forms can be heard throughout Appalachia, and this variety of forms helps to make it distinct from other regions. There are preferred regions of Appalachia for each form, with *y'inz* being used in and near the Pittsburgh area and *you'uns* being historically used more heavily in the Smoky Mountain region. *Y'all*, though, tends to be the preferred term nowadays throughout much of the southern Appalachian region, replacing *you'uns*, which is found mainly among older White residents if at all.

Another grammar feature in White Appalachian varieties that receives a good deal of attention from outsiders is the use of *was* in place of *were*. This use of *was* for *were* is called leveled *was*, and it has been present in Appalachia since European settlement. However, use of this feature among White Appalachians has started to decline because of negative social associations (Hazen 2014).

We can also find the use of regular past-tense forms like *growed* for the standard irregular *grew* in Appalachia. While irregular past tense forms are not unique to White Appalachian speech and occur in vernacular Englishes around the world, their persistence over time in the speech of White Appalachians is noteworthy.

This section highlights some important trends in White Appalachian Englishes. First, we see that the White Appalachian varieties exhibit great variation across the subregions, especially between southern Appalachia and northern Appalachia. Secondly, we see that age and community type are significant factors in the use of specific variables among White Appalachian speakers. Finally, we see that the historical ties to older donor varieties are rapidly receding (or completely gone!). These trends underscore the dynamic nature of White Appalachian varieties, and they continue to undergo significant, socially meaningful linguistic change. At times, they have moved towards more widespread English norms, as noted in Hazen's (2006) work on the adoption of the quotative *be like*, as in *She was like, "Yes, let's go!"* At other times, they have shown linguistic differences based on social characteristics.

AFRICAN AMERICAN APPALACHIAN ENGLISH

Despite persistent myths about a homogeneously White Appalachia, African Americans have been present in the region since the eighteenth century (Inscoe 2001; Dunaway 2003). With most information about slavery focused on the plantations of the South, institutions not found in the mountains, it is often forgotten that there were enslaved people in Appalachia. Appalachian African American communities have existed since these early times, and many have been maintained up to the present day. The African American presence in these long-standing communities has had significant social impacts in local subregions within Appalachian. There are many places where these influences can be seen, from the African American influence on bluegrass music to the noted influence and popularity of the Affrilachian poets. The impact and long-standing presence of African Americans in Appalachia is significant and widespread across the region.

Much of the linguistic work on African Americans in Appalachia has focused on varieties found in the Smoky Mountain region of North Carolina. The linguistic analysis has considered the relationship of African American Appalachian English to White Appalachian varieties and to other African American English varieties in an effort to more accurately describe and place it within a regional and sociocultural framework (Wolfram 2013). Linguistic analysis of speech in Beech Bottom, NC (Mallinson and Wolfram 2002), and Texana, NC (Childs and Mallinson 2004; Mallinson and Childs 2004), forms the basis for this chapter's explanation of African American Language in Appalachia.

Sounds/Phonology

Unlike some White Appalachian varieties, where the /aɪ/ diphthong (as in the words *bite* and *bide*) is reduced to one vowel sound before voiced and voiceless consonants, lowland African American English varieties tend to only reduce the /aɪ/ sound before voiced consonants (as in *bide*). Despite a widespread African American pattern, African American Appalachian speakers in southern Appalachia tend to follow the local pattern reducing the glide before both voiced and voiceless sounds (Childs 2005). Hazen (2006) found that older African American Appalachians in northern Appalachia also followed this pattern, but younger African American residents had patterns more similar to African American English norms if they were from more urban locales.

Similarly, African American Appalachians also participate in the *r*-ful pronunciation of words like *car* typical of the Appalachian region. Rather than participating in more *r*-less pronunciations such as *cah* for *car*, which are typical of more lowland and urban African American English varieties (Childs and Mallinson 2004), African American Appalachians follow regional patterns.

Looking more closely at pronunciation, Childs (2005) found that African American residents of Texana produced more characteristically Appalachian vowel sounds for the /u/ (e.g., *boot*) and /o/ (e.g., *boat*) vowels, saying them as *bewt* and *bowt*. These pronunciations follow a pattern of back vowel fronting that is happening across White Appalachian speech and more general Southern White speech (see chapter 3) but not happening in other varieties of African American English (Thomas 2007).

Grammar/Syntax

We begin to see more variability in regional and ethnic alignment when looking at grammatical features for Appalachian African Americans. Looking at third-person plural –s attachment as in the sentence *Several kids walks now*, studies have found that African American Appalachian community members that affiliate more specifically with the region tend to use this feature at much higher rates—similar to that of White Appalachians—than African American community members who do not have strong local ties (Mallinson and Childs 2005; Mallinson 2006). When looking at grammatical variables more closely aligned with African American English vernaculars, such as third-person singular –s absence (e.g., *She walk_*), research shows a pattern where older and younger residents pattern similarly to local speech norms, while middle-aged residents tend to align more closely with core African American English norms. Similar to plural –s attachment, third-person singular –s absence rates also show sensitivity to local affiliation, with those speakers who are most rooted in the local community having patterns similar to White Appalachian speakers. Finally, *is* copula absence (e.g., *She_ the boss*), a noted core feature of African American English, occurs at low rates among older and more locally rooted residents, while it reaches rates similar to that of African American English elsewhere among middle-aged and less locally affiliated community members.

Although limited in number when compared to studies of White Appalachian varieties, these analyses of African American Appalachian English highlight some important trends. First, we see that sound systems and grammatical systems are behaving in different ways in these communities. African American speakers in Appalachia tend, for the most part, to share many of the sound characteristics of White varieties from the region. In fact, perception tests where speech samples of African American Appalachian speakers were played for listeners to identify race were misidentified a majority of the time as a result of listener assumptions about what an Appalachian speaker and an African American speaker should sound like (Childs and Mallinson 2006). When given sample recorded speech of African American residents of the Smoky Mountains and asked to identify ethnicity, age, gender, and several other social categories, respondents were very good at identifying the age and gender of the Appalachian African American speakers but not nearly as accurate at identifying their ethnicity.

Secondly, it must be noted that factors of identity and affiliation work in tandem with language to help speakers construct their identity. This complex identity work is clear not only in the linguistic studies of speech of African American residents of this region but also in their written language. Childs and Mallinson (2006) look at the use of language by young African American Appalachians in online messaging situations and uncover patterns of written language performance that do not correspond to their spoken language data. For example, we find young male residents writing *brotha'* for *brother* in online messaging platforms. The patterns for online language follow more typical African American English patterns, while the spoken data from the same speakers is similar to White Appalachian patterns. There is no doubt that these rhetorical moves are tied to the desire to affiliate with broader African American culture (Childs 2016).

LATINX

The Latinx community is the newest and fastest growing ethnic group in the Appalachian region. Research into Latinx language in Appalachia is in its beginning stages. To date, the linguistic work on this ethnic variety in the region has examined both its alignment with mainstream Southern and Appalachian varieties. For example, Kohn (2019) finds that Latinx community members, especially young community members in Hickory, North Carolina, are beginning to participate in the fronting of the /o/ sound as in the word *boat*. Meanwhile when looking at /aɪ/ ungliding in Hickory, Kohn finds that no community-wide patterns emerge. Some young speakers may resist accommodation of the locally unglided pattern, while others may adopt it based primarily on individual orientation to the surrounding community. Similar to White Appalachian varieties, the emergence of quotative *be like* is also on the rise among the young Latinx community in Appalachia (Kohn and Franz 2009). Thus, like the other ethnic varieties of Appalachia, the Latinx community shows great variation and variable participation in regional language norms and patterns based on social characteristics.

CONCLUSION

Appalachia has always been an ethnically diverse region. With each wave of migration and settlement across the mountains and hollows, new language features and cultures have been brought to the area and shared. Linguistic research shows some of these shared features have been widespread across multiple ethnic groups, while other language features have remained insular within the group that brought them. Although some features have persisted throughout their time in the region, others have started to fade and are in decline. These changes are all natural processes in the life of dialects and speakers.

What persists, though, across Appalachia and across all ethnic groups and Englishes of the region is a strong sense of place. This place, Appalachia, is looking toward its future and its possibilities, socially and linguistically, as we see in the development of Cherokee language schools, African American youth using online language, and in the emerging Latinx populations of the region. Now, Appalachia is a place where speakers are considering their identity and language practices and aligning themselves with the norms that best suit their identity. As a result, residents and scholars are seeing Appalachian language and identity in the modern frame: a people with language varieties that do not have to be like that of their grandparents or their neighbors. This is the new Appalachia, a region that continues to grow more diverse.

References

Anderson, Bridget L. 1999. "Source-Language Transfer and Vowel Accommodation in the Patterning of Cherokee English /ai/ and /oi/." *American Speech* 74: 339–68.

Catte, Elizabeth. 2018. *What You Are Getting Wrong about Appalachia*. Cleveland, OH: Belt Publishing.

Childs, Becky. 2005. "Investigating the Local Construction of Identity: Sociophonetic Variation in Smoky Mountain African American Women's Speech." PhD diss., University of Georgia.

Childs, Becky. 2016. "Who I Am and Who I Want to Be: Variation and Representation in a Messaging Platform." In *English in Computer-Mediated Communication: Variation, Representation, and Perception*, edited by Lauren Squires. New York: Mouton de Gruyter.

Childs, Becky, and Christine Mallinson. 2004. "African American English in Appalachia." *English World-Wide* 25: 1–27.

Childs, Becky, and Christine Mallinson. 2006. "The Significance of Lexical Items in the Construction of Ethnolinguistic Identity: A Case Study of Adolescent Spoken and Online Language." *American Speech* 81, no. 1: 3–30.

Coggshall, Elizabeth L. 2006. "Differential Vowel Accommodation among Two Native American Groups." MA thesis, North Carolina State University.

Coggshall, Elizabeth L. 2008. "The Prosodic Rhythm of Two Varieties of Native American English." *University of Pennsylvania Working Papers in Linguistics* 14, no. 2.

Cramer, Jennifer. 2014. "Is Shakespeare Still in the Holler? The Death of a Language Myth." *The Southern Journal of Linguistics* 38, no. 1: 195–207.

Dunaway, Wilma. 2003. *Slavery in the American Mountain South*. Cambridge: Cambridge University Press.

Hazen, Kirk. 2006. "The Final Days of Appalachian Heritage Language." In *Language Variation and Change in the American Midland*, edited by Beth Simon and Thomas Murray, 129–50. Varieties of English around the World series. Philadelphia: John Benjamins.

Hazen, Kirk. 2008. "(ING): A Vernacular Baseline for English in Appalachia." *American Speech* 83, no. 2: 116–40.

Hazen, Kirk. 2014. "A New Role for an Ancient Variable in Appalachia: Paradigm Leveling and Standardization in West Virginia." *Language Variation and Change* 26, no. 1: 77–102.

Hazen, Kirk. 2018. "The Contested Southernness of Appalachia." *American Speech* 93, no. 3–4: 374–408.

Hazen, Kirk, Paige Butcher, and Ashley King. 2010. "Unvernacular Appalachia: An Empirical Perspective on West Virginia Dialect Variation." *English Today* 26, no. 4: 13–22.

Hutcheson, Neal. 2014. *First Language: The Race to Save the Cherokee Language*. North Carolina Language and Life Project, Raleigh, NC.

Inscoe, John C. 2001. *Appalachians and Race: The Mountain South from Slavery to Segregation*. Lexington: University Press of Kentucky.

Kohn, Mary. 2019. "Latino English in New Destinations: Processes of Regionalization in Emerging Contact Varieties." In *Mexican American English: Substrate Influences and the Birth of an Ethnolect*, edited by Erik Thomas, 268–90. Cambridge: Cambridge University Press.

Kohn, Mary, and Hannah Franz. 2009. "Localized Patterns for Global Variants: The Case of Quotative Systems of African American and Latino Speakers." *American Speech* 84, no. 3: 259–97.

Mallinson, Christine. 2006. "The Dynamic Construction of Race, Class, and Gender through Linguistic Practice among Women in a Black Appalachian Community." PhD diss., North Carolina State University.

Mallinson, Christine, and Becky Childs. 2004. "The Intersection of Regional and Ethnic Identity: African American English in Appalachia." *Journal of Appalachian Studies* 10, no. 1–2: 129–42.

Mallinson, Christine, Becky Childs, Bridget Anderson, and Neal Hutcheson. 2004. "Smoky Mountain Speech." *Do You Speak American*. http://www.pbs.org/speak/seatosea/americanvarieties/smokies/.

Mallinson, Christine, and Walt Wolfram. 2002. "Dialect Accommodation in a Bi-ethnic Mountain Enclave Community: More Evidence on the Earlier Development of African American English." *Language in Society* 31: 743–75.

Montgomery, Michael. 1991. "The Roots of Appalachian English: Scotch-Irish or British Southern?" *Journal of the Appalachian Studies Association* 3: 177–91.

Montgomery, Michael. 1999. "In the Appalachians They Speak like Shakespeare." In *Language Myths*, edited by L. Bauer and P. Trudgill, 66–76. New York: Penguin.

Montgomery, Michael. 2009. "Historical and Comparative Perspectives on *A*-Prefixing in the English of Appalachia." *American Speech* 84, no. 1: 5–26.

Montgomery, Michael, and Connie Eble. 2004. "Historical Perspectives on the *Pen Pin* Merger in Southern American English." In *Conversations between Past and Present*, edited by Anne Curzan and Kim Emmons, 433–50. Vol. 2 of *Studies in the History of the English Language*. Berlin: Mouton de Gruyter.

Montgomery, Michael, and Joseph S. Hall. 2004. *Dictionary of Smoky Mountain English*. Knoxville: University of Tennessee Press.

Montgomery, Michael, and Paul Reed. n.d. MULTIMO: A Database of Multiple Modals. Accessed 18 February 2018. https://artsandsciences.sc.edu/multimo/welcome.

Neely, Sharlotte. 1991. *Snowbird Cherokee: People of Persistence*. Athens: University of Georgia Press.

Sauceman, Fred. 2015. "Immersion School Works to Save the Cherokee Language." *Our State Magazine*, 13 May 2015. https://www.ourstate.com/cheerokee-language-atse-kituwah-academy/.

Thomas, Erik. 2007. "Phonological and Phonetic Characteristics of AAVE." *Language and Linguistics Compass* 1: 450–75.

Thorton, Russell. 1990. *The Cherokee: A Population History*. Lincoln: University of Nebraska Press.

Williams, Cratis. 1992. *Southern Mountain Speech*. Berea, KY: Berea College Press.

Wolfram, Walt. 1980. " 'A'-Prefixing in Appalachian English." In *Locating Language in Time and Space*, edited by William Labov, 107–42. New York: Academic Press.

Wolfram, Walt. 1998. "Reconsidering the Semantics of *A*-Prefixing." *American Speech* 63: 247–53.

Wolfram, Walt. 2013. "African American Speech in Southern Appalachia." In *Talking Appalachian: Voice, Identity, and Community*, edited by Amy Clark and Nancy Hayward, 81–93. Lexington: University of Kentucky Press.

Wolfram, Walt, and Donna Christian. 1976. *Appalachian Speech*. Arlington, VA: Center for Applied Linguistics.

PART III

Language in the Wider World

CHAPTER 8

Redneck Memes as an Appalachian Reclamation of Vernacular Authority, Language, and Identity

Jordan Lovejoy

SUMMARY

This chapter explores the intertwining lives of folklore and English in Appalachia. Although contemporary researchers approach folklore as something with both traditional and dynamic aspects, folklorists used to see the folk as those quaint, unmodern, illiterate, and quickly disappearing people from mostly rural areas. Likewise, Appalachians are almost always stereotyped as exactly that type of ancient folk. In addition to these hillbilly representations, they're also classified as rednecks in popular imaginings. Because outsiders to the region have classified Appalachians as a specific type of redneck—what I call Type 1—folks within the region are speaking back through social media groups to create a different type of redneck that is more historically accurate and promotes a prideful authority over both language and identity. This model is used by what I call Type 2 Rednecks. Through the creation of memes that employ classic words and features associated with Appalachia, these folk groups embrace regional pride while also promoting critical thought and conversation on control over framing master narratives and recognizing and celebrating language variation.

INTRODUCTION

The field of folklore studies has been working toward a definition of folklore for quite some time. As you have might have noticed, many academic disciplines create extremely nuanced definitions within a field of study, and experts in those fields are always providing new angles and approaches to definitions, which continue to evolve alongside the field. Folklore is no different here, and neither is the ever-evolving way we define and understand the Appalachian region. Since the word *folklore* was coined by William Thoms in 1846—meaning then popular antiquities and literature, or "the uncivilized element in a civilized society"—the definition has continuously evolved (Dundes 1980; Thoms 1999). William Wells Newell, the founder of the American Folklore Society in 1888, saw folklore as the traditions of quickly vanishing groups, traditions that needed to be collected—before they disappeared—from low culture groups who possessed customs and knowledge that more modern and advanced people had outgrown (1888). Along with their fear that traditional customs were disappearing, scholars used to think of the folk in *folklore* as mainly rural and illiterate peasants who held the true voice, soul, and language of a nation within their cultural creations, like folk poetry (Wilson 2006b, 114). Some people still conflate folklore with backwardness and uneducated groups: "For many, the term folklore still conjures up images of European peasants spinning tales of olden times or of Appalachian hillbillies strumming happily away on their banjos" (Wilson 2006c, 204). Rosemary Hathaway, in her study on the history of the West Virginia University Mountaineer, notes how folklore in the United States predictably (though problematically) focused on Appalachia:

> In Europe, this meant that collectors focused on peasants; however, since the United States lacked a comparable group of people, collectors instead swarmed to Appalachia, that "margin of civilization," populated, as emerging definitions of Mountaineer implied, by those who appear to be refreshingly but safely uncivilized. Consequently, Appalachia became a hotbed of folklore collection, especially by the ballad hunters who were convinced that those "old-fashioned" Scots and English settlers in "marginal" Appalachia held the purest repository of traditional British ballads to be found anywhere in the world. (2014, 20–21)

We can see, then, why Appalachians are heavily stereotyped as backward, rural, and uneducated. In addition, they are homogenized as poor Whites and continue to be connected to folklore in popular imaginings. Both usually hold a bad rap with the general public: Appalachians are considered hillbillies or rednecks—specifically Type 1, which I discuss in more detail later. Folklore is made up of simply fictional beliefs that don't really mean much beyond fairy tales and urban legends. As we explore further, neither of these raps hold up, for both Appalachians and folklore (and the folk—i.e., all of us—who make it) are diverse, complex, creative, and *fun*.

To understand folk groups, we might approach them through how they use language as a form of what Toelken calls *cultural logic*: tacit knowledge that allows us to know something and its context (1996, 22). Dell Hymes's concept of the *ethnography of communication* helps us approach language in folklore, which he defines as "the study of communicative behavior with an esthetic, expressive, or stylistic dimension" (1974, 133). The ethnography of communication explores "what a person knows about appropriate patterns of language use in his or her community and how he or she learns about it" (Farah 2008, 125). The ethnography of communication also aims "to investigate directly the use of language in contexts of situation, so as to discern patterns proper to speech activity, patterns that escape separate studies of grammar, of personality, of religion, of kinship, and the like" (Hymes 1974, 3–4). Hymes urges us to investigate a community's "communicative habits as a whole" (1974, 4) and look "beyond those [abilities] of producing and interpreting grammatical sentences" and into the abilities required "to be a competent member of [a] community, knowing not only what may possibly be said, but also what should and should not be said" (1974, 26).

Now that we know who the folk are and how they interact in and out of groups, we can finally move to what folklore is. As noted above, there have been—and continue to be—many different definitions of folklore. One of the most popular and easy to remember definitions comes from Dan Ben-Amos: "Folklore is artistic communication in small groups" (1971, 13). Other common buzzwords of folklore include *unofficial*, *traditional*, and *informal*. Lynne S. McNeill (2013) tells us "folklore is informal, traditional culture," and she notes the importance of both parts of the word: "Without the folk (people sharing an informal culture), we wouldn't have dynamic variation, and without the lore (the stories, beliefs, and customs), we wouldn't have anything to pass on traditionally" (14). William A. Wilson divides folklore into three categories: *verbal lore* (what folks say or use words for, like songs, folktales, and jokes), *material lore* (what folks make, like food, quilts, or chairs), and *customary lore* (what folks do, like dances, rituals, and celebrations) (2006a, 85). Scholars following Wilson have also added a fourth category to this list: *belief lore* (what folks believe, like superstitions, legends, and supernatural events) (Thursby 2006, 116). Appalachian Studies scholar and folklorist Mary Hufford tells us that "folklife is community life and values, artfully expressed in myriad forms and interactions" (1991, 1). Folklore tells us who we are and how we make meaning through informal, person-to-person expression as we live our lives in both traditional and dynamic ways.

In Appalachia, as in every part of the world, folklore occurs in various forms and among radically different groups. It might pop up through an individual word, like *redneck*, or through a variety of internet memes created and shared through social media groups and pages, like *Cornbread Communism* and *The Ghost of Ol Dale Earnhardt*. But one thing folklore and the study of it certainly accomplish is helping us understand how a group sees itself, defines itself, and creatively responds to the world around it.

APPALACHIA AND REDNECKS

The Appalachian region of the eastern United States is 205,000 square miles and follows the Appalachian Mountain range from northern Mississippi to southern New York; 42 percent of the population is considered rural, and the region exhibits higher than average rates of poverty (ARC 2017). Although the region is historically known for an economy of agriculture and extractive industries like mining and timbering, the Appalachian Regional Commission now sees it as "one of economic contrasts: some communities have successfully diversified their economies, while others still require basic infrastructure such as roads and water and sewer systems" (ARC 2017). Despite the dynamic and diverse nature of this region, popular imaginings often depict Appalachia and its people through cruel stereotypes. Appalachians are usually homogenized and stigmatized as poor, rural, uneducated, White conservatives who, among other negative traits, are racist, homophobic, and sexist. One example of a stereotypical hillbilly from pop culture is Kenneth Parcell from NBC's sitcom *30 Rock*. Kenneth doesn't believe menstruating women should be in the workplace, he refers to science as the Christian Bible's Old Testament, and the mayor of his hometown of Stone Mountain, Georgia, is a meth addict. He often uses folksy sayings, and although he clearly speaks a variety from Appalachia on the show, he is very conscious of what will happen if he switches out of the standard English variety expected of him as an NBC page: "Oh no! When I get upset, my accent come out, and when it gets to comin' out, I can't get to talkin' nuh-uh!" (Brock 2009). Further, other characters on the show often mock his cultural background, language use, and naivete of experience. This treatment of such Appalachian characters is quite common in pop culture.

Because of these stereotypes—which are often the only versions we see in popular media representations—Appalachians are usually summed up into one word: *rednecks*. Because of this outsider label placed almost universally on the folks of the region, certain groups who wish to gain control over how they're represented are reworking what the word *redneck* actually means. Though there are certainly more ways of defining a redneck, this chapter breaks the word into two distinct categories: Type 1 Rednecks, which follows the more stereotypical version, and Type 2 Rednecks, which claims a more radical, progressive identification of the word.

Type 1 Rednecks are often seen as Southerners or Appalachians who are racist, homophobic, xenophobic, and sexist conservatives. They are assumed to be overtly masculine men who are working class, enjoy outdoor sports like hunting and fishing, and promote the Confederate flag. This usage is usually applied in a derogatory or negative manner by outsiders, but some insiders do self-proclaim as this type and express pride in its use, although they often "do boundary work around this identity label because they are conscious that they want to identify as redneck on their own terms and not others' terms, which they know or at least expect to be derogatory" (Shirley 2010, 55). Many scholars argue that the term traces back to class and race-based images of a sunburned neck:[1] "The prevailing view is that southern plantation owners and the urban White professional and middle classes coined the epithet to describe those White dirt farmers, sharecroppers, and agricultural laborers who had sunburned red necks from working fields, unprotected, under a scorching sun" (Huber 1995, 147). Patrick Huber (1995) notes that this Type 1 Redneck understanding "emerged as a class slur in the lower Mississippi Valley region sometime in the latter half of the nineteenth century" (146), and "for approximately the last one hundred years, the pejorative term redneck has chiefly slurred a rural, poor white man of the American South and particularly one who holds conservative, racist, or reactionary views" (145).

In internet culture today, we can quickly see Type 1 Rednecks as they appear in popular memes like Almost Politically Correct Redneck and Redneck Randal. The Almost Politically Correct Redneck features a shirtless White male with a mullet leaning against an older red truck; the text pasted over the image usually involves the man attempting to be politically correct or respectful but still missing the mark by saying something problematic or offensive (Don

2012a; 2012b). For example, one Almost Politically Correct Redneck meme says, "There should be no wage discrimination, no matter if you are working in an office, a factory, or doin' woman's work" (Don 2012b). We see the redneck attempt to be progressive by combatting wage discrimination, but he still differentiates labor based on backwards gender dynamics.[2]

The Redneck Randal meme features another White male holding a beer with an American-flag, bald-eagle shirt with cut-off sleeves (Brad 2001). Redneck Randal is usually depicted as an uneducated, racist, and sexist homophobe who often plays into the worst stereotypes about the region. A lighter example of this meme is one in which the text over the image reads, "So I stood up and told that teachin' lady the only 3 letters I need to know are U, S, and A" (Austin 2011).

A Type 2 Redneck, on the other hand, is a union-supporting leftist who embraces intersectional identity. These rednecks are often associated with progressive politics and Appalachian pride and have zero tolerance for racism, homophobia, xenophobia, and sexism. Type 2 Rednecks almost always use the term *redneck* as a positive self-identification that is reclaimed as an identity feature defined from within Appalachia and born from historical leftism in the region. Type 2 Rednecks likely pinpoint the origin of the term in the 1920s West Virginia Mine Wars, where union supporters tied red bandanas around their necks for group identification. Patrick Huber (2006) notes that rednecks were sometimes conflated with communists in the 1920s and 1930s, and that the term also referred to a labor union miner who "appropriated both the term redneck and its literal manifestation, the red bandana, in order to build multiracial unions of White, Black, and immigrant miners in the strike-ridden coalfields of northern and central Appalachia between 1912 and 1936" (2006, 195). Huber (2006) further suggests this "now-obsolete meaning of the word provides insight into how local leaders and organizers of the United Mine Workers used language and symbols to foster union solidarity among racially and ethnically divided miners" (2006, 195). Since Huber's exploration, though, the usage of *redneck* that he calls "now-obsolete" has come back into folk usage, especially within the social media groups that use the Type 2 Redneck category to speak back to the Type 1 Redneck category that has been placed on the entire region by outsiders.

The remainder of this chapter looks at how leftist folks in the region are creating online folk groups and pages to share and express identity through language features that differentiate themselves not only from Type 1 Rednecks but also from outsiders, condescending intellectuals, and liberal elites. As they might say, they're "raising hell and praising Dale."

FOLK GROUPS: *CORNBREAD COMMUNISM* AND *THE GHOST OF OL DALE EARNHARDT*

Folklorist Dorothy Noyes describes folk groups as "the complex networks of contacts and influences feeding into and emerging from an apparently bounded community" (1995, 449), where "the network lets us get rid of those boundaries . . . and gives us a structure for talking about long-distance and mediated relationships. It addresses our concerns with multivocality and complexity by understanding actors as both interrelated and uniquely positioned agents" (1995, 465–66). As an imagined community, the group "exists as the project of a network or some of its members. Networks exist insofar as their ties are continually recreated and revitalized in interaction" (1995, 471–72). Seeing groups as complex networks that create community through interaction is especially helpful for exploring social media groups, whether those interactions occur through individual agents or interrelated actors. Some social media groups about Appalachia have formed as a way to connect a variety of folks both within and outside the region, and individuals are able to choose their level of engagement with others. Several groups and social media pages have formed as a purposeful way to express the Type 2 Redneck identity, and this chapter looks at the work of two of them, the Facebook page *Cornbread Communism* and the Facebook page *The Ghost of Ol Dale Earnhardt*.

A visit to *The Ghost of Ol Dale Earnhardt*'s "About" section on its Facebook page provides a quick glimpse into the world Type 2 Rednecks are building: "There's a haint in the foothills of NC; the haint of the #3 chevy. The rich have formed a holy alliance to exorcise it but they'll never fucking catch him" (n.d.). We are meant to quickly realize that this section is mirroring the opening lines of *The Communist Manifesto*: "A spectre is haunting Europe—the spectre of communism. All the powers of old Europe have entered into a holy alliance to exorcise this spectre" (Marx 2012, 73). Quite beautifully, though, this page incorporates stigmatized features and words from Appalachia into its version of *The Communist Manifesto*, claiming this revolutionary text as its own. The short narrative also complicates the stereotype that Appalachians are uneducated folks who can't speak a standard variety of English and foolishly allow rich outsiders to exploit them by embracing celebrated Appalachian dialect words (like *haint* for *ghost*) through a piece of critical theory.

The figure of deceased NASCAR driver Dale Earnhardt is also an interesting and purposeful move, as a love of NASCAR (which is usually viewed as a boring and repetitive source of entertainment where rednecks are extra rowdy) is typically associated with Type 1 Redneck culture. Here, Type 2 Rednecks are speaking back by reclaiming this figure as a progressive, fascist-bashing leftist, and his association with the Type 2 Redneck world is carefully denoted by placing a feature like coronal stop deletion, which is commonly found in Appalachian varieties, in front of the ghost's name. Coronal stop deletion is when word-final coronal stops, /t/ and /d/, are deleted from a word like *old* (Tanner, Sonderegger, and Wagner, 1). Coronal stop deletion is especially recognizable to and stigmatized by outsiders to the Appalachian region; sociolinguist Kirk Hazen (2011) notes, "[Coronal stop deletion] rates are relatively high, marking these speakers as vernacular in the ears of listeners from other parts of the country" (135). Type 2 Redneck and Appalachian social media groups that purposefully use stigmatized language features like coronal stop deletion to speak back to outsiders do seem actively aware of this vernacular feature, though, as suggested by coronal stop deletion usage in the name of *The Ghost of* Ol_ *Dale Earnhardt*, where the <d> is dropped from *old*.

The *Cornbread Communism* Facebook group also highlights words and features associated (negatively) with Appalachia in conversation with critical theory that is often assumed to be intellectually inaccessible to rednecks. Speaking a nonstandard variety of English is usually associated with a lack of education or intellectual ability. There is a sense that uneducated folks, who don't even speak "proper English," cannot understand Communist teachings, let alone employ them; however, this Facebook group challenges this idea by showing that Appalachian speakers can access the depth of Marxist thought. These Type 2 Redneck efforts foreground and combat the assumption that ideology and critical theory solely belong to elite institutions like universities, and are—of course!—intellectually inaccessible to those who don't enter into that environment (for whatever reason). The "Cornbread Communist Manifesto," written by Cornrad Joey Aloi[3] and available on the group's Facebook page, states, "Cornbread communism is a contested space, and the embrace of it as a platform is an attempt to forge Appalachian worker unity across these contestations" (2018). The manifesto also reads,

> There are anarcho-Maoists, moonshine-swilling Wobblies, pawpaw-fisted syndicalists, ginseng and ramp Diggers, Bolshevik mothmen, agrarian mutualists, androgynous & hairy ecoanarchists, apple-farming autonomists, freegan feminist freedom fighters, Soupbean Social Ecologists, Kentucky Black Panthers, actual Kentucky panthers, antiauthoritarian haints, snake-handling preachers of the Social Gospel, strippers against strip mining, guerrillas in the war on coal, banjo-playing Trotskyists, situationist coal miners, gramscian raft guides, and even (I hear) Clinch Mountain stirnerists. . . .

... It also means that so-called illegitimate economic actors—the lumpenproletariat with a still, the quilting Meemaw, musicians—are as important revolutionary actors as the traditional or service-industry proletariat. (Aloi 2018)

This Type 2 Redneck group uses institutionally and intellectually recognized jargon, but they insert colloquial Appalachian words, like *haint* (a spirit or specter) and *still* (a distillery for making alcohol, historically moonshine), into the manifesto. Because of this blending, you might be able to somewhat understand the manifesto if you're not a group insider or Appalachian, but you won't understand all of it. This blending is a purposeful attempt to turn the tables on who holds knowledge and who it belongs to, especially when it comes to progressive and radical critical thought.

While there are several Type 2 Redneck groups floating around the internet, I've chosen these in particular because they are public and open groups where anyone is welcome to share. Internet research allows us to see how people who might never meet interact and cocreate new modes of expression that set up the identity of the group in general, including through the use of language variation. One of these cocreated artistic modes of expression that involves Appalachian dialect variation is, of course, the meme.

Lynne S. McNeill (2009) describes memes as "aspects of Internet experience (images, videos, phrases, exchanges, etc.) that are propagated via the tools of the Web (e-mail, blogs, forums, etc.)" (85). Internet memes are cultural units that are created, co- or re-created, and transmitted or shared via the web, usually offering cultural critique or reflection on some cultural trend. Because the meme is a beautiful example of folklore and because the Type 2 Redneck social media groups often communicate with memes, the next section of this chapter will explore how these groups employ stigmatized language features Appalachians have been historically mocked for. Although the features are often seen and stereotyped as a nonstandard use of English and, therefore, backwards, wrong, and ignorant, Type 2 Redneck groups use them to take control over the construction of their identity with cultural pride, to celebrate regional dialect features, and to collectively speak back to stereotypes that all Appalachians and rednecks are Type 1 Rednecks.

SEIZE THEM MEANS: LANGUAGE, TYPE 2 REDNECKS, AND MEMES

In this section, I focus on easily recognizable Appalachian dialect features and how they are used in memes generated by Type 2 Redneck social media groups. The most common features and words found in the memes include demonstrative *them*, leveled *was*, and alveolar *–ing*. Hazen, Butcher, and King (2010) explore both fading and enduring features of Appalachian dialects. Demonstrative *them* and leveled *was* are included in the fading features. In their discussion of demonstrative *them*, the authors state, "Demonstrative pronouns in modern English generally have four forms: *this, that, these, those* . . . For vernacular dialects, there is another option for the plural form: *them* as in *Them apples are the best*" (18). They also note, "This dialect feature has been prominent in the stereotype of English in Appalachia and is strongly associated with stigmatized social perceptions. . . . [but] as this dialect feature became a regular part of the stereotype of various vernacular varieties, its usage decreased in West Virginia" (18). The next meme, however, gives us an example of demonstrative *them* making a comeback as a performative feature, employing its stigmatized status to impart more impactful social meaning in a single word. Most interestingly, we are revisited by the Almost Politically Correct Redneck meme image, but instead of being problematic, this Type 2 Redneck is ready for a proletariat revolution, as he asks, "Yunz bout ready to seize them means?" (*Cornbread Communism* 2017c).

Leveled *was* is also widely stigmatized. Hazen (2014) notes this dialect feature is a form of paradigm leveling, which "occurs when the verb paradigm changes from a more diverse set of forms (e.g., *was, were*) to a less diverse set of forms (e.g., *was*)," and it might occur in a sentence like *We was walking* (77). Leveled *was* seems to be declining in contemporary Appalachia, especially as "West Virginians [have gone] through important social changes in the twentieth century, including regular migrations, enhanced institutional education expectations, and generally increased awareness of sociolinguistic norms from other parts of the country" (Hazen 2014, 99).

Again, however, the Type 2 Redneck groups are repopularizing this feature as a social desire to differentiate redneck identity and Appalachians from more problematic and homogenized depictions of the region and its folk. The next meme includes leveled *was* (among other features) alongside celebrations of union identity and heritage and traditional culture like flat-footing and fiddling. The image is a group of Union soldiers dancing (flat-footing) in a circle while other soldiers watch and one plays the fiddle. The text over the image reads, "Share if your ancestors was them flat-footin' unionists" (*Cornbread Communism* 2017a). Here we see multiple intersections of the folklore process with features found in Appalachian varieties: group members are encouraged to share the meme (which is important, as likely not all of their social media connections are Type 2 Redneck group members), and the meme exhibits leveled *was*, demonstrative *them*, and alveolar *–ing*.

Hazen (2008) notes, "The sociolinguistic variable (ING) accounts for the variation of the production of two phonetic forms: an alveolar nasal /n/ and a velar nasal /ŋ/, as in *I was walki*[n]/[ŋ] and *Walki*[n]/[ŋ] *is fun*" (117). In discussing alveolar *-ing*'s enduring nature in Appalachia, Hazen, Butcher, and King (2010) state, "As a widely recognized dialect feature, its steady continuation in West Virginia is an indication of this dialect feature's lower vernacular status within the region. Yet the differences between the social groups, including sharp stratification by social class, points towards West Virginia's speakers' awareness of this dialect feature's social meaning as a stylistic and social marker" (21). Two memes suggest the validity in the suggestion that Appalachians are aware of the feature's social meaning as a marker. The first meme depicts a shirtless Dale Earnhardt wearing a cowboy hat and riding a horse amidst a crowd of people; the text (in rainbow-colored font) over the image reads, "Saddle up, comrade! We're seizin' them means!" (*The Ghost of Ol Dale Earnhardt* 2017b). This meme, which also includes demonstrative *them*, seems to be a purposeful use of alveolar *-ing*, as the creator made sure to include the apostrophe at the end of *seizin'* to let us know there used to be a *g* there but it is no longer needed.

The second meme shows a picture of a White man in a suit looking into a house through an open window. There is a text bubble coming from an unseen person inside the house that says, "Shut the winder! Yunz'r lettin the WArSPs in!" The White man has a text bubble that says, "bzzzzz . . . I could develop this land real good" (*Cornbread Communism* 2017b). This meme, I feel, truly encompasses what the Type 2 Rednecks are trying to get at through their social media groups. It shows how the region has various types of people within it: those problematic, business-type White men who would develop land people live on,[4] and the progressives who reject the WASPs (White Anglo-Saxon Protestants) but still embrace and celebrate language variation in Appalachia with alveolar *-ing* in *lettin*, the use of *yunz* (plural *you*), the intrusive <r> in *WArSPs* (WASPs) and *winder* (window), and the *-ly* absence in the adverb *real* (see chapters 2 and 3). All these vernacular language features cast the meme as powerfully subversive. Interestingly, we only see one of the people speaking: the problematic one. The Type 2 Redneck is inside the house that someone else wants to change and have power over. But the Type 2 Redneck is also speaking back, even though we can't—or choose not to—see her, which we might be able to accomplish by simply looking a little closer. From within the house (which we might characterize here as a space similar to the Type 2 Redneck social media folk groups) we hear and see someone speaking back, rejecting what has come mainly from outside, and reclaiming vernacular authority and language through very purposeful identity politics.

CONCLUSION

Because mainstream institutions have not spent much time combating identity erasure, celebrating an ignored leftist regional history, or reclaiming Appalachian language features that continue to be treated negatively, leftist Type 2 Redneck social media groups have formed to do that work. If more mainstream institutions properly focused their resources on such complex identities, histories, and language features, the content these social media groups distribute through internet forms like memes might also exist more formally—and therefore more accessibly. Not only that, but this content might be known by a wider audience, including those people within Appalachia who have limited access to a variety of content about themselves, their histories, and their places, as well as folks outside the region who need more nuanced, complex, and complicated stories about Appalachia. Folklore methodology of collecting cultural productions in groups, applying discourse analyses, conducting interviews and ethnography, exploring how groups creatively form and respond to such institutional gaps, and simply talking with people can be useful for approaching such issues like those above both inside and outside of institutional settings. Folklorists might also help bridge the gap between institutions and such vernacular groups by focusing on the joint desire for Appalachians to be prideful of their region while also encouraging a critical approach to the world and a questioning of who frames master narratives, who decides what is a standard variety of English, and who benefits from larger, institutional structures. With the rise of internet culture and digital discourse, researchers of language and folklore must be willing to explore group language and communication as they vernacularly and organically emerge in new and creative forms.

Appalachia is a complicated and complex region with a rich and diverse history of language features and progressive movements. Some within the region are attempting to highlight this richness, which has typically been ignored or appropriated as something to mock.

The question for us, then, is whether we will listen, look, or attend to the voices from inside Appalachia that are telling us they're here, they exist, and they're a complex, heterogeneous network of folks. In recent decades, Appalachians have been associated with their use of the word *y'all*, which is a blend of the words *you* and *all*. As a smiling Dale Earnhardt, who is floating in a futuristic place of outer space,[5] in the last meme tells us, "All is for y'all" (*The Ghost of Ol Dale Earnhardt* 2017a). The Type 2 Rednecks are also trying to tell us this message, to persuade us that there are a lot of different folks from Appalachia as well as a lot of different ways to use English. As the Type 2

Rednecks suggest, all of these folks and their language varieties are worth understanding as nuanced and complex. If we take their creations to heart and mind, we just might join them in that psychedelic and futuristic world they are building—fighting fascists, language discrimination, and neoliberal exploitation right alongside cornrad Dale Earnhardt, smiling from inside his #3 Chevy.

Notes

1. Thanks to Andrew Carter of World Sound Entertainment in Scioto County, Ohio, for first bringing this argument to my attention while we were working together on the Center for Folklore Studies at Ohio State's Ohio Field School project.
2. All of the memes discussed in this chapter can be found on the companion website: https://dialects.wvu.edu/appalachian-englishes.
3. *Cornrad* is a cornbread-based pun on the Communist use of *comrade*. Cornbread (especially when cooked in a cast-iron skillet) is a celebrated food in Appalachia and the South.
4. Note that this problematic type of person exists both inside and outside the region, breaking down the insider/outsider binary often employed in regional studies and claims to Appalachian authenticity, an essentialist argument that often excludes people living outside of central Appalachia as well as people who move to the region or work in Appalachian Studies.
5. Thanks to Cassie Patterson, Sarah Craycraft, Katherine Borland, Amy Shuman, Michael Gallimore, and Kirk Hazen for deeper discussions and thoughtful feedback on memes and their meanings.

References

Aloi, Joey. 2018. "Cornbread Communist Manifesto." Cornbread Communism: Our Story. Facebook. 11 April 2018. https://www.facebook.com/pg/cornbreadcommunism/about/.

Appalachian Regional Commission (ARC). 2017. "The Appalachian Region." Accessed 5 December 2017. https://www.arc.gov/appalachian_region/theappalachianregion.asp.

Austin. 2011. "So I stood up and told that teachin' lady the only 3 letters I need to know are u, s, and a." Redneck Randal. Digital image. Know Your Meme. Accessed 17 April 2019. https://knowyourmeme.com/photos/122863-redneck-randal.

Ben-Amos, Dan. 1971. "Toward a Definition of Folklore in Context." *The Journal of American Folklore* 84, no. 331: 3–15.

Brad. 2001. Redneck Randal. Know Your Meme. Accessed 17 April 2019. https://knowyourmeme.com/memes/redneck-randal.

Brock, Tricia. 2009. "The Bubble." *30 Rock*. 19 March 2009. New York: NBC Studios. Accessed from Hulu.

Cornbread Communism. 2017a. "Share if your ancestors was them flat-footin' unionists." Digital image. Facebook. 15 August 2017. https://www.facebook.com/cornbreadcommunism/photos/a.967942186681069/986592814816006/.

Cornbread Communism. 2017b. "Shut the winder! Yunz'r lettin the WArSPs in!" Digital image. Facebook. 12 July 2017. https://www.facebook.com/cornbreadcommunism/photos/a.855378974604058/967335056741782/.

Cornbread Communism. 2017c. "Yunz bout ready to seize them means?" Digital image. Facebook. 5 March 2017. https://www.facebook.com/cornbreadcommunism/photos/a.855378974604058/870466413095314/.

Don. 2012a. Almost Politically Correct Redneck. Know Your Meme. https://knowyourmeme.com/memes/almost-politically-correct-redneck.

Don. 2012b. "Woman's Work." Almost Politically Correct Redneck. Know Your Meme. Accessed 17 April 2019. https://knowyourmeme.com/photos/305447-almost-politically-correct-redneck.

Dundes, Alan. 1980. "Who Are the Folk?" In *Interpreting Folklore*, 1–19. Bloomington: Indiana University Press.

Farah, Iffat. 2008. "The Ethnography of Communication." In *Research Methods in Language and Education*, edited by Nancy H. Hornberger and David Corson, 125–27. Vol. 8 of *Encyclopedia of Language and Education*. Dordrecht, NL: Springer.

The Ghost of Ol Dale Earnhardt. n.d. Facebook. Accessed 29 May 2018. www.facebook.com/pg/the.ghost.ofolddale/about/.

The Ghost of Ol Dale Earnhardt. 2017a. "All is for y'all." Digital image. Facebook. 17 June 2017. https://www.facebook.com/the.ghost.ofolddale/photos/a.1360056464032733/1453325938039118/.

The Ghost of Ol Dale Earnhardt. 2017b. "Saddle up, comrade! We're seizin' them means!" Digital image. Facebook. 27 March 2017. https://www.facebook.com/the.ghost.ofolddale/photos/a.1360056464032733/1370981522940227/.

Hathaway, Rosemary V. 2014. "From Hillbilly to Frontiersman: The Changing Nature of the WVU Mountaineer." *West Virginia History* 8, no. 2: 15–46.

Hazen, Kirk. 2008. "(ING): A Vernacular Baseline for English in Appalachia." *American Speech* 83, no. 2: 116–40.

Hazen, Kirk. 2011. "Flying High above the Social Radar: Coronal Stop Deletion in Modern Appalachia." *Language Variation and Change* 23: 105–37.

Hazen, Kirk. 2014. "A New Role for an Ancient Variable in Appalachia: Paradigm Leveling and Standardization in West Virginia." *Language Variation and Change* 26: 77–102.

Hazen, Kirk, Paige Butcher, and Ashley King. 2010. "Unvernacular Appalachia: An Empirical Perspective on West Virginia Dialect Variation." *English Today* 26, no. 4: 13–22.

Huber, Patrick. 2006. "Red Necks and Red Bandanas: Appalachian Coal Miners and the Coloring of Union Identity, 1912–1936." *Western Folklore* 65, no. 1–2: 195–210.

Huber, Patrick. 1995. "A Short History of Redneck: The Fashioning of a Southern White Masculine Identity." *Southern Cultures* 1, no. 2: 145–66.

Hufford, Mary. 1991. *American Folklife: A Commonwealth of Cultures*. Washington, DC: American Folklife Center, Library of Congress.

Hymes, Dell H. 1974. *Foundations in Sociolinguistics: An Ethnographic Approach*. Philadelphia: University of Pennsylvania Press.

Marx, Karl. 2012. *The Communist Manifesto*. Edited by Jeffrey C. Isaac. New Haven, CT: Yale University Press, 73–102.

McNeill, Lynne S. 2009. "The End of the Internet: A Folk Response to the Provision of Infinite Choice." In *Folklore and the Internet: Vernacular Expression in a Digital World*, edited by Trevor J. Blank, 80–97. Logan: Utah State University Press.

McNeill, Lynne S. 2013. *Folklore Rules: A Fun, Quick, and Useful Introduction to the Field of Academic Folklore Studies*. Logan: Utah State University Press.

Newell, William Wells. 1888. "On the Field and Work of a Journal of American Folk-Lore." *The Journal of American Folklore* 1, no. 1: 3–7.

Noyes, Dorothy. 1995. "Group." *The Journal of American Folklore* 108, no. 430: 449–78.

Shirley, Carla D. 2010. " 'You *might* be a redneck *if* . . .': Boundary Work among Rural, Southern Whites." *Social Forces* 89, no. 1: 35–62.

Tanner, James, Morgan Sonderegger, and Michael Wagner. 2017. "Production Planning and Coronal Stop Deletion in Spontaneous Speech." *Laboratory Phonology* 8, no. 1: 1–37.

Thoms, William. 1999. "Folk-Lore and the Origin of the Word." In *International Folkloristics: Classic Contributions by the Founders of Folklore*, edited by Alan Dundes, 9–14. Lanham, MD: Rowman and Littlefield.

Thursby, Jacqueline S. 2006. "Scholarship and Approaches." In *Story: A Handbook*, 115–40. Westport, CT: Greenwood Press.
Toelken, Barre. 1996. "The Folklore Process." In *Dynamics of Folklore*, 19–54. Logan: Utah State University Press.
Wilson, William A. 2006a. "Documenting Folklore." In *The Marrow of Human Experience*, edited by Jill Terry Rudy, 81–103. Logan: Utah State University Press.
Wilson, William A. 2006b. "Herder, Folklore, and Romantic Nationalism." In *The Marrow of Human Experience*, edited by Jill Terry Rudy, 107–23. Logan: Utah State University Press.
Wilson, William A. 2006c. "On Being Human: The Folklore of Mormon Missionaries." *The Marrow of Human Experience*, edited by Jill Terry Rudy, 201–20. Logan: Utah State University Press.

CHAPTER 9

Intersections of Literature and Dialect in Appalachia

Isabelle Shepherd and Kirk Hazen

SUMMARY

In this chapter, we illustrate some of the ways language variation has been used in Appalachian literature. Our chapter explores how self-identified Appalachian authors use grammatical and spelling variation to bring life not only to their characters but to the language and dialect itself. Rather than working from author to author, or from vernacular feature to vernacular feature, we have extracted some literary examples from various works of fiction and poetry to show how they have been used to signify and shape identity, age, and place. Rather than providing an exhaustive survey of Appalachian literature, the chapter focuses on a few authors to provide examples that illustrate linguistic variables and how including this variation enhances the work as a whole, in addition to providing some insight from West Virginian authors as to how they craft dialogue and utilize dialect in their writing. Appalachian literature is multifaceted, and its complexity is reflected in the language variation authors bring to its pages.

INTRODUCTION

It would be folly for us to provide a concise definition of Appalachian literature. To do so would raise questions too broad—and far too controversial—for this chapter. Instead we analyze literary texts that exude Appalachian themes (e.g., mountains, home, family history, and the imprint of industry) written by Appalachian authors, focusing on a few examples from fiction and poetry. Some of these examples show vernacular dialect features, while others seem more standard, emphasizing the range of what can be considered

Appalachian. Just as some dialect varieties in Appalachia demonstrate more vernacular features than others, Appalachian literary works show different levels of vernacularity.

An excerpt from Glenn Taylor's *The Ballad of Trenchmouth Taggart* provides several good examples of vernacular features found in Appalachia: "'Anse Pilcher *going to* testify against Sid,' Kump said. . . . 'Anse *been* running his mouth, claims he *seed* Sid blow up the *tipple* at Tomahawk way back'" (107). Authors portray variation not only in what they write but also in what they decide to leave out. In two places (italics added), the auxiliary verb is left out, a common vernacular pattern that is establishing *going to* as its own modal verb in many English varieties. The regularized past form, *seed* for *saw*, serves to indicate vernacularity and a lower level of education. Lastly, there is *tipple*, mining jargon for a device to load mined materials into some kind of transportation. Language variation can be layered seamlessly in tight constellations to provide texture and a continuously updated context.

Examining dialect variation in literature is a superb way to experience language in context as it actively merges with people's lives. This chapter covers some select themes that appear in Appalachian literature: the realm of authenticity, representations of age and generational change, connection to place, the author's consideration of dialects, and lastly, why real voices in literature matter. The writers of Appalachia create a diverse, collective literature that serves as a lens, refracting all they have experienced and echoing the myriad voices of their families and communities. Taking into account the critical role of the author's voice, Shepherd also interviewed two authors from West Virginia (Scott McClanahan and Matthew Neill Null) to gather their views on their craft, Appalachia, and the language therein. This chapter brings together their commentary with the chapter's themes.

SIGNALING AUTHENTICITY

For many authors, the term *Appalachian writer* can seem claustrophobic; there is a pressure to fit into and convey a certain identity—Write mountains! Write poverty! Where's the coal? But in "The Dangerous Myth of Authenticity," C. B. George observes that "authenticity is the child of that colonial pastime exotification, and sibling to the bigotry of essentialism." There is no one, distilled Appalachia—and therefore no singular Appalachian literature or Appalachian writer. Indeed, Matthew Neill Null, whose debut novel *Honey from the Lion* depicts a logging company and union uprising at the turn of the twentieth century, finds the term to be too expansive to really have much meaning at all:

I don't really believe in using the term "Appalachian" for anything, and it puts me at odds with the rest of my generation. I like thinking of Appalachia, the mountain chain, but I chafe against its use as an adjective. Until I entered college, I never heard anyone use that term. It really was handed down from on high, when the Appalachian Regional Commission was founded in 1965. It's the language of bureaucracy. Before that, you said, "I'm from Nicholas County," or "I'm from out North Fork." It was a localized sense of geography and identity. I don't really believe in Appalachia. I don't know anything about North Carolina, you know? The term just stretches a group identity farther than I find plausible. I don't see enough commonalities to make it stick.

Here, Null's views align with the insights of other chapters (such as 1, 3, and 5) that mention the role of the term *Appalachia*. The bureaucratic language that accompanies so many representations of the region (and casts it as a singular, homogenous, cultural region) is at times at odds with how communities view themselves. The importance of localized identities, crafted for characters as well as real people in the context of local economies and social realities, resonates with all communities through connections to vernacular varieties of English. Broad regional designations established through government bureaucracy do not encapsulate the local differences between communities.

In talking about the types of fiction people usually consider to be Appalachian, Scott McClanahan, author of *Crapalachia* (among many other novels and short story collections), finds the term *Appalachian writer* just as conflicted and unhelpful:

You have these tropes that people use: the Appalachian frontier novel that deals with the nineteenth century and the conflicts between Native Americans and settlers; the Appalachian sawmill novel, pre-coal; the Appalachian coal mining novel. If we're going to write about our region, why write about a region that doesn't exist and probably never existed? . . . My West Virginia—I mean, I come from coal mining people on both sides, union people on both sides. My family's been on strike, both parents, multiple times. But at the same time, my West Virginia was in TV, Nintendo, Nirvana in the same way as a kid growing up in New Jersey or Minnesota. Are there elements about my life that are regional? For sure. But you never hear someone from Minnesota talk about, "What does it mean to be a writer from Minnesota?" It boggles the mind. Appalachian writing is a form that's used to sell in the same way as a crime novel, or a coming-of-age novel. These are things to be sold to a particular audience who is looking for something, something they already believe in, before they read the book.

McClanahan strikes at the heart of what *authenticity* might mean for Appalachia. As with many qualities outside language, audiences come with prepackaged expectations of what they want to consume from the region. It is the differences in language and other cultural traits that are highlighted, and the spotlighted dialect differences are taken as "authentic."

To better understand the role dialects play in how authors negotiate authenticity, it is important to understand that authenticity is not out there to be discovered, found like a treasure buried far back near a creek in some remote hollow. Instead, it is a value that people construct through their daily language by using dialect features that are part of their family and community. For Appalachian literature, there is no explicit publisher's standard for a work of literature to be seen as authentic, but if an author wants to develop dialogue with Appalachian dialect patterns, they toe a fine line: using some vernacular features that match an outside reader's expectations of regional speech while also not playing into a false conception of the Appalachian dialect as dated and old-worldly. If authors include features that are out of line for a character's social class or anachronistic to the time period being depicted, the language choices can veer into the problematic territory of exotification and/or othering. To use an example from chapter 3, a young female from a town in the 2000s should not be using a lot of demonstrative *them* as in *Them boys will chase you*. This usage has been much more prevalent among males and rural speakers since the start of the twentieth century. Appalachians are often depicted as out-of-step with the times culturally, economically, and linguistically. But as other chapters have shown, the Appalachian varieties are as fluid as any other and indeed are changing in line with national trends.

Another route that some writers use to signal authenticity among rural speakers is with the concept of *eye dialect*, the use of nonstandard spelling for speech to draw attention to pronunciation. Null says, "Often, when I see people render dialogue from the South or West Virginia, the quick and easy way (the lazy way) is to use misspellings or drop the –g off the end of participial phrases." While it may get the point across quickly, Null finds certain spelling tricks to be problematic: "It makes their speech different, and some readers will automatically deduct 20–30 IQ points off of that character. I don't think that's the best way. I think the best way to render dialect is to pay great attention to the use of syntax and diction, tweaking it that way." McClanahan is as hesitant as Null when depicting the speech of his characters, aware that sloppy depictions of dialect can be "used as a sign post for class or some sort of lower breeding." His solution? "You do it through word choice and the way people speak."

There is no prepackaged list of dialect features, country words, or witty idioms that grant stories, their characters, or authors authenticity. It is doubtful that any writer does a linguistic study of a community or reads up on sociolinguistic scholarship to figure out the patterns used to craft dialogue in a work. (If you know of one who does, please let us know, as we would really love to buy that writer a drink.) Rather, writers examine language in use, paying attention to the speakers in their communities. They form their language landscape much as birds gather together their nests: picking up a story told at the bar, a snippet of conversation overheard by the gas pump, a phrase their aunt always used to say.

Authenticity has long been a sought-after quality in sociolinguistic studies, and it is something that many Appalachian authors have wrestled with in depicting their communities, both past and present. In a review of sociolinguistic theory, Bucholtz (2003, 404) notes that researchers have traditionally assumed that the supposedly most authentic speakers belonged to the isolated, "static, and relatively homogenous social grouping that is closed to the outside." These assumptions led researchers to search out people who most embodied these qualities, ignoring others and diversity in communities. In this way, sociolinguistic researchers searching for "authentic" speakers were themselves crafting their subject pool in restricted ways. Bucholtz (2003, 405) also remarks that researchers traditionally preferred everyday, mundane language as more authentic. Because of the emphasis placed on daily conversations, it is this type of language that researchers coveted most often. Like this academic desire for a narrow set of qualities deemed as "authentic," in the past, readers and publishers have required certain qualities of Appalachian literature for it to be considered authentic. In contrast, most modern writers have a more diverse understanding of what fits under the moniker of *Appalachia*.

Since there are many ways to represent Appalachia, authors do not have to pile up vernacular features to highlight a speaker's dialect, but they can craft the "language-scape" of their characters through a socially marked word that represents an Appalachian variety. "You can have a very standard English sentence," Null explains, "but if you use a regionally inflected word like 'catawampus' or 'sigodlin,' it implies a particular dialect without relying upon misspellings, etc." For those scratching their heads, *catawampus* means "cockeyed, uneven, or not centered," and *sigodlin* is "askew." In what is possibly his most famous short story, "Trilobites," Breece D'J Pancake employs this strategy: " 'I would wager on Colly's agreement,' he says. I can still hear a hill twang in his voice." Appalachian communities will not all employ the same terms for their varieties, instead choosing differing ways to represent their authenticity.

SIGNALING AGE OF SPEAKER

Reverence for the wisdom of elders is not unique to Appalachian culture, nor is a reliance upon the passing down of stories to help guide the next generation. That said, this relationship is certainly highlighted in Appalachian literature. Wizened characters may pass along life lessons or touch upon the story's main themes off-handedly, perhaps while spreading manure or pouring Splenda packets into their coffee. In sharing anecdotes, they frequently speak with more vernacular flourish and embellishment. In *Crapalachia*, the character of Grandma Ruby (closely based on McClanahan's grandmother of the same name) exhibits stigmatized dialect features more routinely than any other character—and possibly shows the most insight as well. "That's how the world works," Grandma Ruby observes, watching Scott play checkers with his Uncle Nathan. "Just one thing after another and no plan about it at all. Then something happens and it don't mean nothing."

Language variation is often held up as a set of endearing traits that distinguish older characters from younger ones. Since language change is a natural part of any living dialect, authors use older dialect patterns to remind readers of generational differences and to assign identities to certain speakers. For Appalachian dialects, words used less often by younger folk are regularly noted as the most vernacular ones. At times, younger characters will overtly comment on how they remember the language of older folk. In "Trilobites," Pancake writes:

> [the mother]: "He had some funny names all right. Called a tomcat a 'pussy scat.'"
> I think back. "Cornflakes were 'pone-rakes,' and a chicken was a 'sick-un.'"
> We laugh.
> "Well," she says, "he'll always be a part of us."

Here, the father's vocabulary is remembered as distinctly different, but its fond recollection serves to keep his memory alive and a part of their lives. It is mentioned only twice that Colly's father served in World War II. When Ginny asks Colly what killed his father, he answers: "'Little shell fragment. Been in him since the war. Got in his blood . . .' I snap my fingers. I want to talk, but the pictures won't become words." As the family recalls his language, they illustrate an important period of language change: the transition from the pre–World War II to post–World War II generations. As seen across several variables, stigmatized dialect features declined in frequency after World War II (Hazen 2018b).

In his interview, McClanahan says, "It comes down to word choice. An older person just speaks differently. In my family, the older people would call a brown paper bag a 'poke.' We don't say that anymore. Around here in southern West Virginia, you talk about 'polecats' rather than skunks. You'll still hear people saying that, but it's usually somebody who is older. Those words have changed and almost lost their meaning." As McClanahan notes, one of the levels of language that varies most widely between generations is the flux of vocabulary. Even a single word difference provides not just slightly different meaning, as in the semantic spread between *dating* and *courting* below from *Crapalachia*, but the social meaning of "older folk" is also carried with the term *courting*.

> "Hey, Paw," [Bill] said. "Hey, Paw. How you doing?"
> Grandpa couldn't even hear at all so Bill started shouting at him louder.
> He said, "Hey, Paw. I'm courting this girl." He stopped. "Yeah, I'm still going to school."
> I laughed to myself at his use of the word *courting*. Bill saw that I was laughing at him. He laughed too but he kept right on talking.

The contrast of terms creates the humor for the characters, but also endears them to the grandfather. Other generational differences can be more stigmatized than cute for many readers unfamiliar with them. In the following passage from Pancake's "Trilobites," the main character's mother displays several different vernacular dialect features:

> "It ain't that at all," she says, and I watch her brow come down a little. "It's like when Jim called us askin' if we wanted some beans an' I had to tell him to leave 'em in the truck at church. I swan how folks talk when men come 'round a widow."
> I know Jim talks like a dumb old fart, but it isn't like he'd rape her or anything. I don't want to argue with her. "Well," I say, "who owns this place?"
> "We still do. Don't have to sign nothin' till tomorrow."
> She quits bobbing Jesus to look at me. She starts up: "You'll like Akron. Law, I bet Marcy's youngest girl'd love to meet you. She's a

regular rock hound too. 'Sides, your father always said we'd move there when you got big enough to run the farm."

In the mother's speech are five features of rural dialects, including Appalachian varieties (Hazen 2018a). Of them, *ain't* has the highest profile as a vernacular feature. Another salient feature is the multiple negation of "don't have to sign nothin'." In addition, the alveolar nasal [n] is a relatively unmarked figure in regular speech, but it becomes more prominently displayed when conveyed through written speech because of the punctuation of the apostrophe in words such as *askin'* and *nothin'* (see Hazen chapter 3). Slightly more subtle yet still detectable in writing is the absence of consonants on the words *an'* and *Law*. In the one case there is an apostrophe, but with *Law* for *Lord* there is both the dropping of the last two sounds and a different form to represent their loss. Word initial <th> loss happens with *'em*, and this feature is often marked as Appalachian (see Reed chapter 2). More general contraction takes place in numerous words like *'round, girl'd, she's, 'sides,* and *we'd*; note that contraction might be seen as more vernacular in some contexts, like *girl'd*, than in others, like *she's*. Other dialect traits are layered in this short passage, including the Southern and Appalachian feature of using *swan* (or *swanny*) as a euphemism for "I swear." All of these language qualities, plus cultural themes like religion and agriculture, contribute to the layered meanings of this passage. The impacts of dialect features are not rendered in isolation but instead build together to form a constellation of meanings resonating with other themes found in the story. These features are concentrated around older characters, adding a texture to their language identity.

SIGNALING PLACE

Beyond depictions of Appalachian syntax and diction, semantic features and themes also signal place in Appalachian writing, even while using standard forms of language. Breece D'J Pancake begins "Trilobites" with this meditation:

> I open the truck's door, step onto the brick side street. I look at Company Hill again, all sort of worn down and round. A long time ago it was real craggy, and stood like an island in the Teays River. It took over a million years to make that smooth little hill, and I've looked all over it for trilobites. I think how it has always been there and always will be, least for as long as it matters. The air is smoky with summertime. A bunch

of starlings swim over me. I was born in this country and I have never very much wanted to leave.

In this one paragraph, describing Company Hill, Pancake covers many interwoven themes that appear often in Appalachian literature: mountains, nature, and rurality; the industrialization of the landscape (the hill itself is named for the coal company); the passage of time; and the (sometimes difficult) connection to place.

In reviewing the life and work of Pancake, John Burnside of *The Guardian* observes that a "sense of powerlessness haunts these rural tales" and, while Pancake's characters may make plans to leave, "it is both the hard-won sense of identity and the curse of belonging to a specific place that mercilessly defines them." Burnside cites a letter that Pancake wrote to his mother: "There's something ancient and deeply rooted in my soul. I like to think that I have left my ghost up on one of those hollows, and I'll never really be able to leave for good until I find it. And I don't want to look for it, because I might find it and have to leave" (Burnside 2014).

Being drawn back to—or even haunted by—place is a theme also echoed in the work of Crystal Wilkinson, an Affrilachian novelist and poet from rural, south-central Kentucky. From her poem "Terrain":

> the map of me can't be all hills and mountains even though i've been geographically rural and country all my life. the twang in my voice has moved downhill to the flat land a time or two. my taste buds have exiled themselves from fried green tomatoes and rhubarb for goats' milk and pine nuts. still i am haunted by home. i return to old ground time and again, a homing black bird destined to always return.

The connection to land is an extension of the connection to family. In "Trilobites," the narrator (Colly) struggles with the loss of his father and subsequent loss of the family farm, which he is unable to carry on. In much of Appalachia, the success of the family is dependent upon the land in one form or another—what can be grown upon it, or what can be extracted from it. Crystal Wilkinson touches on this connection in her introduction to her section of *Hick Poetics*:

> Our house was heated by coal and wood-burning stoves and we lived so far back in the woods that we could only get one television station. We were proud and hardworking. Our livelihood was an extension of the

land. I am a Black. I am Appalachian. People don't often acknowledge our presence but we are here. There are many Black mountain folks in small towns, up hollers and across knobs. They are scattered all over Appalachia. These poems are from these places.

In Wilkinson's places, "Black mountain folks" are part of life as much as mountains. Along with writers such as Wilkinson, poet Frank X Walker (2000) has embraced the blended term *Affrilachian* to denote Black Appalachians as a normal part of the region's life. Wilkinson's writing also highlights how the land is not only connected to family but also interconnected with the body: "i can't say the landscape of me is all honeysuckle and clover cause there have always been mines in these lily-covered valleys" (from "Terrain"). We see this connection in *Crapalachia* too:

> We crossed the bridge and Ruby looked out across the river. It had been raining really hard that summer so the river was up and rolling all full of mud and roots. So she looked out over the river and said: "Oh look out there. That river is nothing but a river of blood." She repeated: "It looks like nothing but a river of blood and hearts."

Again, the connection between a body of land and the bodies of its people is not unique to Appalachia, but it certainly can be traced as a thematic element. We consume and are nourished by what is grown or raised on our hills and pastures. We are filled with water from our rivers and reservoirs—whether it be clean spring water rolling down from the mountain or well water polluted by industry. Our blood, inextricable from the mud beneath our boots. And what is buried within our land, and then exhumed—it may as well be our hearts.

WRITERS' COMMENTARY ON DIALECT

The place of dialects in literature certainly reflects the authors' experiences with the world. As authors put recognizable dialect differences into their work, social lines are made visible and social groups become real. The critiques of Appalachian language play into everyday life, and authors want to make their readers feel the sting of those critiques on people. The speaker in *Crapalachia* learns early on the implications of dialect, reading about how civilization was built:

> They built the Hawk's Nest Tunnel by digging a big ass hole in the side of a mountain. They used a bunch of poor people to dig it. A poor person

means either their skin was dark or their accents were thick. That's the best way to do anything—get a bunch of poor people to do it.

Despite the abundance of mineral wealth in Appalachia, the communities above ground have historically been and remain impoverished, with the value of extraction benefiting outside corporations and the revenues generated untaxed for local benefit (Catte 2018). In a way, this history of disenfranchisement is intricately linked with dialect and the language of those who have had the ground literally pulled from beneath them. As *Crapalachia*'s narrator reflects:

> I sat in school and I read about how everything changes even in Crapalachia. I read about how the miners became machines, and the loggers became the machines and the tiny roads turned into interstates and the towns became fast food drive thru's and gas stations and the people became people to serve tourists and let the tourists laugh at their accents.

Poet Tim Earley directly confronts, embraces, and then plays with vernacular language in his introduction to his section of *Hick Poetics*, taking up words marked as Appalachian. These include idioms such as *jab it with a stick* (with a vowel shift), grammar variation with the highly stigmatized *we is* (shared with African American Vernacular English), and *whistle pig* (noted by Carver 1987 as one of the few terms actually used across the entire length of Appalachia):

> Whistle Pig, peaked, job it with a stick, job that shit with a stick, catched that tree frog, I knowed to throw it back, Jesus face, Sissy Holler, we is just folks and these is just some cultural interstices, "the absence of teeth, and the compromised nature of the gums, give the tongue freer range, and indeed, create an almost limitless field for linguistic play and invention. Teeth have everything to do with the Lord and social Darwinism and distract the poet from his orphic emptiness," gum it up in the Berkeley, gum it up in the New Yorks City, POETRY! POETRY! POETRY!

It is unclear who or what Earley is quoting in this passage, but regardless, while it relies upon a stereotype regarding the oral hygiene of Appalachian folk, it also celebrates their linguistic creativity. While Berkeley Springs, West Virginia, might be thought to be distanced both geographically and socially from New York City, Earley connects the two, proclaiming the Appalachian dialect worthy of poetry anywhere and everywhere.

In making connections from local varieties, Wilkinson uses dialect and voice "as weapons, as conduits to the ancestors" in order to "create truths through the eyes and mouths of ordinary people" (Wilkinson 2018). Her strategy: "to lean back into our people—their traditions, myths, dreams, nightmares, secrets, memories, talk—and to place my anchor there." Though readers may approach a piece of Appalachian literature with a certain expectation, they are often greeted with defiance, like in the poem "backtalking a guy who tries to get your number by saying *you're not what i expected out of a west virginian, not a redneck at all*" (Shepherd and Lester 2018):

> What'd you expect? Skinning deer and possums—
> Well, there's that too. Watch one
> try to cross the road. Watch its dead body bloat on the
>   side of the road.
> Watch my hands sketch that in art class in high school.
> Watch me write poems to West Virginia each time I call my
>   mom on the phone.

In preserving the voices from home, writers actively work against the stigmas applied to Appalachian people and their dialects.

THE IMPORTANCE OF REAL VOICES IN LITERATURE

The inclusion of diverse Appalachian voices broadens, enhances, and challenges our literary landscape, which has a tendency to be dominated by the tastes of urban publishers. A great deal of modern rural life, including its impact on language, is controlled by urban trends (see Seale and Mallinson 2018). While relatability is not a necessary quality in literature, or art of any form, it is certainly empowering and affirming to see (and hear) oneself reflected in art. It is a political assertion of the relevance of these voices and stories, and it is also a cry to be heard and respected. As Crystal Wilkinson writes in the *Oxford American*:

> I . . . don't often write directly to politics, but this amalgam of personal memory, historical memory, and imagination—the act of writing these characters, the act of drawing from the oral storytelling traditions of both black and Appalachian communities, and the act of making black, Appalachian vernacular the core—is political. How much more political,

revolutionary really, can you be than to give a country black woman the freedom to tell her own story, from her own mouth, from her own tongue as though she is talking to her own people when much of the world refuses to acknowledge that she even exists?

For Appalachians, getting a stage to tell their own story is invaluable. Many Appalachians have a desire to tell their own stories as a defense against all the negative stereotypes that are stacked against them. Sometimes these stories take the approach of what scholars call *strategic essentialism*. To understand this term, it is necessary to make sense of *essentialism*, a viewpoint that restrictively casts people in categories and assigns them certain supposedly "natural" traits. For example, some educational studies in the 1960s wrongly cast inner-city Black children as having no ability for logical language or speech itself because they had dialect features that differed from mainstream White varieties. Similar assumptions are common about Appalachians. In contrast to basic essentialism, strategic essentialism is when a community itself promotes certain qualities as representative of the group in defense against negative perceptions that others put upon them (Bucholtz 2003). So, a stereotype like "hillbillies are backwards" can be upheld as a positive trait, an emblem of sorts, even when the community itself doesn't consider it to be ubiquitously true.

For example, in the documentary *Mountain Talk*, the Appalachian North Carolina community where the documentary is based warmly promotes their variety of English as a type of Old English. The production team was criticized by other scholars for presenting this myth in an academic documentary (Montgomery 2005). The production team retorted that the community wanted to represent themselves with the Old English storyline and that such stories are ways the community casts themselves as *authentic* (Wolfram, Reaser, and Vaughn 2008). Proudly deploying such beliefs is a form of strategic essentialism. As Bucholtz writes, "Given that the groups studied by sociolinguists are often marginalized politically, economically, and socially and hence may not even be recognized by the academy or by dominant society as legitimate subjects of research, strategic essentialism continues to be a necessary tool for both sociolinguists and the communities we study" (2003, 403).

Writers—similar to the Appalachian communities they originate from or identify with—sometimes use overwrought stereotypes to illuminate and even exalt various aspects of mountain life. Words and phrases generally only used by elder speakers in daily conversation, or which have fallen into disuse entirely, may be called forth and reclaimed: *ain't, coon's age, the old woman is picking her geese*. As was the case in *Mountain Talk*, folk beliefs may be presented as points of pride. Those who view Appalachia from the outside often assume that, if given the chance, these communities would cast off their dialects and ways of life to become mainstream, modern, and urban. But that is quite often not the case, and in utilizing elements of strategic essentialism, speakers in (and writers from) these communities differentiate themselves, pushing back against all that would negate and disparage their local histories and cultures.

By studying how language works and how the complex language patterns that people weave play out in poems, stories, and dramas, we better understand the craft of the writer and the texture of human stories that literature holds. Babies are born to naturally acquire language, and in the same way, we learn to walk and run and dance based on all kinds of natural human qualities. It is not until we study how complex these skills are, and the creative ways artists take these human skills and craft them to certain themes, that we understand the challenges artists have faced and the extent of their accomplishments.

Language variation can be seen in the diversity of dialects at any one time and in the changes between generations. People use and create language variation every day as part of their normal routines and as part of their identity. It is part of their small moments like going to the grocery store—*cart* or *buggy*?—and it is part of their big moments like planning a funeral—*died* or *passed on*? When we can experience the diversity of Appalachian dialect varieties through literature, we experience the lives of Appalachian people.

CONCLUSION

There is a wide variety of literature written by authors from the Appalachian region, and this chapter utilized examples from only a few to illustrate how authors use variability in language to create a topography of dialect and character. Other works have taken different productive approaches to Appalachian literature and dialect, including Ellis (2013) and Locklear (2011). From variation in words to the phrasing of sentences, authors use the language of their childhood, their parents and grandparents, to imbue poems, stories, and drama with life. Many more themes can be found in Appalachian literature, from mountains to family history to the imprint of industry, but this chapter has covered questions of how authenticity gets created through dialect choices. The chapter also delved into how authors represent basic characteristics such as age through choice of generational differences in vocabulary. In addition, the chapter took up a common theme found in so many works from Appalachia: the connection to place and how authors render that relationship through language. We wish we could have explored other worthwhile areas of study in Appalachian literature, including how ethnicity and gender have been represented in different genres, but it is clear there is much research to be done on this area of study. The role of language in Appalachian literature is largely underexplored, and the opportunities for future study are abundant.

References

Bucholtz, Mary. 2003. "Sociolinguistic Nostalgia and the Authentication of Identity." *Journal of Sociolinguistics* 7, no. 3: 398–416.
Burnside, John. 2014. "Breece Pancake: 'Something ancient in my soul.' " *The Guardian*, 8 August 2014. https://www.theguardian.com/books/2014/aug/08/breece-pancake-trilobites-baffled-love.
Carver, Craig. 1987. *American Regional Dialects: A Word Geography*. Ann Arbor: University of Michigan Press.
Catte, Elizabeth. 2018. *What You Are Getting Wrong about Appalachia*. Cleveland, OH: Belt Publishing.
Ellis, Michael. 2013. "The Treatment of Dialect in Appalachian Literature." In *Talking Appalachia*, edited by Amy Clark and Nancy Hayward, 163–81. Lexington: University of Kentucky Press.
George, C. B. 2016. "The Dangerous Myth of Authenticity." *Literary Hub*, 18 August 2016. https://lithub.com/the-dangerous-myth-of-authenticity/.
Hazen, Kirk. 2018a. "Rural Voices in Appalachia." In *Rural Voices: Language, Identity, and Social Change across Place*, edited by Elizabeth Seale and Christine Mallinson, 75–90. Lanham, MD: Lexington Books.
Hazen, Kirk. 2018b. "The Contested Southernness of Appalachia." *American Speech* 93, no. 3-4: 374–408.
Locklear, Erica A. 2011. *Negotiating a Perilous Empowerment: Appalachian Women's Literacies*. Athens: Ohio University Press.
McClanahan, Scott. 2013. *Crapalachia: A Biography of Place*. Columbus, OH: Two Dollar Radio.
McClanahan, Scott. 2017. Personal interview with Isabelle Shepherd, 25 April 2017.
Montgomery, Michael. 2005. "Review of *Mountain Talk*: Language and Life in Southern Appalachia." *Appalachian Journal* 32: 389–94.
Null, Matthew Neill. 2015. *Honey from the Lion*. Wilmington, NC: Lookout Books.
Null, Matthew Neill. 2017. Personal interview with Isabelle Shepherd, 16 May 2017.
Pancake, Breece D'J. 1977. "Trilobites." *Atlantic*, December 1977. https://www.theatlantic.com/magazine/archive/1977/12/trilobites/376288/.
Seale, Elizabeth, and Christine Mallinson, ed. 2018. *Rural Voices: Language, Identity, and Social Change across Place*. Lanham, MD: Lexington Books.
Shepherd, Isabelle, and Keegan Lester. 2018. "Backtalking a guy who tries to get your number by saying *you're not what i expected out of a west virginian, not a redneck at all*." *Powder Keg* 12. https://www.powderkegmagazine.com/keegan-lester-isabelle-shepherd/.
Taylor, M. Glenn. 2009. *The Ballad of Trenchmouth Taggart: A Novel*. New York: Ecco Press.
Walker, Frank X. 2000. *Affrilachia*. Lexington, KY: Old Cove Press.
Wilkinson, Crystal. 2018. "Shit, We're All Consequences of Something." *Oxford American*, 13 March 2018. https://www.oxfordamerican.org/magazine/item/1437-all-consequences-of-something.
Wilkinson, Crystal. 2015. Excerpt from *Hick Poetics*, edited by Abraham Smith and Shelly Taylor, 356–65. Jackson, WY: Lost Roads Publishers.
Wolfram, Walt, Jeffrey Reaser, and Charlotte Vaughn. 2008. "Operationalizing Linguistic Gratuity: From Principle to Practice." *Language and Linguistic Compass* 2, no. 6: 1109–34.

CHAPTER 10

Teachers and Teens Making Sense of Identity, Place, and Language in Appalachian Secondary Schools

Audra Slocum

SUMMARY

This chapter explores how adolescents in Appalachia engage in identity work through their language practices in secondary schools. In this chapter, I explore the ways in which language, identity, and culture intersect for adolescents in Appalachia using available research on adolescent and adult language usage in the region, as well as studies of vernacular adolescent speakers outside of the region. Given the significance of schools and teachers in co-constructing language use, I discuss the role that schools as social institutions have had in regulating adolescent speech, and I review research on teacher attitudes towards and sociolinguistic knowledge about vernacular and non-standardized speech. I describe findings from recent qualitative research with adolescents on their language practices of monitoring each other's speech. At the end, I describe current research being conducted in West Virginia on adolescent speech, their perceptions of speech, and their academic identity. The chapter concludes with a discussion of areas for further study.

INTRODUCTION

As soon as you're old enough to talk and know stuff, there's just the basics. It's like you're born with it; you're born with people stereotyping against you. So, it's not like you're just walking into this kind of hatred, it's been there your whole life. . . . If you like where you live, you're going to like growing up there. And I like where I live. We're going to be the next to make this region. Hopefully, we're going to make something of it.

Chayla, the seventeen-year-old high school senior from eastern Kentucky speaking in the quote above, describes the way stereotypes of the Appalachian region shape existence for residents from birth. Discourses of Appalachian deficiencies constantly circulate in her community. Yet, accustomed to the politics of language, place, culture, and identity, Chayla claims space for self-love and her generation's ability to keep the region moving forward.

We grow up immersed in language communities. As a result, we grow up talking like those around us: our families, neighbors, and community. We learn how to say things, do things, and be certain types of people through language. These "ways with words" are culturally specific (Heath 1983; Lave and Wenger 1991; Eckert 2008). These language communities are complex. As humans are situated within intersecting and interacting social categories—like race, gender, and social class—we are socialized to use language and other social practices to index our membership within these groups (Crenshaw 1991; Bucholtz and Hall 2005; Collins and Bilge 2016). Language acts as a marker of social position; "It symbolizes our social experience in an intimate way and locates us within significant social groups from which we draw our identities" (Luhman 1990, 332).

Inherent to our ties with social groups are our connections to places. Sociolinguists see a powerful local orientation among speakers within a speech community (Eckert 2008; Greene 2010; Moore and Carter 2015). That is, there is a lot of social pressure to sound like people who share membership in social groups. In this way, language is a social tool that provides information to the people in and outside of your community. Mac Ruairc (2011) frames the connections between social tools, contexts, and identity. He writes that the "key cultural, linguistic and symbolic meaning-makers [are] provided within the context of the neighborhood. It is with these constituents that individuals come to a sense of themselves within the boundaries of a particular setting" (539). In part, it is the social history of a community in relation to other communities that shapes the meaning associated with speech variables and language practices.

For many communities in Appalachia, the relationship with other areas has been fraught. Appalachia has been constructed as a place in need of assistance, a place that is always "less than" other areas. In particular, Appalachia has been portrayed in media and public policy as a "backwards" place, a place of generational poverty and educational deprivation. On the other hand, northern, middle-class, cosmopolitan areas have been shaped as the sources of aid, the social model to which Appalachia is supposed to aspire and to which it should be compared. This social hierarchy has also been applied to language practices, marking varieties often used in Appalachia as "incorrect" and signals of poor schooling. Speech variables such as leveled *was* (e.g., *We* was *working on a new project*) and *a*-prefixing (e.g., *I've been* a-fixing *to come by your house*) have a social history. They have been and continue to be used to mark difference, not just geographically, but also by social class, education, and more (see Hazen chapter 3). Thus, we come to the question: For adolescents in Appalachia, a region socially marked by its particular language varieties, what does it mean to "come to a sense of themselves" *here*?

Chayla, the young woman opening the chapter, and her peers around the region are coming to a sense of themselves here in Appalachia. As they do, they are signaling this sense of identity and place through their discourse and speech features. Their *here* in Appalachia is wide-ranging, includes urban areas like Knoxville, Tennessee, and rural areas like Mud Creek, Kentucky. Their *here* is also at a particular time, as highways throughout rural areas have shortened traveling distances between urban centers, allowing young people to travel for team competitions and extracurriculars like Future Farmers of America and Science Olympiad. Even at home, kids are playing multiplayer video games with peers around the world. In the meantime, they might also be spending significant time with grandparents, aunts, uncles, and cousins. All of this social exchange across space and time continues to shape their identities, their sense of *here*.

These exchanges and identity shaping are ongoing and significant. Attending to the language practices of adolescents is important, as they are the leaders of linguistic change (Eckert 2003). Hazen, Flesher, and Simmons (2013) have documented language change in West Virginia, noting the maintenance and change of particular dialect features across age groups. Features like *a*-prefixing and demonstrative *them* (e.g., *Them books are heavy*) are recorded significantly less frequently in younger adults (born between 1980 and 1989) than in older adults (Hazen et al. 2013). They note that while usage rates of these features from older to younger speakers have fallen, some of these features persist in middle-aged populations, with additional variability by location, education, and social class.

However, there is no documentation of contemporary adolescent speech in central Appalachia. Because of this gap in the research, we can only hypothesize on the patterns of language maintenance and change. Additionally, we wonder, for contemporary Appalachian adolescents, what would it mean to demonstrate one's cultural place-affiliation linguistically while also responding to schooling demands and participating in broader social groups and pop culture (Eckert 2003)? In the next part of this chapter, I examine the context of schooling and teachers' perceptions of language varieties, as these contexts and relationships hold significant power on adolescent life. I then turn towards adolescents' perspectives on language varieties and current research on these topics.

LANGUAGE DEMANDS OF SCHOOLING

In the United States, school takes a predominant institutional role in adolescent life, so consequently, schools have significant impacts on identity and language. Not only are young people spending eight hours a day in schools, but schools also serve as a gatekeeper for postsecondary options. The social institution of school is based on White middle-class language norms, and these norms powerfully shape the linguistic context of schooling (Anyon 1980; Heath 1983; Wolfram and Christian 1989; Reaser 2013; Gee 2014). Tied to these norms, standard language ideology is the idea that there is a "standard" language that is superior to other variations of that language (Dunstan and Jaeger 2016; chapter 11 this volume). Through policies and curricula based on standard language ideology, the promotion of "school English" creates "codes of power" (Delpit 1995), which are linguistic rules that dictate what is deemed appropriate or correct within that institution.

The determination of which variety of English is the standard is not based on any linguistic quality; rather, it is based on the prestige of the social group. As a result, because White middle-class communities have entrenched institutional power, speech varieties associated with these groups have widespread prestige and are considered the "standard" variety. The enforcement of this standard is revealed in an examination of many state English content standards. There is a clear institutional bias towards "standard" English. The West Virginia College and Career Readiness Standards, based on the Next Generation Common Core Standards used across the country, explicitly call for instruction on the use of "standard English" in written and oral forms in academic contexts (West Virginia Department of Education 2016). This expectation can be seen in the language standard's first set of indicators for "conventions of standard English," in which the first English language arts (ELA) standard includes the demonstration of "command of the conventions of 'standard English' grammar and usage in writing or speaking."

Interestingly, the ELA standards include qualifiers that create space for teaching the contextual variation of language forms. For example, in the speaking and listening standards for "presentation of knowledge and ideas," the ELA standard states: "Adapt speech to a variety of contexts and communicative tasks, demonstrating command of formal English when indicated or appropriate." Similarly, in the realm of "knowledge of language," the ELA standard states: "Apply knowledge of language to understand how language functions in different contexts, to make effective choices for meaning or style, and to comprehend more fully when reading or listening" (West Virginia Department of Education 2016).

In both instances, the use of different forms of English are suggested as contextual—"when indicated or appropriate." How teachers might navigate teaching the rhetorical aspect of language is shaped by school policy and curriculum and the teachers' own beliefs and understanding about standard and vernacular speech forms. Rather than making these possibilities an afterthought or subject to individual teachers' knowledge, Souto-Manning (2013) proposes, "We must refashion curricula that foregrounds the language and cultural practices of children from linguistically and culturally diverse backgrounds." She continues, "Educators still have the responsibility to socialize all children into the discourse of power, but do not need to take a subtractive stance to do so" (313).

How schools, particularly those schools in low-status, linguistically marginalized communities, enacted these ideologies through "naturalized" prescriptive school practices was the subject of significant sociolinguistic research throughout the 1970s, '80s, and '90s. This line of research documented the continuities and discontinuities between home and school language and literacy practices. Shirley Brice Heath's (1983) classic decade-long sociolinguistic study across three neighboring communities in the Piedmont of North Carolina provided detailed documentation of the ways in which working-class White children, working-class Black children, and middle-class White children were socialized to use language in their cultural communities.

For example, young children in Trackton, the working-class Black community, were immersed in the storytelling practice of "talking junk," in which the storyteller creatively exaggerated stories from life around town. Adults and children alike were celebrated for their skills in talking, and children attempted talking junk from an early age. Quite differently, young children in the White working-class community of Roadville were discouraged from "telling stories" or exaggerating personal experiences for rhetorical effect; rather, parents instructed their children to report events factually. In different ways, the language practices expected within their schools did not align with the language practices they were socialized into in the working-class White and Black communities. The discontinuity of expectations for discourse from the context of home to that of school, when interpreted through a frame of "school readiness," which is built on the White middle-class practices of teachers and the school, was not simply a matter of difference. Rather, teachers viewed the working-class White and Black children and their families as less intelligent and less academically capable than their White middle-class peers, whose home language and literacy practices aligned with those expected at school. Importantly, speaking a dialect different from the variation expected in schools does not set up cognitive barriers; the barriers are social ones (Reaser 2013).

Teachers play a central role in schools' enactment of the institution's ideological system (DeYoung 1995). Many rural schools in Appalachia are staffed primarily by teachers who are from the same or neighboring counties as their students. In these cases, it is likely that these teachers have been socialized into local language practices and ideologies. However, the concept of "local" is complex, as there are not homogenous practices or ideologies within a community. Furthermore, with experience in college, teachers may have secondary socialization into middle-class institutional language practices and ideologies that affirm the stigmatization of vernacular speech. As a result, teachers sit at the intersection of multiple communities in ways that may or may not reflect the same intersectional identities as their students. For example, a teacher may have come from a middle-class family, perhaps in the county seat, yet be working in a school that primarily serves working-class families, perhaps in more rural areas in the county. Might their use of stigmatized speech features be based on their age, gender, social class, education level, and affiliation with the community? According to Reck, Reck, and Keefe (1987), "Appalachian teachers did not identify overtly with the rural, Appalachian group that they perceived. Despite their shared origin—the mountains—they distanced themselves from the group" (12). They reasoned that "middle-class status provides Appalachian people the means and the inclination to negotiate themselves out of a largely forced, negative identity" (12). Given these social positions, what might their language ideologies include?

While avoiding a forced negative identity has strong social influence, so does the maintenance of social connections to one's community. Many teachers seek to show affiliation with their students and their community, and they can do so through the use of locally valued speech features. Greene's (2010) dissertation on the adult language use in an eastern Kentucky county demonstrated tensions in adult speakers' interests in both "sounding local" and "sounding educated." She found that "all of the Wilson Countians in this study use phonological features in part to signal their local identity, but that they avoid local grammatical features in an effort to appear competent, intelligent, and modern" (Greene 2010, 132). An example of "sounding local" might be the use of /aɪ/ ungliding in words like *mine* (see chapter 2). Note that there is a finely tuned scale of more or less local based on whether the vowel is closer to [aː] or [aɪ]. This pattern of using local phonological features while avoiding local grammatical features was intensified for people who work in the school systems and with college degrees. Greene found that adults with college degrees who work in schools "use particularly low rates of *was*-leveling, apparently reflecting the high value that schools place on correct grammar" (Greene 2010, 132). Leveled *was* can be seen in the sentence *They was going to the store*, as opposed to *They were going to the store*. This grammatical feature is available in local discourse; however, she found that "retired teachers used *was*-leveling at an average rate of 9 percent" (120). Variations in the rate of adult use of these features are seen across gender, geography, social class, and education levels. There are no linguistic studies specifically of teacher language varieties within Appalachia. Such a study might reveal interesting patterns across grade levels and content areas as well as interesting patterns regarding the frequency of grammatical versus phonological variations. For example, do English teachers use fewer stigmatized grammatical features than teachers of other content areas?

Whether responsible for direct English language instruction or not, and regardless of their own speech variations, teachers regulate student language (Godley, Reaser, and Moore 2015). Teachers' negative judgment of vernacular speech can limit students' access to educational opportunities, as a teacher may associate particular speech forms as indicators of intelligence and academic capability, or lack thereof (Wolfram and Christian 1989). Problematically, teacher knowledge of sociolinguistic principles and sociolinguistic pedagogy are often limited. Godley, Reaser, and Moore (2015) found that "many teachers erroneously believe that standardized English is more grammatical than vernacular dialects and form negative opinions of students, particularly minority students, when they use vernacular dialects in school" (42). The majority of English teachers have only had one linguistics course at most during their preparation; other teachers most likely have had no linguistic coursework. Even for English teachers, a course specifically on the teaching of language is rare; more typical is the integration of some aspects of teaching language embedded in one or maybe two methods courses. Often, the focus of these courses or units is about vocabulary or grammar instruction decontextualized from sociolinguistic principles. As a result, many teachers, even those with a specialization in the teaching of English, are underprepared to teach using findings from sociolinguistic research. If a teacher brings with them negative associations of vernacular speech forms, it is unlikely that these ideas will be substantively countered by the curriculum in their teacher preparation program (Godley, Reaser, and Moore 2015). In a region where residents are characterized as "sounding illiterate," examining how teachers understand themselves as speakers and as caretakers of young people in the region may open up powerful insights into how codes of power are reproduced and rationalized, modified, or resisted by teachers.

APPALACHIAN ADOLESCENT LANGUAGE USE

Despite the limited research specifically on adolescents in Appalachia, it is not hard to extrapolate from patterns of adult usage to predict those of adolescents. After all, adolescents are members of many of the same communities of practice as adults. There are, however, specific pressures and possibilities acting upon adolescents, particularly in school contexts (Eckert 2003). Where vernacular speech is predominant in the community, there can be tension between the standard language variety valued in schools and the vernacular varieties used locally (Chisholm and Godley 2011; Souto-Manning 2013). In practice, most spaces are porous; the school doors do not hold back the use of language variation. Mixing and meshing varieties is common in schools (Mac Ruairc 2011; Brady 2015). For example, adolescents may alternate between vernacular varieties and "standard" varieties moment to moment, between the classrooms, the hallways, and the restrooms, depending on the social dynamics of the speakers. While the schooling context is highly regulated, adolescents respond in ways that may take up, modify, or resist these ideologies and practices in complex, sometimes contradictory ways (Souto-Manning 2013). Kirkland (2010) points out that adolescents who are culturally and linguistically marginalized are attuned to the political nature of using codes associated with schooling, saying, "It is also about relevance in a world that requires certain ways of speaking, certain sounds and social postures pronounced in various sociopolitical accents" (294). Examining how adolescents, particularly those who use stigmatized dialects, respond to the linguistic regulation of school is important for understanding how adolescents view schools as a speech context and the depth and variety of their linguistic repertoires.

Even as adolescents engage in complex use of language variations, they also can hold prejudices against particular dialects, including ones that they use themselves (Chisholm and Godley 2011; Cramer chapter 5). Contrary to perceptions of relatively racially and economically homogeneous rural schools (and not all schools in Appalachia are rural or homogenous!), there are diverse language ideologies circulating in the hallways. Just as with adults (Greene 2010), adolescents in different social positions have been immersed in and have adopted a range of language ideologies regarding language diversity and the expectations of schools around language instruction. Generally, adolescents may share beliefs that vernacular speech is incorrect, a sign of the speaker's ignorance or poor schooling, or conversely that they represent cultural pride and community affiliation. Regarding school-based language instruction, adolescents may hold beliefs that teachers should be teaching "proper" grammar, along with the contingent belief that it is only through the use of "proper" grammar that students will succeed academically. In Brady's (2015) study of working-class adolescents in the United Kingdom, 21 percent reported viewing people using vernacular speech as "not very intelligent." Further, 60 percent of the adolescent participants agreed or strongly agreed that "teachers should correct the use of nonstandard English in the classroom." Such attitudes amongst some adolescents might reflect an internalization of the hierarchical system that locates vernacular speech into a lower status marked by region, class, and race. It also may demonstrate the belief that learning and using standard English varieties leads to academic and, therefore, economic success. On the other end of the spectrum, some students maintain stigmatized speech features as a way to signal a strong stance of affiliation towards their local community. Some students who reject schooling, with its restrictions and its dismissive stance against vernacular discourse, might demonstrate their resistance by maintaining the use of stigmatized speech features.

To illustrate ways that some adolescents in Appalachia respond to perceptions of local speech, I draw from my ethnographic study of adolescent social positioning around language and literacy situated in a single English high school classroom in rural eastern Kentucky (Slocum 2014; Slocum 2019). The participants were White working- to middle-class high school seniors. Half the class had planned to attend college after high school; half intended to enter the workforce or military. I found three key discursive practices adolescents used for social positioning around language and identity. First, talking about talk was common. Among the students, there was ongoing social commentary in school about language variation, particularly regarding how their own language was viewed as a marker of a lack of intelligence outside of their community.

Chayla, the young woman quoted at the beginning of this chapter, related to the English class a story from her experience at a prestigious statewide summer camp for young artists. A peer from a suburban area outside of the region persistently teased Chayla about her speech. Chayla frequently used phonological features like unglided /aɪ/ (as in *mahl* for *mile*) and morphological features like the alveolar form of *–ing* (e.g., *walk*in') that clearly marked her as a "country," southern Appalachian speaker. She explained to the class how one camper identified herself as Chayla's interpreter, as if Chayla would be otherwise unintelligible. This girl followed Chayla around restating things Chayla said for their peers. While hurt by the implication and social isolation, Chayla was also profoundly angered, as were her classmates. Her response was not to erase her dialect features; no, Chayla explicitly celebrated her speech. In my interview with her, she stated, "Like, people here talk about the way I talk. I *like* the way I talk. So, I mean, I guess I take on that one [stereotype]. Or, like, we're redneck, and stuff, but I mean, I embrace it!" Chayla took up her speech as a cultural symbol signaling her identity as a person from eastern Kentucky. Significantly, Chayla maintained socially recognized rates of stigmatized speech features *and* was a leader in her senior class. She led several extracurricular groups, served as an editor for the school newspaper, and took all honors-level courses. She did not subscribe to the ideology that vernacular speech indicates a lack of intelligence or prevents academic success.

In addition to this particular story, students in the class frequently commented on their own, each other's, and "outsiders'" language. They indexed two ends of a spectrum of speech as "proper" and "country" speech, a reflection of community perception of language variation (Luhman 1990; Agha 2007). They associated proper speech with White, middle-class, college-educated speakers from nonrural backgrounds, more widely accepted and of greater value in the broader society. However, proper speech had limited value locally. Country speech, on the other hand, was associated with White working-class speakers from rural communities and was perceived as familiar and relatable. There was a strong local value assigned to country speech.

At times, socially powerful girls in the study's focal class labeled peers' speech as "too proper," "country," or "too country." While they were not specific about a particular feature or a frequency of use of a feature, there is a socially recognizable point of disrupting local norms. Mac Ruairc (2011, 39) similarly found that,

> Any submission to these [standardized] codes and practices, just as any transgression, is immediately the object of commentary; a norm exists that defines those who are not or do not act "like us". This exerts a normalizing force on the group and is supported by a stringent yet informal

panoptic gaze which reveals how the power of the norm permeates all levels of social existence (Foucault 1977). The consensus within this perspective is that in general, individuals are presented with a strong sense of what is expected in particular cultural spaces.

Importantly, the "particular cultural space" in this study has the speech norms that reflect at least some southern Appalachian stigmatized speech features. There was a single Appalachian-heritage student in the class who had grown up in the North and whose speech patterns fell outside of local norms. With peers still commenting on her speech a year after her arrival, this student felt the "panoptic gaze" and its "normalizing force." In fact, she intentionally adapted her speech to sound more like her peers. Her intentional speech modifications were socially recognized, as multiple students in the class commented on the change in her pronunciation (Slocum 2019). Her adaptation also signified the role of the local context and her adolescent peer group in shaping linguistic decisions (Greene 2010). Her adolescent peer group's expectations for language flipped the mainstream sociolinguistic hierarchy, such that "country" speech features were more valued, while speech features associated with White northern speakers were mocked in these peer groups. As Greene (2010) notes, the adolescents in this study had expectations for community members who attended college outside of the region to continue to use locally valued speech features. Such maintenance was interpreted as a stance signifying allegiance to the local cultural community.

Evident within these findings is the significance of language as a social tool for mediating social relationships, monitoring community practices, and, consequentially, co-constructing identity and place. In complicated ways, some participants took up elements of the discourses of proper and country binaries to create local expectations for speech that were broad enough to include some variation but also marked speakers using features (or frequency of features) that fell outside of the norms. While "country" speech was locally valued, it did not hold the same meanings outside of the community. Locally, it meant community affiliation. To the participants, many forms of "country" speech did not seem to indicate anything socially significant about social class or education level, suggesting space for an individual to participate both in local speech norms and in a variety of social groupings. Indeed, contrary to discourses that assign identities of being poor and uneducated to the region's residents, there was qualitative evidence that students with strong academic performance and high engagement in school activities used "country" features, as did students with average academic performance with goals of entering the workforce directly out of high school. This range of interests and orientations is left out of most representations of the region, and many adolescents that see the simplistic and uninformed representations critique them while also striving to work around them. Importantly, the adolescents' ability to work within and against these representations is not to suggest that experiences like Chayla's at camp are acceptable or without consequence. Rather, these findings indicate that scholars and those working with young people in the region must listen closely to young people: listen for how they populate meaning into an identity position and for how they make sense of and navigate the discourses circulating through their communities.

CURRENT AND FUTURE RESEARCH

In this final section, I draw on the work discussed above to inform a series of current and future research projects that would more fully develop understanding of contemporary sociolinguistic issues for adolescents in Appalachia. For a broader review of language variation work in education, Hazen (2017) reviews the development of pedagogical perspectives on dialects in the classroom. In particular, there are two categories of research needed. First, in research that centers on Appalachian youth, documentation of their language practices, ideologies, and knowledge is needed to provide a stronger empirical knowledge base for this region and the leaders of linguistic change here. Second, research that attends to the language practices, ideologies, knowledge, and instructional practices of teachers in the Appalachian region is needed to better understand the key context for intersections of standardized and vernacular speech, how access to educational opportunities is shaped by language, and the identity negotiations of those involved.

Attention to adolescent language use in Appalachia has been scant (Slocum 2014, 2019); however, some research is in progress to document adolescent language in schools in West Virginia. The new research builds on the research about adult speakers' language variations across the northern and southern parts of the state and across towns and rural areas (Hazen, Butcher, and King 2010; Hazen et al. 2013). The project includes four secondary school sites across the state of West Virginia, with the goal of documenting variation by geography and community demographics. Specifically, "in order to address questions of language change, we examine how adolescent speakers deploy both changing and stable linguistic variables to create anew the sociolinguistic fabric of their community" (Hazen and Slocum 2016). Based on ongoing analysis of interview data with twenty eighth-grade students from northern Appalachia, adolescents show keen awareness of language stereotypes and control the production of grammatical variation so as not to produce vernacular features in formal situations. Appalachian dialect features like *a*-prefixing (e.g., *She was a-studying*) and demonstrative *them* (e.g., *Them cars raced all night*) were not found in sociolinguistic interviews. The widest range of variation appears with sounds. For example, variation with the vowels in words like *beat, bit,* and *bite* shows some social correlation but is also part of the social awareness of what sounds "country," even for rural areas.

In addition to documenting language variations, the project also addresses adolescent perceptions of dialect. This aspect of the study seeks to qualitatively examine the metalinguistic awareness about code-switching practices, referring to views of vernacular speech and its "appropriateness" in various contexts, including formal schooling. A third element of the study is analysis of the adolescents' academic identities: how they see themselves as learners within formal schooling contexts and how these are informed by and inform their social identities within these contexts.

Future studies need to be attentive to the diverse identities and ideologies of these adolescents to continue to account for the variations that exist in a region that is typically and inaccurately represented as homogenous. As Greene (2010) notes, there are complex linguistic variations that are impacted by ideologies, and in turn, the ideologies are informed by things like an individual's inward and outward orientation, relationships with people from outside the region, and cultural affiliation. Further, Mallinson and Childs's (2004) research on the use of African American Vernacular English within rural Appalachian contexts is a critical reminder about intersections of race, rurality, and dialect that are often left out of studies on these speakers and dialect studies in Appalachia. As their study includes only one adolescent participant, there is ample room for more research in this area. What social and linguistic resources do young people of color in Appalachia draw upon to mediate their identity positioning? As an example, given the range of communities children of color grow up in within Appalachia—from predominantly African American towns to historically African American neighborhoods within predominantly White counties and cities—the social and linguistic resources and available identity positions also range greatly. Additionally, documenting adolescent language practices outside of school will better account for the rich and complicated social contexts that compose adolescent life. For example, many young people interact verbally through online spaces like multiplayer games with speakers from across the world, and these spaces pose interesting intersectional communities of practice.

Similarly, studies that account for the intersectional identities of teachers in the region open up opportunities to better theorize the situated relationships between language ideologies and language use. For example, how might an intersectional analysis of teacher sociolinguistic identity add to our understanding of them as actors in institutional language ideologies, particularly relative to their relationships with students from the same or differing social classes, race, or community? As research moves forward, there are many questions to be answered about how language use connects with language identity and educational orientation.

CONCLUSION

As leaders of language change, adolescents need to be a part of our conversation about the Appalachian region and education. They are engaging in complex work that simultaneously reproduces some social and linguistic practices, even as they disrupt other ones, therein creating new perspectives for what it means to be from this region.

References

Agha, Asif. 2007. *Language and Social Relations*. Studies in the Social and Cultural Foundations of Language 24. Cambridge: Cambridge University Press.
Anyon, Jean. 1980. "Social Class and the Hidden Curriculum of Work." *Journal of Education* 162, no. 1: 67–92.
Brady, Jude. 2015. "Dialect, Power and Politics: Standard English and Adolescent Identities." *Literacy* 49, no. 3: 149–57.
Bucholtz, Mary, and Kira Hall. 2005. "Identity and Interaction: A Sociocultural Linguistic Approach." *Discourse Studies* 7, no. 4–5: 585–614.
Chisholm, James, and Amanda Godley. 2011. "Learning about Language through Inquiry-Based Discussion: Three Bidialectal High School Students' Talk about Dialect Variation, Identity, and Power." *Journal of Literacy Research* 43, no. 4: 430–68.
Collins, Patricia Hill, and Sirma Bilge. 2016. *Intersectionality*. Key Concepts. Cambridge, UK: Polity Press.
Delpit, Lisa. 1995. *Other People's Children: Cultural Conflict in the Classroom*. New York: The New Press.
DeYoung, Alan J. 1995. "Constructing and Staffing the Cultural Bridge: The School as Change Agent in Rural Appalachia." *Anthropology and Education Quarterly* 26, no. 2: 168–92.
Dunstan, Stephany B., and Audrey Jaeger. 2015. "Dialect and Influences on the Academic Experiences of College Students." *Journal of Higher Education* 86, no. 5: 777–803.
Godley, Amanda, Jeffrey Reaser, and Kaylan Moore. 2015. "Pre-service English Language Arts Teachers' Development of Critical Language Awareness for Teaching." *Linguistics and Education* 32: 41–54.
Greene, Rebecca. 2010. "Language, Ideology, and Identity in Rural Eastern Kentucky." PhD diss., Stanford University. http://purl.stanford.edu/fh361zh5489.
Hazen, Kirk. 2017. "Variationist Approaches to Language and Education." In *Research Methods in Language and Education*, 3rd ed, edited by Kendall King, Yi-Ju Lai, and Stephen May, 145–57. Vol. 10 of *The Encyclopedia of Language and Education*. New York: Springer. https://doi.org/10.1007/978-3-319-02249-9_10.

Hazen, Kirk, Paige Butcher, and Ashley King. 2010. "Unvernacular Appalachia: An Empirical Perspective on West Virginia Dialect Variation." *English Today* 26, no. 4: 13–22.

Hazen, Kirk, Jaime Flesher, and Erin Simmons. 2013. "The Appalachian Range: The Limits of Language Variation in West Virginia." In *Talking Appalachian*, edited by Amy Clark and Nancy Hayward, 54–69. Lexington: University Press of Kentucky.

Hazen, Kirk, and Audra Slocum. 2016. "Community Studies of Sociolinguistic Change in Appalachia." Funded National Science Foundation Proposal (BCS-1651003). https://nsf.gov/awardsearch/showAward?AWD_ID=1651003.

Kirkland, David. 2010. "English(es) in Urban Contexts: Politics, Pluralism, and Possibilities." *English Education* 42, no. 3: 293–309.

Luhman, Reid. 1990. "Appalachian English Stereotypes: Language Attitudes in Kentucky." *Language in Society* 19, no. 3: 331–48.

Mac Ruairc, Gerry. 2011. "They're My Words—I'll Talk How I Like! Examining Social Class and Linguistic Practice among Primary-School Children." *Language and Education* 25, no. 6: 535–59.

Mallinson, Christine, and Becky Childs. 2004. "The Intersection of Regional and Ethnic Identity: African American English in Appalachia." *Journal of Appalachian Studies* 10, no. 1–2: 129–42.

Reaser, Jeffrey. 2013. "Dialect and Education in Appalachia." In *Talking Appalachian*, edited by Amy Clark and Nancy Hayward, 94–109. Lexington: University Press of Kentucky.

Reck, Una Mae, Gregory Reck, and Susan Keefe. 1987. "Teachers' Perceptions of Appalachian and Non-Appalachian Students." Paper presented at American Educational Research Association Annual Meeting, Washington, DC.

Slocum, Audra. 2014. "Look What They Said about Us: Social Positioning Work of Adolescent Appalachians in English Class." *English Teaching: Practice and Critique* 13, no. 3: 191–209.

Slocum, Audra. 2019. "Exploring Identity through Literature and Language: Adolescents' Identity Positioning in Rural Appalachia." *Journal of Language, Identity, and Education* 18, no. 5: 283–96.

Souto-Manning, Mariana. 2013. "Competence as Linguistic Alignment: Linguistic Diversities, Affinity Groups, and the Politics of Educational Success." *Linguistics and Education* 24, no. 3: 305–15.

West Virginia Department of Education. 2016. *West Virginia College and Career Readiness Standards*. https://wvde.us/tree/middlesecondary-learning/english-language-arts/.

Wolfram, Walt, and Donna Christian. 1989. *Dialects and Education: Issues and Answers*. Englewood Cliffs, NJ: Prentice Hall.

CHAPTER 11

Appalachian Englishes and the College Campus

Stephany Brett Dunstan and Audrey J. Jaeger

SUMMARY

Research suggests that feeling a sense of belonging at a college or university is an important factor in academic success, persistence, and graduation. Many factors have been identified as influencing what makes us feel as if we belong, but there has been little research on the role dialect plays in feeling a sense of belonging in college. In this chapter, we discuss a study on the role of language and belonging for students from rural Appalachia who attend college in the urban South. For many of these students, coming to college was the first time they realized that their speech made them different, even to other Southerners. We discuss how dialect shaped their experiences fitting in on campus and implications for creating inclusive campus environments.

INTRODUCTION

When students come to college, most are looking for a good fit. They want a place where they feel comfortable learning and engaging on their pathway to a degree and career. Research suggests that there are a number of components that influence the extent to which students feel like they fit or feel a sense of belonging on campus, such as making friends, finding social outlets, connecting with instructors, enjoying their classes, and more. However, what role a student's dialect plays in their sense of belonging on campus has not been well documented. Nonetheless, a sense of belonging may be affected if the student feels that their dialect makes them in some way the "other." This situation can be especially true for students from rural Appalachia whose dialect features may mark them as different, even when attending college in the South. In this chapter, we describe a study conducted on this topic at a large research institution in the southern United States.

College campuses, like any organization, hold certain values and norms, which influence the culture of the organization and its members. Also like any organization, these values and norms are influenced by dominant, mainstream culture. On campus, linguistic hegemony and standard language ideology (we will talk more about these terms later) influence the rules of what Lisa Delpit (1995) calls "codes of power" (in other words, the rules for participation in dominant culture). French philosopher Pierre Bourdieu (1991) notes that an emphasis on the prestige of the linguistic norms of dominant groups is particularly strong in educational institutions. Colleges and universities have been noted as being discourse communities in their own right, as they have "unique and specialized discursive practices" (White 2005, 371). These institutions have a distinctive scholarly culture that is unique and different from other organizations. White suggests that not all students will come to campus understanding the rules of its discourse community and will subsequently feel excluded from participation. Because language, culture, and identity are closely intertwined (Vygotsky 1999), those students whose language differs from typical academic discourse norms may feel a lessened sense of belonging or have trouble fitting in. Strayhorn (2017, 4) defines a sense of belonging as "students' perceived social support on campus, a feeling or sensation of connectedness, and the experience of mattering or feeling cared about, accepted, respected, valued by, and important to the campus community or others on campus such as faculty, staff, and peers." In a sense, students' dialects can contribute to the notion Schlossberg (1989) refers to as marginality and mattering. Schlossberg suggests that marginality is a sense of feeling unimportant and "can be a temporary condition during transition, a description of a personality type, or a way of life." Conversely, when a person feels that they "matter," they feel accepted, important, and included.

Marginalization on college campuses is perhaps not a unique phenomenon for students from rural Appalachia. Fewer students from rural Appalachia attend and graduate from college than from any other region in the United States (Haaga 2004; Shaw, DeYoung, and Rademacher 2004; Pollard and Jacobsen 2014), and as such, students from Appalachia are underrepresented on most non-Appalachian college campuses. Further, Appalachia has historically been subject to numerous stereotypes throughout our nation's history, particularly stereotypes associated with backwardness and otherness (Eller 1999). Appalachians are a small group on this study's campus, and when non-Appalachians mark rural Appalachian students as "other," their college experiences are compromised and devalued.

OUR FRAMEWORK

In this chapter, we frame our discussion (fig. 11.1) using three concepts based on our previous work. The first, standard language ideology, is the notion that there is a single, standard variety of English that is more correct than others (Lippi-Green 2012). The second concept, linguistic hegemony, is a form of cultural hegemony that uses standard language ideology to convince members of nondominant groups that the preferred linguistic variety of the dominant classes is more correct or superior to nondominant varieties. Speakers of nonstandardized varieties of English are taught in dominant institutions, like colleges and universities, that their native variety is inferior or lacking compared to the preferred, standardized variety of speech used by members of dominant groups.

The third concept, codes of power in education (Delpit 1995), works together with linguistic hegemony. Delpit asserts that codes of power are the specific rules required for participation in the culture of power. Included in the codes of power are the correct or preferred types of language to be used. The preferred variety of language is an element of the culture of power of dominant groups. Institutions of higher education can be viewed as communities that have their own codes of power, which usually reflect the codes of power of society at large, since educational institutions are often controlled by dominant groups. Participation in the culture of power and/or the academic discourse community requires knowledge of linguistic norms associated with codes of power. In our model, the three concepts work together to influence how students perceive the openness of the campus environments, its tolerance for linguistic diversity, and their subsequent sense of belonging on campus. In our model, identity and a sense of belonging are in flux and are shaped differentially by all of the elements included in the model (in addition to many others). Thus, a student's sense of belonging could be increased in social environments where they associate with others like them and in which less standardized speech is accepted (for example, in a student club) and decreased in environments in which they do not have control of the membership and in which there may be implicit expectations of use of standardized language (such as in an academic course).

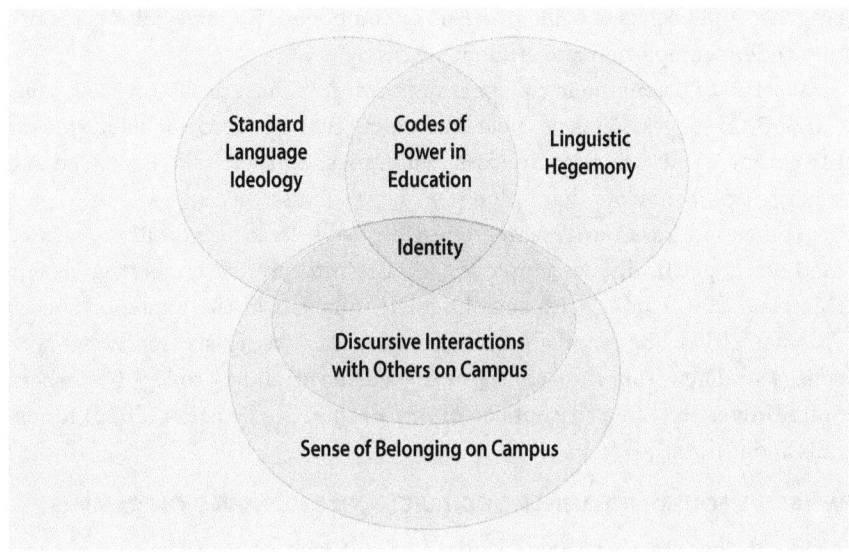

Figure 11.1. Conceptual Framework: Factors Influencing Sense of Belonging on Campus. Illustration by Stephany Brett Dunstan and Audrey J. Jaeger.

BACKGROUND

Previous research on Appalachian college students has focused on different parts of their college lives: attitudes toward higher education (Wallace and Diekroger 2000; Kinney 2018); attitudes toward multicultural education within higher education institutions (Asada, Swank, and Goldey 2003); the role of family in college student success (Wilson et al. 2018); first-generation Appalachians (Hand and Miller-Payne 2008; Bryan and Simmons 2009); first-year transitions (Bickel, Banks, and Spatig 1991; Carter and Robinson 2002; Dees 2006; Bradbury 2008; Bush 2015); and persistence (Hunley 2015; Hlinka 2017; Swafford 2017). However, no existing studies focus solely on the influence of language within the college experiences of rural Appalachian students. Some studies do touch upon language and the broader topic of higher education for Appalachian students (McBride 2006; Greene 2010) and the influence of language on college experience for Lumbee students (Scott 2008). These studies support the idea that language is influential in shaping college experiences, and they highlight that standard language ideology and linguistic hegemony influence how speakers with stigmatized varieties experience college. In our study, we build on previous work by specifically focusing on language and a sense of belonging—a key component in conversations regarding student completion and student success.

A sense of belonging in college is important, because as Ostrove and Long (2007, 381) suggest, "it is possible that feeling that one does not belong affects the extent of participation in class, willingness to seek help as needed and other critical behaviors that influence college success."

To best address our research question, we selected qualitative research methods. Specifically, we employed a basic interpretive qualitative design (Merriam 2002) along with sociolinguistic analysis of the students' speech (Thomas 2011). The population of this study was twenty-six traditional-aged college students from rural southern Appalachia attending college ("Southern State University") in a city outside of Appalachia. See Dunstan (2013) for details about the study.

WHAT WE FOUND: INFLUENCE OF DIALECT AND BELONGING ON CAMPUS

Academia has its own rules for discourse. It prefers standardized speech, and students are expected to modify their speech to fit into the academic discourse community. Students in our study presented conflicting views on language and belonging on campus. On one hand, they remark that, in general, standardized language is expected in the academic discourse community on campus. Yet because the university is large and diverse, they note that language diversity is tolerated overall. However, in certain subcultures, they have found that language diversity can become an issue in whether they feel a sense of belonging.

Students in our study, regardless of level of vernacularity, say that the campus environment at Southern State University is one that supports notions of linguistic hegemony on a large scale—in other words, in order to be taken seriously as a student and accepted as "intelligent," one must conform to a preferred variety of speech. The students often referenced notions of "proper" speech, noting that the way members of their home community speak is *not* proper, using terms like "hick," "hillbilly," and "country" to describe their speech. They believe that their native dialect would not be considered proper on campus, particularly in the classroom. Some students indicate that, on campus, there is an implicit idea that the language used should be standardized:

> It's like there are a lot of settings where people I'm sure do think carefully about what they say. And then there are a lot of settings where people just kind of spout things off. But I think as a general rule people

are pretty careful what they have to say because they want to participate in the intellectual environment maybe. (Joseph)

I kinda wanted to pronounce things that they did–the way they did [peers on campus]. Generally it's kinda like a peer pressure type kinda situation. (Thomas)

I feel like I focused more on making sure the way I dictate the things I'm trying to say are very clear, very grammatically correct and supporting the fact that I—my language is not an issue . . . I just want them to not necessarily be impressed but not have any sort of questions on whether or not I'm competent. (Robert)

'Cause being here and around certain people, you don't really take many people seriously if they really drawl, like have a real serious drawl as you would somebody who was like more—what's the word I'm looking for—enunciates better. (Jessica)

Some students were proud of not sounding southern Appalachian, whether or not they sounded that way normally or because they have made attempts to sound more "standard." These students suggest that there is an advantage on campus to not sounding Appalachian, which points again to standard language ideology and linguistic hegemony's pervasiveness on campus. As several students in our study suggest, to belong in the academic community, there are certain expectations about a person's speech. Some students suggest that because their speech is more standardized, they have had little trouble fitting in. For example, Sara, whose speech is a standardized Southern variety, notes that she is aware of the stigmatization of southern Appalachian speech and has tried "not to have an accent."[1]

Because of perceived standard language ideology and linguistic hegemony, several students say that they feel a need to code-switch, or switch between language varieties in certain situations to fit in or accommodate the norms of that community. Beebe and Giles (1984, 8) suggest that speakers will "attempt to converge linguistically toward the speech patterns believed to be characteristic of their recipient when they (a) desire their social approval and the perceived costs of so acting are proportionally lower than the reward anticipated; and/or (b) desire a high level of communication efficiency and (c) social norms are not perceived to dictate alternative speech strategies." Some of the more vernacular students indicate code-switching, meeting all three of these conditions, particularly at times when using socially preferred varieties of speech would help them "fit in" in certain environments:

> I guess it really matters who I'm around 'cause if I'm around friends or people I know real good, I don't really think about it at all. But if I'm talking to a professor or presenting or something like that, then I really try to talk a lot differently from where I was raised. (Jason)

> I would say in a typical day at Southern State, I would change the way I speak at least 80 percent of the time. If I was in a class or around people I have never met before or if I am in a professional setting, I always change the way I speak and try to drop the accent as much as possible. I do it without even realizing it . . . When I first meet someone I lose my accent, and the more comfortable I get the more my accent will come out. (Lauren)

Students whose speech does not contain stigmatized features (apart from those like Robert and Landon whose speech is standardized because of an admitted effort) did not mention feeling a need to code-switch on campus. Additionally, as Jason and other students mention, being around friends is a time when students do not feel a need to code-switch. These findings suggest that standard language ideology and linguistic hegemony operate in certain environments on campus but may be less pervasive in others. In other words, language use and a sense of belonging seem to vary depending on the environment.

Beliefs about Campus Environments and Language

Standard language ideology and linguistic hegemony can influence students' perceptions of the campus climate in relation to linguistic diversity. On one hand, students say that they believe that campus is a place where standardized speech should be used. On the other hand, many students suggest that linguistic diversity is generally tolerated on campus. This view may seem somewhat contradictory based on students' statements that highlight linguistic hegemony and standard language ideology on campus. However, because these processes are so ensconced in educational institutions and so pervasive in society as a whole, students have likely already accepted and internalized them. For example, Lauren notes, "I've just always been taught or I've always heard that we've been looked down upon because of that . . . I guess it's just frowned upon the way we normally talk." However, when asked about the university broadly, students, regardless of level of vernacularity, generally indicate that the university is rather accepting of student diversity, including dialects:

> Here it's like so many different cultures it's fun to learn, you know, and like everyone speaks different. Sometimes you'll hear different languages and not just accents. (Megan)

> I think for the most part the campus is accepting on a larger scale, when you get to the smaller scale like in individual classes and majors I think it is different. But overall, it's pretty good. (Kelly)

Kelly raises a point that other students echo: there is a difference on campus between feeling accepted linguistically on a large scale than on a smaller scale. With a student population of over thirty thousand, Southern State University hosts a diverse student population with speakers of many languages and dialects. When thinking of the institution on a large scale, Appalachians agree that their dialect situation is similar to international students or students from other dialect regions. However, students make distinctions on the smaller scale, noting that some departments, majors, and courses seem to be more tolerant of nonstandardized dialects than others. Southern State University has a strong agriculture and engineering tradition, and the agricultural programs draw many rural students to the university. Students suggest that programs related to agriculture and life sciences (as well as some engineering programs) may be more tolerant of nonstandardized dialects because of the student population that has traditionally been drawn to those areas. Other students suggest that outside of agriculture and life science departments, there may be less tolerance for nonstandardized speech:

> I guess in soc[iology] classes it's kind of backwards the way I mean it's supposed to be. I guess in the soc classes I've noticed more of the professors they think I'm a little slower and stuff like that. (Christopher)

> Like, I've made more friends in the mechanical engineering department or from the agricultural department than I have in aero [her major] or biomedical departments. You do see people from different areas pretty much like separating themselves out. Which is why I guess people find it so odd that there's rural kids in the aerospace program. (Kelly)

> I would think that the agricultural department is probably [more accepting] and life science, it seems to me at least, it's why we're called Moo U I guess. I mean, most of the people that I know didn't come here to study education or something like that, they were in life sciences or some engineering too I guess. (Brandon)

Based on these statements from students, it seems that whether students feel like their speech is accepted on macro or micro levels is influenced some by language ideology on campus. Students indicated that language was not a significant determining factor for how well they feel they belong at the institution in general. However, it does play a role in how well students suggest they feel a sense of belonging in certain subcultures:

> I do feel like my accent somewhat affected my sense of belonging in college. If other people had similar accents to mine, I felt more comfortable to be around them because I didn't feel like they would criticize me or anything. I don't think though that my accent solely depended on my sense of belonging though. There are definitely some other factors that go into that but I do know that the more I get to know someone and the more I am around them, the more I become comfortable using my accent and start talking with it. (Lauren)

> When you find people that kinda talk funny like you do, you feel a little bit better. . . . like Ag people, we have accents and we're wearing plaid. We're just different. And I guess it's just I feel more comfortable around my friends. I got a bunch of friends that are from the mountains and we're all Ag majors together and so it's fun to go do something. (Patty)

Of course, as Kuh (2001) points out, large universities are made of numerous subcultures, and if students are unable to find a sense of belonging in a subculture on campus, they are less likely to feel connected to the university.

WHAT WE LEARNED

The findings from our study support the idea that linguistic hegemony and standard language ideology are present and felt on campus by students. These processes can be influential in shaping how students perceive the campus climate and see themselves as fitting in on campus. In this section, we discuss two main ideas: (1) Students are aware (sometimes for the first time) that their variety of speech is not one that is valued on the college campus, which provides, for some students, an impetus to change their speech either entirely or to code-switch in certain environments. This suggests that the way students view themselves as part of the campus community is indeed influenced by interactions with others that highlight linguistic differences. (2) Students indicate that the effects of language and fitting in or being accepted are different when considering the campus environment as a whole compared to smaller subcultures, such as departments or certain classes.

When they come to college, many students realize that their speech marks them as different. This realization may in turn influence how they see themselves and represent themselves to others. Some of the more vernacular students indicate that they rebel against this restriction by generally retaining their home style of speech. Others, like Robert and Thomas, have accommodated the preferred variety of speech on campus, noting that what might be natural to their native Appalachia is devalued on campus. Students whose speech is more vernacular realize they might not be taken as seriously and that their professors or classmates might judge them unfavorably for their speech. Jason, for example, believes his speech might be viewed less favorably in the classroom than that of his more standardized, urban peers. Although he notes that he is sometimes teased good-naturedly for his speech, he says he does not feel out of place because of it. Still, he suggests that in an academic environment his speech might be viewed less favorably than that of his more standardized, urban peers.

This perception suggests that there are different degrees to which students adapt to the linguistic environment on campus in response to standard language ideology and linguistic hegemony. For example, Jason does not necessarily change his speech but has adopted strategies in certain cases, such as letting his more standardized peers take the lead on oral presentations. Other students, like Robert and Thomas, however, have made conscious efforts to avoid this stigma and adapt their speech to sound "more educated" to be accepted academically on campus. On the other hand, vernacular speakers like Kelly, Hank, and Rachel indicate a confidence in themselves, pride in their speech, and pride in their abilities such that they do not feel that they should have to change their speech for anyone. Some students, like Hank, even carry a sense of resentment about the implicit ideology that they should have to change their speech in order to be accepted. More standardized speakers like Sara, Isabelle, and Rebecca indicate that they do not feel a need to change their speech to adapt to the campus environment but highlight that their more standardized speech is an advantage for them on campus. These adaptation strategies underscore the presence (and the awareness of most students) of a language of power on campus and the role that language plays for students in feeling a need to change to fit in (Hudley and Mallinson 2011).

Language also has an influence on how students negotiate identity and see themselves. For example, some of the students who came to campus and recognized a need to change to fit in perhaps saw themselves (through interactions with others) as being somehow inferior, notably related to others' perceptions of their intelligence. Conversely, students like Kelly or Hank may have seen that their speech marked them as inferior in the eyes of others in some capacity, yet they believe that their abilities and accomplishments will allow them to succeed. They have not been made to feel ashamed of being "country" or being Appalachian despite teasing or being told that their speech is in some way deficient. For example, it was suggested to Kelly, an honors student in aerospace engineering, that she enroll in speech therapy.

Students did make a distinction between campus at large and smaller niches or subcultures on campus in terms of the degree to which standard language ideology/linguistic hegemony are felt. Even if students do not feel that they fit in on a large scale, they feel that they can participate in some subcultures on a smaller scale. Astin (1984) suggested that such student involvement is critical to student learning, development, and retention. If students feel a lowered sense of belonging, they are more likely to become disengaged. As noted, academic institutions can have their own rules for linguistic participation on large and small scales within individual units. Thus, if a student feels that his or her speech influences how well they feel they belong on campus, their level of involvement and decision to persist could be influenced. Although participants in this study indicated that they recognize notions of a formal, standardized language being preferred on a large scale, they also suggest that the university is rather accepting, due in large part to the ability of students to find subcultures on campus where their language is accepted.

Even so, students do indicate that they code-switch in certain situations and in certain environments. Some students have changed their speech altogether. How well students feel like they belong is being influenced to a degree by language in certain environments. For example, Emily notes feeling uncomfortable because of language in several courses and in situations in which others might view her speech as "the entertainment." This unease, in turn, may influence how students' identities are shaped in college; through interactions with others, they may see themselves as lacking in some area and needing to adapt to fit in. Lauren mentions that after she gets to know people she will use her "real accent" but code-switches to a more standardized style at first to avoid stigma. Although code-switching can be an effective strategy for fitting in, one might assume that, if a student feels a persistent need to code-switch on campus, they may feel marginalized. As such, the degree to which they feel they belong could be negatively influenced, as can the way they view themselves, their background, and their culture.

Students suggest that particular departments or courses, such as courses in English, social sciences, and humanities, are less accepting of nonstandardized language and perhaps more imposing of standard language ideology and linguistic hegemony. This situation is perhaps not unexpected in English, but for social sciences, as Christopher notes, it is the opposite of what one would expect. Is it possible that programs in humanities and social sciences at Southern State have perhaps seen fewer rural students than programs in agricultural and life sciences or certain types of engineering? Students from rural backgrounds may stand out more, then, in courses in the humanities or social sciences at Southern State. Many rural students are also first-generation college students, and studies on this student population have found that first-generation students and students from lower social classes typically do not gravitate toward humanities and social sciences but rather take courses in fields they believe to be more lucrative (Terenzini et al. 1996; Davis 2010). Students in this study also note an element of covert prestige within agricultural, life science, and engineering programs (covert prestige is association with a concept or thing because it *is* stigmatized; Trudgill 1972). Students like Patty note that, in those classes, "if you don't have an accent you probably wish you did." Some of the more standardized students suggest that, because they do not sound particularly Southern or Appalachian, these are the courses in which they might feel least comfortable. What is interesting to note here is the connection that students make between being rural, speaking a stigmatized dialect, and being a part of the agricultural program. At Southern State University, despite its agricultural tradition, there seems to be some stigma associated with agricultural academic programs. It is possible that this stigma is due to these programs historically attracting rural, in-state students who are more likely to speak nonstandardized varieties of Southern American English. Thus, as others make assumptions about level of intelligence based on speech (Lippi-Green 2012) and geographic origin, a program with a large population of rural, nonstandardized speakers might be unfairly assessed. Some of the more vernacular students note that others on campus will often assume that they are agricultural science majors upon hearing them speak, and while some note that it is not a completely unfair assumption, they felt that it can also be viewed as somewhat pejorative. So, while there are subcultures on campus in which linguistic diversity is accepted, such as certain departments/programs/classes or among friends, these environments are not necessarily viewed favorably by the institution as a whole. This trend suggests the pervasiveness of standard language ideology, linguistic hegemony, and their influence on campus environments.

The type of language varieties valued by an institution sends a message, intentionally or not, to students about the type of culture and the type of students who are valued on that campus. Whether intentional or not, institutions can be sending messages to potential students about campus culture and excluding some before they even begin. Linguistic diversity is an element of diversity that should be highlighted to foster a truly inclusive campus. Representation is critical for students to feel a sense that they, too, belong in higher education, and this representation must also include language. It is important for speakers of nonstandardized dialects to hear others who sound like them. Language is tied closely to identity and culture and can be closely associated by some with their race/ethnicity, social class, heritage, and many other facets of identity. As such, acceptance of linguistic diversity is of critical importance for low socioeconomic status, rural, first-generation, and minority students (and any combination thereof). It is detrimental for institutions of higher education to unwittingly send a message that, to fit in on campus, one must reject the style of speech that may associate them with their social class, home culture, or racial/ethnic group, but this pressure is more likely to occur when standardized varieties are continually given higher prestige in academia.

CONCLUSION

If students feel like the academic community does not value their language, they may feel a pressure to change, or as they feel an aspect of their identity is rejected, they may reject the institution and be less likely to engage, succeed, or persist (Kuh 2001). The findings from this study suggest that dialect-diversity education for faculty and students alike is critical to create inclusive campus environments, particularly classroom environments. We cannot expect our students to become tolerant and accepting citizens if we send mixed messages about what it means to be accepting of diversity. As some students in this study point out, it is still perceived as "OK" to make fun of others based on language, even on college campuses, and even in the classroom. Several students recount being laughed at or seeing peers with stigmatized dialects being laughed at for speaking in class, with no mention of intervention from faculty members. In some cases, faculty members were the offenders. Language can be used as a proxy for other characteristics used in discriminating against certain populations, and as Lippi-Green (2012, 73) notes, this is considered the "back door" to discrimination, "and that door stands wide open."

Institutions that aim to be inclusive need to ensure that all members of their campus community are educated about the value of linguistic diversity and celebrate the numerous languages and dialects that students, faculty, and staff bring with them to campus. This goal may be achieved through a model such as the one outlined by Dunstan, Wolfram, Jaeger, and Crandall (2015), in which universities would include a dialect-diversity curriculum in university-wide diversity programming for all campus community members and examples of how instructors, student affairs professionals, and student leaders can model tolerance and acceptance in the campus environments for which they are responsible. By acknowledging and understanding this type of diversity, students may feel greater belonging in the academic community, have richer experiences, and achieve greater success.

Notes

1. The common public claim about "not having an accent" means not having a stigmatized accent. All humans who have language have an accent.

References

Asada, Hideko, Eric Swank, and Gregory T. Goldey. 2003. "The Acceptance of a Multicultural Education among Appalachian College Students." *Research in Higher Education* 44, no. 1: 99–120.

Astin, Alexander W. 1984. "Student Involvement: A Development Theory for Higher Education." *Journal of College Student Development* 40, no. 5: 518–29.

Bourdieu, Pierre. 1991. *Language and Symbolic Power*. Cambridge, MA: Harvard University Press.

Bickel, Robert, Steven R. Banks, and Linda Spatig. 1991. "Bridging the Gap between High School and College in an Appalachian State: A Near-Replication of Florida Research." *Journal of Research in Rural Education* 7, no. 2: 75–87.

Bradbury, Barbara L. 2008. "The Integration of First-Generation, First-Term College Students from Ohio Appalachia: A Multiple Case Study." PhD diss., Ohio University.

Bryan, Elizabeth, and Leigh Ann Simmons. 2009. "Family Involvement: Impacts on Post-Secondary Educational Success for First-Generation Appalachian College Students." *Journal of College Student Development* 50, no. 4: 391–406.

Bush, Jeffrey T. 2015. "The Experience of Transition as Told by First-Year, First-Generation Appalachian College Students." PhD diss., West Virginia University.

Carter, Carolyn S., and Ruby Robinson. 2002. " 'Can We Send Some of the Money Back Home to Our Families?' Tensions of Transition in an Early Intervention Program for Rural Appalachian Students." Paper presented at the American Educational Research Association, New Orleans, LA, 1–5 April 2002.

Dees, David M. 2006. " 'How Do I Deal with These New Ideas?': The Psychological Acculturation of Rural Students." *Journal of Research in Rural Education* 21, no. 6: 1–11.

Davis, Jeff. 2010. *The First Generation Student Experience: Implications for Campus Practice, and Strategies for Improving Persistence and Success*. Sterling, VA: Stylus Publishing.

Delpit, Lisa. 1995. *Other People's Children: Cultural Conflict in the Classroom*. New York: The New Press.

Dunstan, Stephany Brett. 2013. "The Influence of Speaking a Dialect of Appalachian English on the College Experience." PhD diss., North Carolina State University. https://repository.lib.ncsu.edu/bitstream/handle/1840.16/8561/etd.pdf.

Dunstan, Stephany Brett, Walt Wolfram, Audrey J. Jaeger, and Rebecca E. Crandall. 2015. "Educating the Educated: Language Diversity in the University Backyard." *American Speech* 90, no. 2: 266–80.

Gallagher, Janice M. 2019. "First-Generation Central Appalachian Students' Process of Becoming a College Student: A Grounded Theory." PhD diss., Capella University.

Greene, Rebecca Dayle. 2010. "Language, Ideology and Identity in Rural Eastern Kentucky." PhD diss., Stanford University. https://stacks.stanford.edu/file/druid:fh361zh5489/RGreene%20dissertation-augmented.pdf.

Haaga, John. 2004. *Educational Attainment in Appalachia*. Washington, DC: Appalachian Regional Commission.

Hand, Christie, and Emily Miller Payne. 2008. "First-Generation College Students: A Study of Appalachian Student Success." *Journal of Developmental Education* 32, no. 1: 4–15.

Hlinka, Karen R. 2017. "Tailoring Retention Theories to Meet the Needs of Rural Appalachian Community College Students." *Community College Review* 45, no. 2: 144–64.

Hudley, Anne H. Charity, and Christine Mallinson. 2011. *Understanding English language Variation in US Schools*. New York: Teachers College Press.

Hunley, Richard. 2015. "Understanding Factors Contributing to the Persistence of First-Generation College Students from Appalachian Distressed Counties: A Phenomenological Study." PhD diss., Liberty University.

Kinney, Wayne T. 2018. "Appalachian College Students' Perceptions on Attainment of Higher Education: An Action Research Study." PhD diss., Capella University.

Kuh, George D. 2001. "Organizational Culture and Student Persistence: Prospects and Puzzles." *Journal of College Student Retention: Research, Theory and Practice* 3, no. 1: 23–39.

Lippi-Green, Rosina. 2012. *English with an Accent: Language, Ideology and Discrimination in the United States*. 2nd ed. London: Routledge.

Ostrove, Joan M., and Susan M. Long. 2007. "Social Class and Belonging: Implications for College Adjustment." *The Review of Higher Education* 30, no. 4: 363–89.

Pollard, Kelvin, and Linda A. Jacobsen. 2014. *The Appalachian Region: A Data Overview from the 2008–2012 American Community Survey*. Washington, DC: Appalachian Regional Commission.

Scott, Christopher E. 2008. "An Investigation of the Impact of Speaking the Lumbee Dialect on the Academic Achievement and Identity Development of Native American College Students." PhD diss., University of North Carolina at Chapel Hill. https://cdr.lib.unc.edu/indexablecontent/uuid:585e7ca6-6fda-4c89-846a-99744bbfc805.

Schlossberg, Nancy K. 1989. "Marginality and Mattering: Key Issues in Building Community." *New Directions for Student Services* 48: 5–15.

Shaw, Thomas C., Allan J. DeYoung, and Eric W. Rademacher. 2004. "Educational Attainment in Appalachia: Growing with the Nation, but Challenges Remain." *Journal of Appalachian Studies* 10, no. 3: 307–29.

Strayhorn, Terrell L. 2017. "Using Intersectionality in Student Affairs Research." *New Directions for Student Services* 2017, no. 157: 57–67.

Swafford, Stacy J. 2017. "Factors Affecting Retention of First-time, Full-Time Freshmen Students at Higher Education Institutions within the Appalachian College Association." PhD diss., University of Tennessee at Chattanooga.

Terenzini, Patrick T., Leonard Springer, Patricia M. Yaeger, Ernest T. Pascarella, and Amaury Nora. 1996. "First-Generation College Students: Characteristics, Experiences, and Cognitive Development." *Research in Higher Education* 37, no. 1: 1–22.

Thomas, Erik. 2011. *Sociophonetics: An Introduction*. New York: Palgrave Macmillan.

Trudgill, Peter. 1972. "Sex, Covert Prestige and Linguistic Change in the Urban British English of Norwich." *Language in Society* 1, no. 2: 179–95.

Vygotsky, Lev. 1999. *Thought and Language*. Cambridge, MA: MIT Press.

Wallace, Lisa A., and Diane K. Diekroger. 2000. " 'The ABCs in Appalachia': A Descriptive View of Perceptions of Higher Education in Appalachian Culture." Paper presented at the Annual Conference of the Women of Appalachia: Their Heritage and Accomplishments 2, Zanesville, OH, 26–28 October.

Wilson, Steffen P., Jonathan S. Gore, Amanda Renfro, Marion Blake, Eric Muncie, and Jodi Treadway. 2018. "The Tether to Home, University Connectedness, and the Appalachian Student." *Journal of College Student Retention: Research, Theory and Practice* 20, no. 1: 139–60.

Afterword: Reflections on the Study of English in Appalachia

Walt Wolfram

Appalachia is a state of mind more than anything else.
—Michael Montgomery, 2000

INTRODUCTION

Almost a half-century ago, sociolinguistics descended on "Appalachian English." Of course, there was already a tradition of language study prior to this early sociolinguistic fieldwork, but it tended to be primarily dialectological (cf. McMillan and Montgomery 1989) or anecdotal (Williams and Beaver 1999). Inspired by some of the pioneering descriptive studies of vernacular African American English (Labov, Cohen, Robins, and Lewis 1968; Wolfram 1969) and the burgeoning analytics of variationism, Donna Christian and I undertook a study based on an extensive set of sociolinguistic interviews conducted in two rural counties in southwest Virginia (Wolfram and Christian 1975, 1976). We were certainly earnest in our focus on vernacular speech, but in retrospect, also a bit presumptuous and naïve. As Christian noted in the foreword to this collection, we looked forward to "the development of AE [Appalachian English] in the years to come," but we were mostly thinking of Appalachian English "as it preserves some features while changing others" (Wolfram and Christian 1976, 162). The essays in this collection do not ignore the changing structures in varieties of English spoken in Appalachia, but they have done much more. For Appalachia, they have expanded the sociolinguistic study of English in much more complete and complex ways that we really didn't imagine at the time.

Little did we realize the multifarious ways and diverse paths that inquiry might take. Issues in the study of language in Appalachia certainly needed to be problematized and expanded. These areas included levels of language structure, diversity in regional, social, and ethnic variation. There were also sociopsychological dimensions of language use such as agency and identity that needed to be confronted and navigated (Reed chapter 2; Cramer chapter 5; Slocum chapter 10). I am indeed grateful for the multidimensional, insightful perspectives that have enabled the study of language variation in Appalachia to come of sociolinguistic age in this collection.

In this essay, I focus on some of the shifting perspectives from the reflexive stance of a long-term investigator in regional, social, and ethnic varieties of English that includes both a research and an engagement perspective. I take the perspective that "knowledge has to be shared to have value" (Semple 2012, quoted in Spiglanin 2012)—not simply with a small cohort of educated researchers for academic understanding but with the communities who enable our research and the public at large who need to know how language affects everyday life. As Dwight Bolinger (1979, 4) noted, "The workings of language are terra incognita to the average person, who daily treads a minefield thinking it is familiar ground. There is no sense of urgency to learn what one thinks one already knows. The linguist's task is double: to infuse complacency with curiosity and to answer the resulting question the best he [sic] can. The public needs to know enough about our specialty to realize how it affects their lives."

LANGUAGE MYTHS, IDEOLOGY, AND THE ENGLISH OF APPALACHIA

Appalachia has suffered more than its share of myths.[1] In fact, a century ago, social researcher John C. Campbell (1921, xxi) noted that the Southern Highlands is "a land of promise, a land of romance, and a land about which, perhaps, more things are not true than of any part of our country." The myths about the people, the language, and the culture of Appalachia run the gamut. For example, perceptions of the language have ranged from a variety that preserves Elizabethan or Shakespearian English (Montgomery 1998; Cramer 2014) to an ungrammatical, corrupt version of English used by backwoods illiterates. The Elizabethan view has persisted over time, notwithstanding linguists' strong objections to the notion that *any* living language can be frozen in time (Montgomery 1998). When I first arrived at North Carolina State University in 1992, I was greeted by a well-intentioned literature professor who advised me to study the speech of the Outer Banks or the mountains where they retained Elizabethan English. In the midst of writing this afterword in the summer of 2019, I was interviewed four times on prominent international radio broadcasts inspired by a BBC article titled "The US Island That Speaks Elizabethan English" (Carlton 2019).

Some linguists may seem obsessed with debunking the Elizabethan myth, but apparently much of the public and journalists in search of intriguing language stories have not made the kind of progress linguists have hoped for. In fact, our documentary *Mountain Talk* (Hutcheson 2004b) has been criticized for not including more linguistic experts who addressed this myth (Montgomery 2005). Without disputing the literal status of this myth, I have to say that we have found it advantageous in persuading communities to embrace their dialect as an essential part of their cultural legacy. Further, I have not found community members and others who espouse this myth resistant in the least to linguistic observations that all language varieties are dynamic and under constant change. Myths about language are not always consistent in populations and can live with conflicting myths. In fact, I wonder if folks are using this Elizabethan reference as a metaphor or metonymic rather than literal reference for so-called *relic forms*, a construct in its own right (cf. Hazen chapter 3). After all, the reference is based on a valid observation that some lexical, phonological, and morphosyntactic features are retained in these communities vis-à-vis their loss in mainstream varieties of English.

So is the claim that Shakespearean English is spoken in isolated communities a bald-faced lie or a questionable metonymic reference to a valid observation with respect to relic forms? Perhaps linguists—who certainly use similar kinds of language metonymy when they refer to notions such as the "genetic" relationships between languages—might be a little more tolerant and understanding when they hear such references. At least it's a positive myth that can be amended and nuanced and, perhaps more importantly, used to help community members embrace the legitimacy of their linguistic heritage. The intersection of absolute truth, negotiated accuracy, and metaphorical reference needs to be taken into account when we consider statements by the community about its language. As I recently posted on the Ocracoke Facebook page (July 19, 2019) about the article on Elizabethan English, "They didn't get it all right but at least it was all positive." There are lots of myths more seriously detrimental to the language of Appalachia that deserve greater priority in addressing than this one.

It is also important to recognize that varied myths are associated with different communities or communities of practice. These include myths from those outside the community, representing popular culture, writers, and the media who often view the area as a remnant place and language. But there are also myths generated and disseminated from within the community. While outsiders may often homogenize the unitary nature of Appalachian speech, insiders may offer an opposite extreme—that "every holler or cove has its own dialect." Is one correct and the other erroneous, or do both engage in some mythmaking based on differential perceptual lenses? Furthermore, sociolinguists are hardly immune from the construction of convenient myths about the nature of language varieties, as discussed in Wolfram (2007). For example, several myths about African American Language were inadvertently advanced by sociolinguists (including the author), such as the "supraregional" or "homogeneity" myth related to African American Language. As Bonfiglio (2002, 62–63) observes, "The illusion of homogeneity is largely a function of secondary revision that glosses over differences and constructs a linear metanarrative, an overgeneralization that suppresses differences and unites the percepts in a structure of wish-fulfillment; i.e. there is something in the popular consciousness that desires to see a unity of geography, ethnicity, and language."

To some extent, sociolinguists have done the same thing in their study of the speech of Appalachia as they did to African American Language. In this context, I suspect that one of the rationales for the pluralization of English(es) in the title of this book is due to the cautions about the homogenization myth for Appalachia. And Hasty certainly confronts this notion in chapter 1, along with other authors in this collection. Appalachian varieties have further suffered from the sociolinguistic preoccupation with vernacular versions of the variety, reflecting a kind of sociolinguistic nostalgia for the authentic vernacular speaker (Bucholtz 2003). Again, I plead mea culpa with respect to some of our publications (Wolfram and Christian 1976) and documentaries (Hutcheson 2004a, 2004b), as pointed out by Montgomery (2005). Happily, research in the twenty-first century, including the comprehensive work of Hazen (e.g., 2008, 2011, 2014) and the authors of the articles in this book, offer strong counterevidence to this myth. At the same time, let me caution that scholarship should be sensitive to Johnson's (2001, 606) warning that "Linguists—like all other interested social actors—are 'ideological brokers' bidding for 'authoritative entextualization,' that is, trying to influence those readings of language debates which will eventually emerge as dominant." Just sayin': we ain't as objective and pure as we think we are.

DIVERSITY

Most of the papers in this volume explore diversity in the English of Appalachia, although Reed's chapter 2 and Hazen's chapter 3 certainly recognize a common core of vernacular structures. To some extent, the focus on diversity is part of a natural extension of language variation studies over the past half century, but there also seems to be reaction to the homogeneity myth that had been embedded in the term *Appalachian English*. We were not insensitive to this generic label in our introductory discussion in *Appalachian Speech* when we noted (Wolfram and Christian 1976, 29):

> Ultimately, we would have to restrict our use of the term to a particular variety of English which we have found in the region of Appalachia we studied. Even within this context, however, the designation needs to be qualified since there are obviously differences within the region we are discussing. Our focus has been on the rural working class population, so that our restricted interest would preclude many middle class speakers who do not use the forms we describe here. Specifically, then, we use the term AE to refer to the variety of English most typically associated with a working class rural population of the Appalachian range.... In our designation we have chosen to err in the direction of generality, realizing that we have created a somewhat fictitious designation.

Admittedly, we succumbed to a version of the homogenization myth, as well as the "exotic vernacular syndrome"—the sociolinguistic nostalgia for the authentic vernacular speaker that sociolinguists embraced in their descriptions of vernacular varieties such as African American Language (Wolfram 2007). Contra this generalization, Hazen and Fluharty offered the observation that "because of this problem of defining a single Appalachian English, we have seen it not as one dialect with a particular set of features, but as a number of dialects" (Hazen and Fluharty 2006, 19), hence the term *Appalachian Englishes* for this book. Further, the compilation of chapters counters the generalization trend by including a more representative array of speaker groups and regions than our singular study. That is certainly a welcome and significant contribution to the understanding of language use in the region. But it still begs the questions of what is Appalachia and who speaks a variety from this region, as set forth by Hasty in chapter 1. The dominant focus of papers in this collection is clearly the Southern Highland region of the South, which is only half of the region officially defined as Appalachia that stretches geographically from southwest New York to northeast Mississippi. The construct of Appalachia, however, is more than geography and more than a mountainous place separated by physical and social distance. As Shapiro (1978, 18–19) put it, "The process of reification, by which the perception of Appalachian otherness became transformed into conception as a thing in itself, occurred within the context of southern color-writing, and in particular of the claims of that genre to verisimilitude." Or, as Montgomery (2000) put it in more accessible language, "Appalachia is a state of mind more than anything else. While Appalachia has precise boundaries for geographers, it does not for lay people."

I understand the reaction to the homogenization myth, but I admit that I have been puzzled to explain the lay observation that "every holler has its own dialect," an equally extreme proclamation at the other end of the spectrum. This impetus is not peculiar to Appalachia, and I have found similar observations by residents of the Outer Banks as they refer to different small islands having their own dialect at the same time that linguists document an overwhelming number of shared distinctive features across islands. While linguists might be prone to dismiss the every-holler-has-its-own-dialect myth, the consideration of language regard (Preston 2018) should compel us to look for an explanation of this observation (Cramer 2016). Queries to those who offer such claims suggest that the kinds of dialect features that lay people are referencing in these remarks are limited to a relatively small set of lexical differences for local places and occasionally a pronunciation item or two. Perceptually, these may have iconic, indexical status for those who live in the respective communities, while linguists might overlook them in their focus on phonological and grammatical systems. Linguists, of course, have their own biases about the significance of the differences they scrutinize for dialect differentiation. I often say, when asked by people about the number of dialects in North Carolina, "Anywhere from two to 200; depends on how many pieces you want to cut in your language pie." Perceptions themselves are valid data and require explanation.

One final caveat about the label *Appalachia*. Over the years, I have found that the vast majority of people who use this term are outsiders or those who have status as experts. In all of our discussions with lay people in and around the Smoky Mountains of North Carolina during our filming for the documentary *Mountain Talk* (Hutcheson 2004b), lay speakers rarely if ever referred to the phenomenon we were talking about as "Appalachian English(es)." As one interviewee said, "The only people who talk about Appalachia are those who aren't from here." Perhaps we should pay closer attention to the terms that the residents and ordinary speakers use for their language variety and worry more about defining these constructs vis-à-vis those that have dominated the academic community of practice. As famed moonshiner Popcorn Sutton put it in the documentary, "Well, the way people talks around here would be more of what you call hillbilly style, I guess. It's just mountain talk" (Hutcheson 2004b). The reappropriation of the term "hillbilly" and the construct "mountain talk" as a dialect entity seem to be just as worthy—if not more so—as the scholarly, outsider construction of the notion of Appalachia. It is indeed encouraging to see linguistic regard (Preston 2018) and the linguistic perceptions of the people of this region highlighted in this collection by Cramer (chapter 5), Lovejoy (chapter 8), Slocum (chapter 10), and others.

COMPLEXITY

The papers in this collection symbolize the complex journey that sociolinguistic scrutiny of Appalachia has taken over the last half century. Admittedly, our study (Wolfram and Christian 1975) was focused almost exclusively on documenting and describing the structural and variable language foundation of vernacular structures. The influence—and linguistic biases—of previous studies in African American Language (Labov et al. 1968; Wolfram 1969) and other vernacular varieties of English (Wolfram 1974) at the time seem quite transparent in retrospect. The structural focus gave rise to a number of sophisticated descriptive accounts that have certainly embellished our understanding of the structures of English in Appalachia that include *a*-prefixing (e.g., Wolfram 1980; Montgomery 2009), irregular verbs (Wolfram and Christian 1975), personal datives (e.g., Christian 1991; Webelhuth and Dannenberg 2006), and many other structures (e.g., Tortora 2006; Hasty 2012; Zanuttini and Bernstein 2014; Wood, Sigurðsson, and Zanuttini 2015; Johnson 2018) that are cited in Hazen's overview (chapter 3) of grammatical structures as well as the phonological structures surveyed in Reed's overview (chapter 2) of phonology. Overall, the structural description of morphosyntactic features has been more extensive than phonological traits. Rarely have linguists paid attention to discourse in studies of Appalachia, so Burkette's chapter 4 is a welcome complement to the traditional structural foci in vernacular language descriptions. Further, Appalachian Englishes have provided a proving ground for the developing subfield of variation analysis, particularly in the research of Hazen and his colleagues (e.g., Hazen 2008, 2011, 2014; Hazen, Hamilton, and Vacovsky 2011) and other variationists (e.g., Reed 2014, chapter 2 this volume; Walker, Southall, and Hargrave 2017).

To be honest, much of the earlier sociolinguistic work demonstrated that sociolinguists were much better linguists than they were sociologists or cultural anthropologists. The social side of variation was often neglected or dismissed in favor of linguistic insight, lagging behind the intersection of social and cultural factors that was taking place elsewhere in sociolinguistics. For example, one of the central observations of Mallinson and Inscoe's review of language and gender in Appalachia (chapter 6) is that "above all, this chapter highlights the need for much more research on language, gender, and sexuality among diverse speakers and communities in Appalachia." Childs's review of language and ethnicity (chapter 7) cites some research on the English of the Eastern Band of the Cherokee Nation (Anderson 1999; Coggshall 2006, 2008), African Americans (Mallinson and Wolfram 2002; Childs and Mallinson 2004; Mallinson and Childs 2004; Wolfram 2013), and Latinx populations (Kohn and Hans 2009; Kohn 2019), but this research tradition is quite sparse for such an expansive region, and most of that research has been conducted since the turn of the twenty-first century. Voices of color in Appalachia remain mostly underrepresented, but there is a growing murmur that should be amplified in the future, countering the notion that Appalachia is a homogenous Anglo-American population. Further, the consideration of the intersection of gender and ethnicity in communities of practice, as exemplified in the work of Childs and Mallinson (Childs and Mallinson 2004; Mallinson and Childs 2004; Childs 2005; Mallinson 2006) is a welcome trend in recognizing the complexities of social and cultural factors needed to unpack sociolinguistic diversity.

On a more macro level, the study of Appalachia by linguists and others has often been simplistically contextualized by the notion of physical isolation. Statements such as the following have been common in setting the social context of Appalachia: "Historically the physical environment has been a very determining factor in the development of [Appalachia]. Although the geographical isolation of the past has become overcome to a large extent with modern transportation, evidence for historical isolation remains" (Christian, Wolfram, and Dube 1988, 2). As Montgomery (2000, 44) rightly points out, "linguists need to move beyond a simplistic, static conception of 'isolation' that provides little insight into the culture of mountain and other peripheral communities and that all too often perpetuates stereotypes." The appeal to a loosely defined notion of isolation as an essential explanation may even contribute to a kind of sociolinguistic myth about the historical development of these varieties.

In Wolfram (2004), I attempted to problematize the notion of isolation and to counteroffer some of the physical, social, and cultural components that needed to be included in the sociolinguistic construction of remnant varieties of a language—the peripheral dialects that retain features of English that have been lost in mainstream varieties of the language. And, of course, identity is implicated as social distinctions between insiders and outsiders are constructed. In this connection, the local construction of "us" versus "them" often results in indexical labeling, such as: *foreigners*, "outsiders"; *halfbacks*, "folks from the North who move to Florida for the winter and 'halfway back' to the mountains in the summer"; *jaspers*, "unknown outsiders"; *peckerwoods*, "obnoxious outsiders"; and so forth in the Smoky Mountains of North Carolina. Differences in norms are also operative, as discussed in Andersen's (1988, 74–75) open versus closed and endocentric versus exocentric communities. As Montgomery (2000) notes, "for many things such as language, physical maintenance to mainstream culture is far less crucial than psychological orientation to change," and "it would not be surprising if this orientation were not reflected symbolically in the maintenance of speech patterns" (50). Physical, demographic, and historical conditions are at play, along with interactional relations, identity work, and ideology when describing and explaining how English works in Appalachia.

ENGAGEMENT

Given the social and linguistic subordination of Appalachia, it is inconceivable—and in my opinion unconscionable—that sociolinguistic research be undertaken without an engagement component that ensures that socially conscious sociolinguists share their findings with the communities and the people who have enabled our research careers. The prejudices and stereotypes about mountain talk are deep and wide, and they are not limited to popular culture. One of the most powerful studies about the pervasiveness of implicit and explicit language prejudice toward mountain dialects is Dunstan's (2013) research on the effect of language prejudice on college students at a southern metropolitan university (see Dunstan 2013; Dunstan et al. 2015; Dunstan and Jaeger chapter 11). The study disclosed that course participation was affected by the perception of vernacular dialect, that a vernacular dialect added barriers in social-academic settings, and that the college experience heightened students' awareness of language stigmatization of their home dialect as the linguistic other. It was also noteworthy that experiences in different departments and colleges varied and that disciplines in the humanities and social sciences, typically known for having the most socially progressive faculty, were associated with students' most prejudicial and oppressive experiences (Dunstan et al. 2015). In fact, language differences may even be a legitimate factor affecting student retention.

Near the beginning of a graduate-level class on variety in language that I have taught for decades now, I routinely play a recording of different phonetic productions of the THOUGHT vowel for the word *bought* using native-speaker productions from different regions of the United States. These include (1) the merger of [a] and [ɔ] as found in an expansive region of the western United

States and northern Appalachia; (2) a raised, monophthongal version of [ɔ] found on the coastal islands of the mid-Atlantic; (3) a raised and inglided [oə] as found in northeastern cities such as New York City and Philadelphia; and (4) a back-upgliding version [aʊ] that is found in the mountains of North Carolina and some other regions of the rural South. Without fail, the back-upgliding production characteristic of Appalachia evokes audible laughter from the class of students. When I ask them why they laughed at the production, they seem slightly dumbfounded, and the first response is usually that "it just sounds funny." When pushed further, they may say that it sounds "country" or "hillbilly," or offer a euphemism for rural or nonnormative. Rarely do the students see this laughter as evidence of linguistic othering, or as a case of linguistic subordination. Instead, they view their response as an innocuous, humorous occasion with no intention of insulting rural Southerners.

To put the response of the class in a broader reflective context, consider the following comment offered by a participant in Dunstan's (2013) study where the back-upgliding [aʊ] variant is commonly used. The student from Appalachia was being interviewed by Dunstan about her language experiences at the large university in the urban South: "I don't really speak up too much in class and stuff like that unless I feel really comfortable . . . 'cause I can hear, you know, people snickering or stuff like that when I talk" (239). When we juxtapose the reactions of the students in my class and the comment of a student who uses this variant, we see that the humorous reaction of the students may not be nearly as harmless as intended, and, in fact, their reaction may be a case of implicit bias. Certainly, their reaction does not align with their declared beliefs or stances that these students would explicitly endorse as earnest graduate students in a course on language variation in English.

The conclusions of Dunstan's study were so significant that this study became the impetus for a comprehensive, university-level language diversity program that has now been initiated at North Carolina State University (Dunstan et al. 2015) and is being instituted at other institutions of higher learning in the United States. When it comes to language, it appears that our universities are institutional agents for reproducing language inequality rather than linguistic egalitarianism. As noted by Greene (2015) for the *Economist*, "The collision of academic prejudice and accent is particularly ironic. Academics tend to the centre-left nearly everywhere, and talk endlessly about class and multiculturalism. . . . And yet accent and dialect are still barely on many people's minds as deserving respect."

Linguists who study and serve populations from Appalachia must assume a leadership role in combating the persistent linguistic subordination of

Appalachian students' language and transforming condemnation into celebration. Since 1998, the editor of this book, Kirk Hazen, has been a model for such advocacy through the West Virginia Dialect Project (https://dialects.wvu.edu/), conducting workshops and media interviews, lecturing, writing, and preparing materials on this topic for students and the public. A similar program is underway at the University of Kentucky, under the leadership of Jennifer Cramer and Allison Burkette, but such programs should not remain the exception if universities in Appalachia are to become agents of language-attitude change. Every college and university in Appalachia should become an advocate and an agent for proclaiming the truth about Appalachian language varieties.

In proactive engagement, it is also essential to work with local communities where we conduct our research. One of the most convenient ways to do this is to combine interviews with the compilation of oral histories. Based on sociolinguistic interviews, and with the assistance of community members, we have put together collections of stories that reminisce, celebrate, and entertain both community residents and outsiders, including several for communities in Appalachia. For example, Christine Mallinson and Becky Childs (Mallinson, Childs, and Cox 2006) conducted sociolinguistic interviews in a small, remote African American community in the Smoky Mountains, then teamed with local community leader Zulu Cox to repurpose passages in their interviews for a well-received oral history compilation for the community. Similarly, Hutcheson has taken audio extracts from his many hours of filming for *Mountain Talk* (Hutcheson 2004b) to compile an oral compilation. This kind of project is most effectively and authentically produced collaboratively by local community members and sociolinguists.

One of the most popular venues we have developed for public and educational audiences over the past couple of decades is through video productions, ranging from posted vignettes on a YouTube channel (https://www.youtube.com/user/NCLLP) to documentary programs for television. Of the thirteen documentaries we have produced for television broadcast, the sale of our documentary *Mountain Talk* has exceeded all of the others, and YouTube views of the vignettes (circa four million) have far surpassed the views of vignettes featuring any other language variety. The public intrigue about language in Appalachia is there to be tapped.

The documentary *Mountain Talk* has been reviewed by Montgomery (2005), who notes that it presents a "story that is simplistic and incomplete" (390), "a shortage of factual information about language," and "promotes some stereotypes while dispelling others." It should be noted, however, that a guiding principle of the documentary was that mountain people should talk for themselves rather than be interpreted by outside experts. In fact, no outside linguistic experts are in the documentary, based on this guiding principle. Some of Montgomery's observations were shared in person at the premiere of *Mountain Talk* for the Appalachian Studies annual meeting in Cherokee, North Carolina, in 2005. Present at the same meeting were a number of the people featured in the film since most of them were from the surrounding regions and curious about the final version of the documentary. After watching the premiere, several of these residents responded by profusely thanking the producer, Neal Hutcheson, for letting them speak for themselves. As one participant said, "This is the first film that lets us talk for ourselves instead of having outsiders interpret us. Thank you." Further, we have never received more positive responses from viewers of any documentary that we have produced. Comments such as the following have inspired us: TV viewers wrote, "I have never been prouder to be from 'over yonder,'" and "This has made me feel really homesick"; handwritten notes stated, "I *loved* your movie, *Mountain Talk*. It makes me homesick for the mountains and the South," and "You don't know how good it makes me feel when I watch your movies. I just want to cry, laugh, sing, it just makes me so happy I could dance."

Such gratitude from the community underscores the need for our engagement projects on the language of Appalachians to involve community members as active collaborators in these productions. Nothing can be properly and adequately accomplished for the community if we do not give community folks a substantive, active voice in celebrating their language.

Finally, we should emphasize the importance of formal education about language diversity in Appalachia. In other publications, Jeff Reaser and I (Reaser 2006; Wolfram, Reaser, and Vaughn 2008; Wolfram and Reaser 2014) have discussed the significant role a dialect curriculum (Reaser and Wolfram 2007) can play in promoting language awareness and changing attitudes about linguistic diversity. In fact, one of our early experimental versions of the curriculum was developed for Appalachia (Wolfram, Dannenberg, and Anderson 1996) and taught in Watauga County in the mountains of Western North Carolina. Formal education from K–16 needs to be included in such educational programs in order for wide-scale change to take place with respect to the language regard in Appalachia. Furthermore the integration of dialect awareness in other curricula, such as the program described by Shepherd and Hazen on this book's companion website (http://dialects.wvu.edu/appalachian-englishes), is an ideal intersection of language and literature.

In the final analysis, there is no singular program or strategy for changing the narrative about varieties of English in Appalachia. A full array of approaches, venues, technologies, and lay and professional opinion have to be actively engaged in this endeavor. But our exploration of outreach and engagement opportunities in Appalachia has indicated that there is a fertile opportunity for folks from within and outside of this region to celebrate its linguistic landscapes as one of the great sociolinguistic traditions within American English.

Notes

This article is dedicated to the memory of Michael Montgomery. No one knew more about Appalachia than Michael, and no one loved it more. From the time he took a class with me at the LSA Linguistic Institute in 1976, to the present article, he has been a keen, supportive critic of linguistic research. He was also the most courageous linguist I ever met in my life. Anyone who ever studies Appalachia is indebted to him for his vast knowledge and love for things Appalachian. Thank you, Michael! You done good!

1. This section was inspired by Jennifer Cramer's session on Appalachian English held at the Southeastern Conference on Linguistics 79, 2012, at the University of Kentucky in Lexington, Kentucky. This is part of the paper I intended to write but procrastinated until now.

References

Andersen, Henning. 1988. "Center and Periphery: Adoption, Diffusion, and Spread." In *Historical Dialectology*, edited by Jaceb Fisiak, 31–89. Berlin: Mouton de Gruyter.

Anderson, Bridget L. 1999. "Source-Language Transfer and Vowel Accommodation in the Patterning of Cherokee English /ai/ and /oi/." *American Speech* 74: 339–68.

Bolinger, Dwight. 1979. "The Socially-Minded Linguist." *The Modern Language Journal* 63, no. 8: 404–7.

Bonfiglio, Thomas P. 2002. *Race and the Rise of Standard American*. Berlin: Mouton de Gruyter.

Campbell, John C. 1921. *The Southern Highlander and His Homeland*. Lexington: University of Kentucky Press.

Carlton, Brian. 2019. "The US Island That Speaks Elizabethan English." *BBC*, 24 June 2019. http://www.bbc.com/travel/story/20190623-the-us-island-that-speaks-elizabethan-english.

Childs, Becky. 2005. "Investigating the Local Construction of Identity: Sociophonetic Variation in Smoky Mountain African American Women's Speech." PhD diss., University of Georgia.

Childs, Becky, and Christine Mallinson. 2004. "African American English in Appalachia." *English World-Wide* 25: 1–27.

Coggshall, Elizabeth L. 2006. "Differential Vowel Accommodation among Two Native American Groups." MA thesis, North Carolina State University.

Coggshall, Elizabeth L. 2008. "The Prosodic Rhythm of Two Varieties of Native American English." *University of Pennsylvania Working Papers in Linguistics* 14, no. 2: 2.

Christian, Donna. 1991. "The Personal Dative in Appalachian Speech." In *Dialects of English: Studies in Grammatical Variation*, edited by Peter Trudgill and J. K. Chambers, 13–19. London: Longman.

Christian, Donna, Walt Wolfram, and Nanjo Dube. 1988. *Variation and Change in*

Geographically Isolated Communities: Appalachian English and Ozark English. Publication of the American Dialect Society 74. Tuscaloosa: University of Alabama Press.

Cramer, Jennifer. 2014. "Is Shakespeare Still in the Holler? The Death of a Language Myth." *Southern Journal of Linguistics* 38, no. 1: 195–207.

Cramer, Jennifer. 2016. *Contested Southernness: The Linguistic Production and Perception of Identities in the Borderlands.* Publication of the American Dialect Society 100. Durham, NC: Duke University Press.

Dunstan, Stephany Brett. 2013. "The Influence of Speaking a Dialect of Appalachian English on the College Experience." PhD diss., North Carolina State University. https://repository.lib.ncsu.edu/bitstream/handle/1840.16/8561/etd.pdf.

Dunstan, Stephany Brett, Walt Wolfram, Audrey J. Jaeger, and Rebecca E. Crandall. 2015. "Educating the Educated: Language Diversity in the University Backyard." *American Speech* 90, no. 2: 266–80.

Greene, Robert Lane. 2015. "The Last Acceptable Prejudice." *The Economist*, Prospero (blog), 29 January 2015. https://www.economist.com/prospero/2015/01/29/the-last-acceptable-prejudice.

Hasty, J. Daniel. 2012. "We Might Should Oughta Take a Second Look at This: A Syntactic Re-analysis of Double Modals in Southern United States English." *Lingua* 122, no. 14: 1716–38.

Hazen, Kirk. 2008. "(ING): A vernacular baseline for English in Appalachia." *American Speech* 83, no. 2: 116–40.

Hazen, Kirk. 2011. "Flying High above the Social Radar: Coronal Stop Deletion in Modern Appalachia." *Language Variation and Change* 23, no. 1: 105–37.

Hazen, Kirk. 2014. "A New Role for an Ancient Variable in Appalachia: Paradigm Leveling and Standardization in West Virginia." *Language Variation and Change* 26, no. 1: 77–102.

Hazen, Kirk, and Ellen Fluharty. 2004. "Defining Appalachian English." In *Linguistic Diversity in the South: Changing Codes, Practices, and Ideology*, edited by Margaret Bender, 50–65. Athens: University of Georgia Press.

Hazen, Kirk, Sarah Hamilton, and Sarah Vacovsky. 2011. "The Fall of Demonstrative *Them*: Evidence from Appalachia." *English World-Wide* 32, no. 1: 74–103.

Hutcheson, Neal, producer. 2004a. *An Unclouded Day: Stories and Songs of Southern Appalachia.* CD. Raleigh, NC: North Carolina Language and Life Project.

Hutcheson, Neal, producer. 2004b. *Mountain Talk.* Raleigh, NC: North Carolina Language and Life Project.

Johnson, Greg. 2018. "The Syntax of Liketa." *Natural Language and Linguistic Theory* 36, no. 4: 1129–63.

Johnson, Sally. 2001. "Who's Misunderstanding Whom? Sociolinguistics, Public Debate and the Media." *Journal of Sociolinguistics* 5, no. 4: 591–610.

Kohn, Mary. 2019. "Latino English in New Destinations: Processes of Regionalization in Emerging Contact Varieties." In *Mexican American English: Substrate Influences and the Birth of an Ethnolect*, edited by Erik R. Thomas, 268–90. Cambridge: Cambridge University Press.

Kohn, Mary, and Hannah Franz. 2009. "Localized Patterns for Global Variants: The Case of Quotative Systems of African American and Latino Speakers." *American Speech* 84, no. 3: 259–97.

Labov, William, Paul Cohen, Clarence Robins, and John Lewis. 1968. *A Study of Non-Standard English of Negro and Puerto Rican Speakers in New York City.* 2 vols. Philadelphia: US Regional Survey.

Mallinson, Christine. 2006. "The Dynamic Construction of Race, Class, and Gender through Linguistic Practice among Women in a Black Appalachian Community." PhD diss., North Carolina State University.

Mallinson, Christine, and Becky Childs. 2004. "The Intersection of Regional and Ethnic Identity: African American English in Appalachia." *Journal of Appalachian Studies* 10, no. 1–2: 129–42.

Mallinson, Christine, Becky Childs, and Zula Cox. 2006. *Voices of Texana*. Texana, NC: Texana Committee on Community History and Preservation.

Mallinson, Christine, and Walt Wolfram. 2002. "Dialect Accommodation in a Bi-ethnic Mountain Enclave Community: More evidence on the Earlier Development of African American English." *Language in Society* 31: 743–75.

McMillan, James B., and Michael B. Montgomery. 1989. *Annotated Bibliography of Southern American English*. Tuscaloosa: University of Alabama Press.

Montgomery, Michael. 1998. "In the Appalachians They Speak Like Shakespeare." In *Language Myths*, edited by Laurie Bauer and Peter Trudgill, 66–76. New York: Penguin.

Montgomery, Michael. 2000. "Isolation as a Linguistic Construct." *Southern Journal of Linguistics* 1: 41–52.

Montgomery, Michael. 2005. Review of *Mountain Talk: Language and Life in Southern Appalachia*. *Appalachian Journal* 32, no. 3: 385–95.

Montgomery, Michael. 2009. "Historical and Comparative Perspectives on A-Prefixing in the English of Appalachia." *American Speech* 84, no. 1: 5–26.

Preston, Dennis R. 2018. "Language Regard: What, Why, How, Whither?" In *Language Regard: Methods, Variation, and Change*, edited by Betsy Evans, Erica Benson, and James Stanford, 3–30. Cambridge: Cambridge University Press.

Reaser, Jeffrey. 2006. "The Effect of Dialect Awareness on Adolescent Knowledge and Attitudes." PhD diss., Duke University.

Reaser, Jeffrey, and Walt Wolfram. 2007. *Voices of North Carolina: From the Atlantic to Appalachia*. Teacher manual and student workbook. Raleigh, NC: North Carolina Language and Life Project.

Shapiro, Henry D. 1978. *Appalachia on Our Mind*. Chapel Hill: University of North Carolina Press.

Semple, Euan. 2012. *Organizations Don't Tweet, People Do: A Managers Guide to the Social Web*. Chichester, West Sussex: Wiley.

Spiglanin, Tom. 2012. "Knowledge Has to Be Shared to Have Value." *Tom Spiglanin* (blog), 27 March 2012. https://tom.spiglanin.com/2012/03/knowledge-has-to-be-shared-to-have-value/.

Tortora, Christina. 2006. "The Case of Appalachian Expletive *They*." *American Speech* 81, no. 3: 266–96.

Walker, Abby, Rebecca Southall, and Rachel Hargrave. 2017. "An Acoustic and Phonological Description of /z/-Devoicing in Southern American English." *The Journal of the Acoustical Society of America* 142, no. 4: 2678.

Webelhuth, Gert, and Clare J. Dannenberg. 2006. "Southern American English Personal Datives: The Theoretical Significance of Dialectal Variation." *American Speech* 81, no. 1: 31–55.

Williams, Cratis, and Patricia D. Beaver. 1999. *The Cratis Williams Chronicles*. Boone, NC: Appalachian State University.

Wolfram, Walt. 1969. *A Sociolinguistic Description of Detroit Negro Speech*. Washington, DC: Center for Applied Linguistics.

Wolfram, Walt. 1974. *Sociolinguistic Aspects of Assimilation: Puerto Rican English in New York City*. Arlington, VA: Center for Applied Linguistics.

Wolfram, Walt. 1980. "A-Prefixing in Appalachian English." In *Locating Language in Time and Space*, edited by William Labov, 107–42. New York: Academic Press.

Wolfram, Walt. 2004. "The Sociolinguistic Construction of Remnant Dialects." In *Sociolinguistic Variation: Critical Reflections*, edited by Carmen Fought, 84–106. Oxford: Oxford University Press.

Wolfram, Walt. 2007. "Sociolinguistic Myths in the Study of African American English." *Language and Linguistic Compass* 2: 292–313.

Wolfram, Walt. 2013. "African American Speech in Southern Appalachia." In *Talking Appalachian*, edited by Amy Clark and Nancy Hayward, 81–93. Lexington: University Press of Kentucky.

Wolfram, Walt, and Donna Christian. 1975. *Sociolinguistic Variables in Appalachian Dialects*. Report for National Institute of Education of the Department of Health, Education, and Welfare, NIE-G-74–0026.M. Arlington, VA: Center for Applied Linguistics. https://files.eric.ed.gov/fulltext/ED112687.pdf.

Wolfram, Walt, and Donna Christian. 1976. *Appalachian Speech*. Arlington, VA: Center for Applied Linguistics.

Wolfram, Walt, Clare Dannenberg, and Bridget Anderson. 1996. *Dialects and Appalachian English*. A dialect curriculum for eighth-graders. Raleigh, NC: The North Carolina Language and Life Project.

Wolfram, Walt, and Jeffrey Reaser. 2014. *Talkin' Tar Heel: How Our Voices Tell the Story of North Carolina*. Chapel Hill: University of North Carolina Press.

Wolfram, Walt, Jeffrey Reaser, and Charlotte Vaughn. 2008. "Operationalizing Linguistic Gratuity: From Principle to Practice." *Language and Linguistic Compass* 3: 1109–34.

Wood, Jim, Einar Freyr Sigurðsson, and Raffaella Zanuttini. 2015. "Partitive Doubling in Icelandic and Appalachian English." In *Proceedings of the 45th Annual Meeting of the North East Linguistic Society* 3: 217–26.

Zanuttini, Raffaella, and Judy B. Bernstein. 2014. "Transitive Expletives in Appalachian English." In *Micro-Syntactic Variation in North American English*, edited by Raffaella Zanuttini and Laurence R. Horn. New York: Oxford University Press, 143–77.

Contributors

Allison Burkette is professor of linguistics at the University of Kentucky. Her research is grounded in the study of language variation and change from both a large-scale historical perspective and a small-scale perspective focused on individual interactions. Her works include two monographs: *Language and Material Culture* (John Benjamins 2015) and *Language and Classification* (Routledge 2018). She is also the editor of the Linguistic Atlas Project, a large-scale survey of American English.

Becky Childs is professor in the department of English at Coastal Carolina University. Her research takes an ethnographically informed approach to language change in phonetic and phonological systems of English. Her recent work has focused on issues of identity, salience, and local language change in Newfoundland and Appalachia. She is a coeditor of *Data Collection in Sociolinguistics*, 2nd ed. (Routledge 2017), as well as other works on sociolinguistic variation.

Donna Christian is senior fellow at the Center for Applied Linguistics, where she held the position of president from 1994 to 2010. Her work has focused on the role of language in education, including issues of second language learning and dialect diversity. She is a coauthor of *Dialects at School* (2017) and a coeditor of *What Teachers Need to Know about Language* (2018).

Jennifer Cramer is associate professor and chair of the department of linguistics at the University of Kentucky. Her research focuses on the perception and production of linguistic variation, with a specific interest in the dialects spoken in Kentucky. Her research utilizes the tools of perceptual and traditional dialectology to investigate connections between language and identity. She is the author of *Contested Southernness: The Linguistic Production and Perception of Identities in the Borderlands* (Duke University Press 2016).

Stephany Brett Dunstan, PhD, is assistant vice provost for assessment and accreditation at North Carolina State University and holds an appointment as teaching assistant professor in the college of education. She codirects the NC State Language Diversity Initiative, a comprehensive approach to addressing issues of language diversity on college campuses. Her research and practice focus on success for students from historically underrepresented populations, notably students from rural areas, supporting them at NC State and across North Carolina.

J. Daniel Hasty is associate professor of linguistics in the department of English at Coastal Carolina University. His research focuses on language variation, especially syntactic variation, in Appalachia and the South, and he investigates both how language varieties vary parametrically as well as how speakers use syntactic variants to construct social identities.

Kirk Hazen is professor of linguistics at West Virginia University, where he is the founding director of the West Virginia Dialect Project and a Benedum Distinguished Scholar in the humanities. His research, teaching, and linguistic service center on social and linguistic patterns of language variation. His most recent book is *An Introduction to Language* (Wiley 2015), and he is a coeditor (with Janet Holmes) of *Research Methods in Sociolinguistics* (Wiley 2014).

J. Inscoe is a PhD student of the language, literacy, and culture program at the University of Maryland, Baltimore County. Their burgeoning list of research interests include the ideological construction of standardized American English, media representations of dialect, and the link between voice, body, and sexual identity. Currently, they are writing their dissertation on radio broadcaster Paul Harvey, American vocal aesthetics, and cultural anxieties in the twentieth century.

Audrey J. Jaeger, PhD, is Alumni Distinguished Graduate Professor, North Carolina State University. Prior to NC State, Dr. Jaeger served in various student and academic affairs administrative positions. Dr. Jaeger directs the Belk Center for Community College Leadership and Research. Her research examines relationships and experiences among faculty and students that illuminate issues of transition, access, climate, agency, and community engagement. Dr. Jaeger is an associate editor for *Research in Higher Education*.

Jordan Lovejoy is a PhD candidate in English and folklore at the Ohio State University. She is also a fieldworker for the Central Appalachian Folk and

Traditional Arts Survey and Planning Project through the Mid Atlantic Arts Foundation and Livelihoods Knowledge Exchange Network. Her dissertation focuses on floods in Appalachian literature and the cultural and environmental memory of the 2001 floods in southern West Virginia.

Christine Mallinson is director of the Center for Social Science Scholarship, professor of language, literacy, and culture, and affiliate professor of gender, women's, and sexuality studies at the University of Maryland, Baltimore County. Her books and edited collections include *Understanding English Language Variation in U.S. Schools*, *We Do Language: English Language Variation in the Secondary English Classroom*, *Data Collection in Sociolinguistics: Methods and Applications*, and *Rural Voices: Language, Identity, and Social Change across Place*.

Paul E. Reed is assistant professor of phonology/speech science at the University of Alabama. His research focuses on the sociophonetic variation and change in the English varieties of the American South, particularly of Appalachia. A primary focus is the analysis of how local identity, what he terms *rootedness*, impacts a variety of phonological features. His work has appeared in the *Journal of the Acoustical Society of America*, *Journal of Speech, Language, and Hearing Research*, *American Speech*, and the *Southern Journal of Linguistics*.

Isabelle Shepherd is a poet from West Virginia. She now lives in Wilmington, NC, where she received her MFA from the University of North Carolina, Wilmington. She has held various positions within the nonprofit sector, as a public radio reporter, social worker, and advocate for historic preservation. She currently runs a small business supporting affordable, accessible housing. Her poetry has appeared in *DIAGRAM*, *The Journal*, *Ninth Letter*, *Redivider*, *Sixth Finch*, and elsewhere. Her work and reading dates can be found at www.isabelleshepherd.com.

Audra Slocum, PhD, is assistant professor of English education and a codirector of the National Writing Project at West Virginia University. Her research is ethnographic and explores how adolescents in marginalized communities discursively navigate school spaces. Her current work examines adolescent identity positioning and language variation in schools across West Virginia. Her work has been published in *English Teaching: Practice and Critique*, the *Journal of Identity, Language, and Education*, and *English Education*.

Walt Wolfram is William C. Friday Distinguished University Professor at North Carolina State University. He has pioneered research on social and ethnic dialects since the 1960s and published more than twenty books and over three hundred articles. Among these are *Appalachian Speech* (1976) with Donna Christian, their comprehensive final research report, *Sociolinguistic Variables in Appalachian Dialects* (1975), and a host of articles on different vernacular structures of Appalachia.

Index

academic community, 165, 172–73, 182
/æ/ breaking, 12
African American(s), 38, 93, 107–11, 157
   Appalachian(s), 108–10
   and Appalachian English, 107–9
   community or communities, 70, 107, 109, 187
   culture, 110
   residents, 100, 108 (*see also* Affrilachia)
   speakers, x, 108–9
   women, 86, 90, 94
African American English, x, 4, 70, 86, 108–10
African American Language, xvi, 108, 180–81, 183
   African American Vernacular English, xvi, 140, 157, 177
Affrilachia, 89
Affrilachian(s), 89, 100, 108, 138–39
/aɪ/ ungliding, 11–12, 28, 87
   prevoiceless, 12, 28
   social marking, 10, 20, 87, 110, 151
   Southern Vowel Shift, 14, 27
Alabama, 5–7, 9–11
allophones, 21
Almost Politically Correct Redneck, 119–20, 124
alveolar
   approximant, 24
   fricative, 24
   nasal, 33; progressive verbs and, 46–47; social marking and, 86, 124–25, 137, 154
   stop, 26
American English, 4–5, 189
   varieties of, 10, 21, 23–25
   vowels in, 27, 29, 100
American Folklore Society, 116
anthropology, xxi, 84
Appalachia, 4–10
   See also Northern Appalachia; Southern Appalachia
Appalachian region
   central, 31
   defined, 8, 74, 116, 118
   ethnic diversity of, 99–100, 108, 110, 184
   and literature, 143 (*see also* Appalachian literature)
   queer, 91
   second-person plural pronoun, 107

   social intersections, 85, 96
   stigmatized, 74, 78, 88, 95, 122, 146
   teachers/students in, 156, 158
Appalachianness, 61, 75
Appalachian Kentuckians, 69–72, 80
Appalachian literature
   authentic, 134
   variation in and of, xxii, 130, 141
   themes in, 131, 133, 135, 138, 143–44
Appalachian Mountains, 6, 9, 91
Appalachian Regional Commission (ARC), 7–8, 46, 118, 132
Appalachian Regional Development Act, 7
Appalachian Speech, xix, 10, 181
Appalachian speech, 32–33, 43, 76, 180; White, 103, 106–8
Appalachian writer, 131–32
a-prefix, 36, 39–40, 59–61, 63–64
a-prefixing
   in discourse, 56–58, 60, 63, 65
   example, xii, 15, 157
   study of, 183
   vernacular (salient) feature, 43, 50, 105, 147
aspiration, 21
Atlas of North American English, 11
Atse Kituwah Academy, 102
authenticity, 70, 127, 131, 133–35, 143

back vowel fronting, 14, 27, 29, 105, 108
Ballad of Trenchmouth Taggart, The (Taylor), 131
boundaries
   identity, 89, 119, 121, 146
   perceptual, 4, 74
   official, 7, 182
   regional, xix, 6, 11

catawampus, 134
central Appalachia, 91, 105, 120, 147
Cherokee, x, xvii, 99–102, 111, 184, 188
codes of power, 148, 152, 161–63
code-switching, 90, 95, 157, 165–66, 168, 170
completive *done*, 105–6
   examples of, xii, 57–58, 106
Conference of Appalachian Governors, 6
connectedness, 89, 161

conservative, 45, 75, 86, 118–19
consonants
   absence of, 137
   additions, 25, 36, 104
   cluster reduction, 26, 38
   consonantal processes, 23–24, 49, 108
   consonantal variation, 23
   defined, 23
   deletions, 25–26
   syllable structure, 101
   voiced, 11, 104, 108
   voiceless, 11, 28, 108
contracted *was*, 42
Cornbread Communism, 118, 121–22, 124–25
"Cornbread Communist Manifesto," 122
coronal stop deletion, 122
cot/caught merger, 30–31. *See also* low-back vowel merger
counterfactual *liketa*, 105–6; examples of, 49, 106
country speech, 154–55
Crapalachia (McClanahan), 132, 135–36, 139–40
cultural logic, 117
cultural region, 74
Cumberland Plateau, 10

"Dangerous Myth of Authenticity, The" (George), 131
deletion, 11, 26, 122
demonstrative pronouns, 43, 124
demonstrative *them*
   frequency of, 43, 85, 147
   usage of, 48, 50, 124–25, 133
dialects, 37, 62, 167
   appreciation of, xiii, 88, 93, 172–73, 179, 188
   Black, 90, 141–42
   boundaries, xix, 4, 74
   cultural significance of, 89, 95, 133, 139, 154, 183
   diversity, 172–73
   donor, 99, 103
   eye, 133
   features of, xx, 121, 123, 130, 137, 147
   grammatical features of, 39–40, 43, 58, 64, 124–25, 157
   landscape, 71, 73–74, 76–77, 81
   language change, 31, 50, 103, 110, 124
   in literature, 131, 133–39
   monolithic, xv, 180–82
   phonological features of, 25–26
   race, 157
   region, 4–5, 27, 80, 89, 94–95
   stigmatized, xxii, 135–36, 141–43, 164, 171–72
   student, 93, 151–52, 156, 161, 166
   Ulster-Scots English, 106
   variation, xix, xxi–xxii, 92, 123
   varieties of, 42, 73, 131, 135, 143, 167
   vernacular, xiii, 38, 95, 106, 150, 185–86
   Washington (state), 75
   White, 101
   words, 121, 135–36

dialectology framework, 69, 71, 75
diphthong, 12, 28, 31, 100–101, 104–5, 108
discourse
   analysis, xxi, 126
   about Appalachia, 80, 91, 146
   a-prefix, 59
   and construction of social meaning, xxi, 55
   defined, xi, 55–56
   and education, 156, 161–62, 164
   and family, 63
   and identity, 147
   local, 155
   and objects, 64, 67
   of power, 149
   in/of schools, 150–51, 153
   strategies, 90
   study of, 55, 57–58, 61, 66, 92, 183
diversity, 172, 181
   of Appalachian speakers, xxi, 84
   in communities, 134
   of dialects, 143, 193
   of Englishes, x, 180
   ethnic, xxi, 99–100, 178
   language, 153, 164, 186, 188, 194
   across levels of language, 3
   in linguistic features, 20, 99
   linguistic, x, xxii, 162, 166, 171–72, 188
   programming, 173
   regional, ix, xiii, 178
   of scholars, xix
   sociolinguistic, 184
   student, 166
   superdiversity, x
double modals, 14–15, 49, 106
drawl, 165
   drawling, 29
   mountain, 30
   southern, 12, 30

Early Modern English, 39, 45, 47, 105
Earley, Tim, vi, 140, 184
Eastern Band of the Cherokee Nation, 99–100, 184
education
   and gender, 92–95
   in Kentucky, 78, 90, 93, 153
   in North Carolina, 188
   perception of, 94, 148, 166, 169
   social groups, 146, 148
   stereotypes, 94, 96, 161–62
   stigma in college, xxii, 163, 169, 171–73, 185
   stigma in high school, 93, 150–55
   variation, xiii, 149–50, 152, 156, 186
   varieties of language, 121, 126, 151, 168, 187
Elizabethan English, 22, 103, 178–79
essentialism, 131, 142–43
ethnicity
   correlation, 26
   intersections, 94, 96

as part of identity, xi, xxi, 143, 172
perception of, 109, 180
social structure, 84, 184
ethnography of communication, 117

Fabulachia, 91
falling pitch, 31
feature clustering, 61
folklore, 116–18
frequency distribution, 59
fricative, 23–25
Future Farmers of America, 147

gender
    and education, 92–95
    and ethnicity, xi, 84–85, 94, 143
    and femininity, 86
    and identity, 86, 89–90, 109
    and language, 84–85, 95, 184
    and language use, 87, 151
    and pronouns, 45
    and region, 87
    and sexuality, x, 84–85, 95–96
    and social class, 146
    stereotypes, 91–92, 95
    stigma, 91, 120, 150
geographers, 7, 11, 182
Georgia, 6–7, 9, 11, 118
Germanic languages, 101
gerunds, 46–47
Ghost of Ol Dale Earnhardt, The, 118, 121–22, 125–26
glide (vowel)
    inglided, 186
    offglide, 28
    onglide, 28
    upglide, 11–12
    unglided, 28, 87, 101, 110, 154
grammar
    African American Appalachian, 109
    Cherokee, 102
    defined, xx, 37–39
    and ethnicity, 103, 105, 106–7, 117
    and language change, 48–50
    and language use, 117
    levels of, 10, 13
    patterns of, 43–44, 47, 49–50
    public perception of, 36
    standard English, 148, 151, 153
    stigmatized, 40–43, 140
    system of, 109, 182
    variation of, 36, 41
    vernacular, 39, 42, 50
Guardian, The, 138

hick, 74, 76, 164
Hick Poetics, 138, 140
hillbilly
    as persona, 70, 115, 118
    as dialect descriptor, 77, 164, 183, 186

homogeneity, ix, 180–81
homogenization myth, 180–82
homonyms, 48
Honey from the Lion (Null), 131

identity, xix–xx
    Appalachian, 9, 12, 14, 76, 85, 89
    racial, 89
    regional, 76, 88, 91, 95–96
    social, 17
identity development, xiii
identity marker, 88
ideology, 122, 154, 169, 178, 185
indefinite determiner, 49
-ing variation, 46–47
interactional context, 58
intonation, 20, 31–33
is copula absence, 109

Kentucky
    education in, 78, 90, 93, 153
    linguistic identities of, 70, 80, 150–51, 154
    as part of Appalachia, 6–7, 9, 11–12, 15–16
    perceptual dialectology framework in, 69
    phonological features in, 12–13, 42, 150–51
    poetry from, 138
    rank of, 81n2
    rural, 90, 138
    stereotypes of, 72, 74, 146
    urban, 16, 76–79, 80
Kentuckians, 69–71, 76, 79–80

L-sound, 15, 24
L-vocalization, 24
labiovelar, 23
language change
    and age groups, xi, 135–36, 147
    and grammatical features, 41, 45, 48
    and language varieties, xv, xix–xx, 3, 99
language communities, 146
language complexity, xvii
language differences, 10, 103, 185
language norms, 101, 110, 148
language use
    in adolescents, 145, 152, 156
    and gender, 86–87, 93–96
    and identity, 119, 158
    and ideology, 62, 86, 158
    patterns of, 96, 117
    in regions, 87, 90, 150
language variety
    Cherokee, 100
    comparison, 4, 71, 182, 187
    education, xiii
    standard, 152
    West Virginia, xii
Latinx, x, 110–11, 184

leveled *was*
  in discourse, 56–58, 151
  and identity, 85, 107, 124, 147
  and language change, 41–42, 45, 48
levels
  of grammar, 10
  of language, xix, 3, 136, 178
lexical, 10, 13, 15, 179, 182
lexical items, 15
LGBTQ, xvii, 45, 91
linguistic distinctions, 14
linguistic feature sets, 99
linguistic hegemony
  and linguistic identity, 81
  and standard language ideology, xxii, 162, 165–66, 170–71
  in universities, 164, 166
linguistic identity, 71, 73, 80, 92
linguistic norms, 124, 161–62
lore, 117–18
low-back vowel merger, 12–13. *See also* cot/caught merger
low-high tones, 87

marginality, 161, 71–73, 80
mattering, 161
mergers, 30
metalinguistic awareness, 73, 75, 157
mid-front vowel, 30
Midland region, 4–5, 75
Midwest, the, 4, 12, 14–17, 33, 49
midwestern, 5, 14, 16, 59, 94
Midwestern English, 5
Montgomery, Michael, xviii, xiii, 177, 189
morpheme, 14, 26
morphology, 26, 38–39
morphosyntactic, 10, 13–15, 179, 183
Mountain Talk (Hutcheson), 142, 179, 187–88
multimodal, 67
multiple negation, 10, 40–41, 56–57, 63, 137
myths, 178

nasals, 30
nasal sound, 24
negative concord, 41
negative inversion, 41
New York
  dialects of, 71, 141, 186
  as part of Appalachia, 6–9, 11, 46, 118, 181
Next Generation Common Core Standards, 148
non-Appalachian, 13, 70–72, 74, 80, 161–62
nonnarrative, 59–60, 64–65
non-Southerners, 75
nonstandard(ized), 145, 162, 167, 170–72
nonstandard past tense, 56–58, 63
North, the, 6, 11–12, 15, 17, 155, 185
North Carolina
  African American communities of, 108, 187
  Cherokee communities of, 100, 102
  education in, 188
  grammatical features of, 42, 48, 56, 63, 65
  Latinx communities of, 110
  as part of Appalachia, 9, 11–12, 55, 87, 142
  as part of the South, 7
  vowels in, 12, 182, 186
Northern Appalachia
  phonological features, 12–13, 15–17, 30, 104, 186
  social markers of, 156
  as subregion, x–xi, 3, 11, 14–17
nucleus, 28

Oxford American, The, 141

Pancake, Breece D'J, 134–38
particular cultural space, 155
past tense *be*, 26
past tense form(s), 49, 57–58, 107
patterns
  grammatical, xi, 36, 38
  qualitative, xx
  quantitative, xx
Pennsylvania, 6–9, 11, 16, 104
perception
  of Appalachia, 10, 142, 183
  in education, 94, 148, 166, 169
  of language, 21, 66, 153, 157, 178
  linguistic, 69, 183
  social, 124
  of speech, 30, 109, 145, 154, 185
  of urbanity, 16–17
perceptual dialectology, 69–71, 73–75, 81
phoneme(s), 21
phonetics, 21
phonological distinctions, 13
phonology, xi, 21, 103, 108, 183
pin/pen merger, 15, 30, 105
poetry, 56, 88–89, 100, 116, 130, 140–41
positive *anymore*, 14
postsecondary, xiii, 148
President's Appalachian Regional Commission (PARC), 6–7
prestige, xii, 71–72, 80–81, 171
progressive verbs, 46–47
pronounce
  consonant, 24–26, 103–5
  distinctions, 10, 21
  merger, 15
  social postures, 152, 165
  vowel, 11–12, 14, 27, 29–30, 101
pronouns
  demonstrative, 43, 124
  personal, 44–45
  plural, 45
  singular, 44–45, 47, 50
proper speech, 154, 164
prosody, 101

qualitative data, 80, 86, 155
qualitative language patterns, xx, 103

qualitative sociolinguistic interviews, 75, 93
qualitative study/research, 90, 94, 145, 164
Qualla Boundary, 100, 102
quantitative language patterns, xx, 11, 103
quantitative research, xx, 36, 87, 93
quotative *be like*, xi, xix, 47, 48, 107, 110

race
    challenges, 94
    discourse strategies, 90
    and gender, 90
    social intersection, 84, 96, 146, 153, 157–58, 172
    locating, 89, 109, 119
R-dropping, 38, 71
redneck
    as a stereotype, 74, 141, 154
    in memes, xxii, 115, 118–20, 124
Redneck Randal, 119–20
reduction, xxii, 11, 26
reflexive(s), 43, 44–45, 178
region(al)
    Appalachian region, central, 8, 31, 74, 116, 118
    Appalachian Regional Commission (ARC), 7–8, 46, 118, 132
    Appalachian Regional Development Act, 7
    boundary, xix, 6, 11
    cultural, 74
    dialect, 4–5, 27, 80, 89, 94–95
    diversity, ix, xiii, 178
    gender, 87
    identity, 76, 88, 91, 95–96
    language, xix, 3, 87, 90, 110, 150
    language use, 87, 90, 150
    President's Appalachian Regional Commission (PARC), 6–7
    speech, 4, 16–17
    urban, xix, 9, 16–17, 147
    variation, xix, 3–4, 11, 13, 15, 106–7
    varieties of language, 5, 13, 17, 165
    vowels, 14
    West Virginia, 6–7, 11
rhetoric of resistance, 63
rising pitch, 31–33, 87
Romance languages, 101
rootedness, 22, 32–33, 87, 195
R sounds (/r/ sound), 71, 104
rural, 16, 76, 138, 186
    Appalachia(ns), 116, 118, 160–61
    areas, xix, xxi, 3, 90–91, 103, 115, 147, 150, 156
    background, 171
    community, 25, 76, 86, 154
    contexts/locales/parts, 31, 104, 157
    counties, 72, 177
    dialect(s)/forms/varieties, 59, 70, 75, 137
    environment, 90
    family, ix
    folk, 33
    Kentucky, 90, 138, 153
    LGBTQ youth, xvii
    life, 39, 141
    literary characters, 39
    man, 119
    peasants, 116
    population, 118, 181
    schools, 150, 153
    South, 186
    Southern Appalachia, xxii, 164
    speakers, 10, 38, 106, 133, 171–72
    speech, 43
    state, 76
    students, xxii, 93–94, 150, 162–64, 167, 171
    tales, 138
    urban distinction/divide, 12, 16, 75, 80
rurality, 10, 75, 138, 157
rural/urban divide, 12, 16, 75

schwa, 100
Science Olympiad, 147
second-person plural, 45–47, 106
self-identification, 120
self-image, xii
sense of belonging, xxii, 22, 93, 160–66, 168, 170
sense of identity, 132, 138, 147
sense of place, 110
sense of self, 22, 146–47
Sequoyah, 102
sexual identities, 87, 91–92
sexuality, x, xxi, 84–85, 91, 95–96, 184
social associations, xx, 107
social class
    correlation with dialect features, 26, 46–48, 125, 133, 147, 151
    indexing of, 89, 146–47
    as a social structure, 84, 96, 172
    and stigmatized speech, 150, 155
social connections, xx, 150
social groups
    and dialect variation, 24, 85, 125, 139
    in education, 146, 148
social meaning
    and discourse, xi, 55, 59, 61–64
    and objects, 64, 66
    and identity, 56, 73
    and vocabulary, 136
    and phonological features, 28, 44, 124–25
social motivations, xx
social reality, 84, 132
social practice, 55, 62
sociolinguistic education, 151–52, 158, 164
sociolinguistic diversity, 95, 184
sociolinguistic hierarchy, 155
sociolinguistic identity, 146, 158
sociolinguistic interviews, 75, 81, 157, 177, 187
sociolinguistic nostalgia, 180–81
sociolinguistic patterns, xvii, 43

sociolinguistics
  methods, xx, 13, 60–62, 93, 178
  myths, 180, 184
  pedagogy, 151
  principles, 151–52
  research, 84–87, 95, 149, 152, 183–85
  scholarship, 134, 142
  studies, 48, 86–87, 134
  tenet of, xvi
sociolinguistic traditions, 189
sociology, xxi, 84
sounding local, 150–51
sound patterns, xx, 21, 101, 103
South, the
  connections, 3, 181, 188
  dialect region, 4, 12
  distinctions, 9, 13–17, 81n3
  education, 92–93, 161
  features of, 103
  food, 127n3
  grammatical features of, 46–47, 49, 106
  LGBTQ, 45
  limits, 6, 11, 76
  perception of, 74
  phonological features of, 28, 30, 104–5
  representation, 133
  slavery, 107
  stereotype, 119
  study of, xvii, 75
  subregions, 5, 186
South Carolina, 7, 9
Southern English
  connections, 5, 10, 13
  differences, 14, 16, 105
  grammatical, 106
  phonological, 11, 25
  speakers, 25
  varieties, 4, 105
Southern Appalachia
  phonological features, 12–13, 27–28, 30–31
  social markers of, 100, 104–8, 154–55, 165
  speech, 12, 165
  as a subregion, x–xi, 3, 11, 14–17, 164
Southernness, 73, 75–79, 193
Southern Vowel Shift, 12, 14–15, 27–29
speech communities, xi, 69–71, 73, 81, 146
speech patterns
  accommodation, 90, 165
  Cherokee, x, 101
  education, 94
  language change, xi, 185
  prestige, xii
  regional, 75, 155
speech regions, 4, 16–17
Standard English(es), xvi, 148
  Appalachian contrast, 95, 103, 134
  varieties, 71, 87, 118, 153
standard forms, 44, 58, 137
standard language ideology, xxii, 148, 161–66, 168–71
standard speech, 78, 86

stereotypes
  awareness of, 89, 156
  as a barrier, 89, 142, 145–46
  believed, 70, 80, 88
  combatting, xvi, 77, 121, 123
  common, 91, 116, 118–20, 124
  dialect features of, 124
  education, 94, 96, 161–62
  folk, xi, 140
  gender-based, 91–92, 95
  identity, xii
  isolation, 184
  language, 70, 156
  mountain life, 142, 185
  and myths, xiii
  ownership of, xxii, 154
  Southern, 12, 76
  West Virginia, 91
stigma
  against Appalachia, 74, 90, 118, 141
  and code-switching, 170
  and college education, xxii, 163, 169, 171–73, 185
  of features, 22, 121, 123, 135–36
  gender/sexual identities, 91
  of grammatical features, 36–41, 43, 50, 124, 140
  and high school education, 93, 150–55
  and nonstigmatized, xvi, 21, 166
  of phonological features, 26, 28, 32, 104, 122
  regional, 9, 22, 74, 90, 165
  strategic essentialism, 142–43
stress-timed language, 101–2
style-shift, 70
subregions, x–xi, 3, 11, 14–17, 164
superdiversity, x
syllable-final positions, 24
syllable-initial positions, 24
syllables, 12, 20–21, 26, 28–29, 31–32
  stressed, 40, 102, 104–5
  unstressed, 42, 104
syllable-timed languages, 101–2
syntax
  defined, xx
  as grammar, 31, 38–39, 105, 109
  as level of language, xi
  as writing tool, 133, 137

talking junk, 149
Taylor, Glenn, 131
Tennessee
  language features of, 30, 40, 75, 81n3
  as part of Appalachia, 6–7, 9–12, 147
"Terrain" (Wilkinson), vi, 138–39
third-person plural –s attachment, 109
third-person singular –s absence, 109
Trail of Tears, 99–100
"Trilobites" (Pancake), 137
Type 1 Redneck, 119–21, 123
Type 2 Redneck, 115, 120–21, 125–26

urban
  African Americans, 90, 108
  economics, 3
  identity, 69–70, 76–77
  language variation, 33
  Latinx community, xxi
  middle classes, 119
  norms, 78–79, 141, 143
  regions, xix, 9, 16–17, 147
  schools, 160, 186
  speech, 25, 43
  stereotypes, 80, 86
  students, 72, 92–94, 154, 169
  tales, 117
urban/rural distinction, 12, 16, 75
US Census Bureau, 16, 81n2

variation
  in Appalachia, 22
  consonant, 23–25
  and education, xiii, 149–50, 152, 156, 186
  ethnic, 110
  and folklore, 115, 117, 123, 125
  grammatical, xx, 41, 46–50, 125, 140
  and identity, xxii, 70, 81, 89, 92
  intonation, 31, 101–2
  language change, 103, 135, 143
  in literature, 131, 143
  needed research, 17
  perception of, 38, 73
  regional, xix, 3–4, 11, 13, 15, 106–7
  stigmatized, 153–55
  social, xxi, 10, 12, 84–85, 95, 178
  study of, xv–xvi, 156–57, 181, 183
  urban/rural distinction, 16
  vowel, 27–33, 104
  word, 39
variationist, xx
varieties of language
  African American, 109
  continuum, xiii, 4, 16
  diversity, xix, 111, 143, 182
  distinctions, 3–4, 42, 118, 134–35, 152, 165
  and education, 121, 126, 151, 168, 187
  ethnic, x, 178
  folklore, 124, 127
  gendered, 85, 87, 96
  historical development of, 38, 43, 45, 131, 184
  home, 72
  and language change, ix, xi, 177, 179
  Latinx, 110
  mainstream, 142
  myths of, 142, 178, 180
  Native American, 100
  perception of, 78, 80–81, 94, 148
  phonological differences, 21–33, 122
  prestige, xxi, 70–72, 148, 169
  regional, 5, 13, 17, 165
  rural, 137, 141
  similarities, 10–11, 36–37, 48–49, 133

  standard, 41, 70–71, 87, 121, 152–53, 172
  stigmatized, xii, 75–76, 147, 162–63, 171
  study of, xv, xvii–xviii, 62, 185, 189
  systematic, xvi, 50
  vernacular, 41, 44, 124, 132, 181, 183
  White varieties, 102–8
  working-class, ix
  world, ix
velar nasal, 33n1, 46–47, 125
verbal expression, 94
vernacular dialect features, 38, 43, 130, 136
vernacular English, xvi, 106, 140, 157
Virginia, 6–7, 9, 11, 15–16
vocal folds, 23, 28
vocal tract, 23
vowel(s)
  breaking, 12, 29–30
  in Cherokee, 100–101
  with consonant variation, 24, 26
  defined, 20, 23, 26–27
  ethnic distinction, 104–5, 108
  fronting, 29, 105, 108
  and identity, 32, 36, 38, 88, 151, 157
  lengthening, 12
  merger, 12–13, 15, 30–31, 105, 185
  perception, 87, 185
  regional distinction, 14
  shift, 27–29, 140
  of standard Englishes, xvi, 49, 102
  system, 23
  ungliding, 11, 28

Walker, Frank X, 89, 139
was-leveling. *See* leveled *was*
West Virginia
  author, 131–32
  Berkeley Springs, 140
  consonants, 24–25, 104
  grammar pattern, 124–25
  language change, 147
  LGBTQ, 91
  miner(s), xii, 120
  as part of Appalachia, 11
  as part of Appalachian Regional Commission, 6–7
  poetry, 141
  population demographics, 40
  representation of, 133
  research study of, ix, xi, 42, 47–48, 85, 156
  southern, 9–10, 12, 15, 136
  urban, 16
  vowels, 13, 105
West Virginia College and Career Readiness standards, 148
West Virginia Dialect Project, 187
West Virginia University, 116
Wilkinson, Crystal, vi, 138, 141
World Englishes, ix

zero plural measurement, 14

www.ingramcontent.com/pod-product-compliance
Lightning Source LLC
Chambersburg PA
CBHW070803230426
43665CB00017B/2467